Economics of Social Relations

Starting from the idea that economic relations are social relations, and every economic fact is first a social fact, this book explores one of the crucial problems within economic science: how to embody the social dimension into the study of economic reality from a critical perspective.

This book opens with an examination of the concept of social capital, incorporating all the approaches from the last 30 years of analysis. It reviews the two main orientations of existing research programmes in social capital: the macro or culturalist perspective and the micro or individual social capital. Furthermore, it proposes a reconstruction of the theory from a micro perspective. Finally, taking this approach, this book explores the link between social capital and the negative aspects of social reality, such as corruption or inequality, and, through the study of so-called relational goods, the influence of social capital on subjective well-being. The analysis of the concept of social capital not only involves economists but also requires a necessary bridge with sociology, anthropology, political science, and even psychology.

This book will, therefore, be crucial reading for anyone engaged in the problem of the interrelation between economy and society.

Atilano Pena-López (Celeiro-Lugo, 1968) is Professor of Economic Policy at the Universidade da Coruña, has a PhD in Economics, and is Member of ECOBAS and OSIM research groups.

Matías Membiela-Pollán (A Coruña, 1981) is Associate Professor of Marketing and Market Research at the Universidade da Coruña (Spain), has a PhD in Economics and Business Administration, with a thesis on Social Capital and Relational Goods, and is Member of the research groups OSIM and iMARKA.

Routledge Advances in Social Economics

Series Editor: John B. Davis, Marquette University

This series presents new advances and developments in social economics thinking on a variety of subjects that concern the link between social values and economics. Need, justice and equity, gender, cooperation, work poverty, the environment, class, institutions, public policy and methodology are some of the most important themes. Among the orientations of the authors are social economist, institutionalist, humanist, solidarist, cooperatist, radical and Marxist, feminist, post-Keynesian, behaviouralist, and environmentalist. The series offers new contributions from today's most foremost thinkers on the social character of the economy.

Publishes in conjunction with the Association of Social Economics.

Human Nature in Modern Economics
Structure, Change and Perspectives
Anna Horodecka

The Economics of Scientific Misconduct
Fraud, Replication Failure, and Research Ethics in Empirical Inquiry
James R. Wible

Virtues, Morals and Markets
Why Moral Identity Matters
Rojhat Avsar

Political Economy, Institutions and Virtue
Alasdair MacIntyre's Revolutionary Aristotelianism
Matías Petersen

Normative Economics in the History of Economic Thought
Marx, Mises, Friedman and Popper
Sina Badiei

For more information about this series, please visit: www.routledge.com/Routledge-Advances-in-Social-Economics/book-series/SE0071

Economics of Social Relations

Critical Perspectives on Social Capital

Atilano Pena-López and Matías Membiela-Pollán

Routledge
Taylor & Francis Group
LONDON AND NEW YORK

First published 2025
by Routledge
4 Park Square, Milton Park, Abingdon, Oxon OX14 4RN

and by Routledge
605 Third Avenue, New York, NY 10158

Routledge is an imprint of the Taylor & Francis Group, an informa business

British Library Cataloguing-in-Publication Data
A catalogue record for this book is available from the British Library

ISBN: 978-1-032-45083-4 (hbk)
ISBN: 978-1-032-45084-1 (pbk)
ISBN: 978-1-003-37530-2 (ebk)

DOI: 10.4324/9781003375302

Typeset in Times New Roman
by codeMantra

Contents

Figures

Tables

Boxes

About the authors

Atilano Pena-López (Celeiro-Lugo, 1968) is Professor of Economic Policy at the Universidade da Coruña, has a PhD in Economics, and is Member of ECOBAS and OSIM research groups. He researches socioeconomics and critical aspects of economics, paying particular attention to the frontiers with other social sciences, with a special accent on social capital and its derivations (social trust, corruption, happiness, etc.), Ethics and Economics, and the Economics of Religion. Among the research on social capital, he has published in international journals like the *Economics Bulletin*, the *Cambridge Journal of Economics*, the *Journal of Business Ethics*, the *Journal of Happiness Studies*, and *Social Networks* and a series of book chapters linked to open questions.

Matías Membiela-Pollán (A Coruña, 1981) is Associate Professor of Marketing and Market Research at the Universidade da Coruña (Spain), has a PhD in Economics and Business Administration, with a thesis on Social Capital and Relational Goods, and is Member of the research groups OSIM and iMARKA. His research interests are socioeconomics and social capital. He has published articles in various international journals and publishers indexed in WOS/JCR and Scopus. He is also the author of books on social capital, such as *Capital Social. Glosario* (2013) and *La Teoría del Capital Social* (2016).

Foreword

From disappointing evidence to articulating a way forward

This book starts from a piece of evidence and aims to answer a problem. In a simple statement: "All economic relations occur amid social relations". Like all evidence, it does not need to be tested; nevertheless, it is astonishing that economic science is built on assumptions that seriously compromise the sociability of human beings.

Economics is based on a deficient anthropology. It is formulated as a formal science focused on optimising utility functions defined by individuals considered in isolation. However, our goals, preferences, and means are fundamentally social, and our actions are socially conditioned. The challenge lies in including human beings' inherent "sociability" in economic models. Efforts to address this issue have been diverse, spanning from the strictest forms of economic reductionism to more anthropologically substantive approaches.

Since the 1980s, the theory of Social Capital has promised to be one of the most balanced proposals in economic theory. Although it does not represent a unified approach, it can be integrated into what has come to be termed "neocapital". This integrative perspective seeks to incorporate various human dimensions as forms of capital, ranging from knowledge and creativity in human capital to social recognition in symbolic capital. In the Social Capital approach, networks of relationships are also considered expressions of capital. However, this promising interpretative framework requires clarification of its internal logic. Anyone who has followed the development of this field has likely felt at some point that it would be desirable to "put order" into it. The theory needs a comprehensive interpretative model of social capital and its functioning. This work aims to contribute to this endeavour.

Thus, the work is structured in three large blocks that attempt to answer a logical sequence of questions.

In the first block, we will critically review the issue's status. That is, we seek to answer two questions: How can the social dimension of the human being be introduced into the economy, and how has the theoretical proposal of social capital evolved?

In the central one, we will rethink the articulation of the two major perspectives on social capital (micro and macro). The general model of "Coleman's boat" serves as a basis for proposing the micro-macro link that social capital theory lacks.

In these chapters, we will answer the following questions: What are the ways of analysing social capital? What does not work in the macro approach? How can we base a macro approach on a solid micro approach?

The final block tries to put this refocusing into practice by applying it to three issues: inequality, corruption, and subjective well-being or happiness. Based on this proposal to reconstruct theory from a micro approach, we answer three questions. The questions to which these chapters respond are: How do networks of relationships structure society? How do networks influence the appearance of corruption problems? How do these individual networks influence subjective well-being?

Lastly, we would like to contribute to finding a way out of the lack of integration of social capital theory and to bring a kind of social realism to economics.

Acknowledgements

To the friends and colleagues who unknowingly contributed to our search for answers during long years of dialogue and discussion.

Introduction

The dissatisfactions of economics

> The homo oeconomicus would behave in this way in a common situation.
> "Where is the railway station?" he asks me.
> "There," I say, pointing at the post office, "and would you please post this letter for me on the way?"
> "Yes," he says, determined to open the envelope and check whether it contains something valuable.
>
> (Sen, 1977, p. 317)

The previous quote is a good example of how the simplifications of human behaviour in economics can become caricatures. The economic literature considers that every person maximises a (their) utility function that depends on their own consumption as if the rest of society did not exist.

This simplified model, referred to as *homo oeconomicus*, which obeys methodological individualism, is justified as a useful theoretical stylisation for its mathematical treatment (Swedberg & Granovetter, 1992). However, it entails a multitude of drawbacks, in particular, the construction of explanations or causal accounts that may be admitted in terms of logic but are weak and biased from the point of view of understanding human behaviour. In this sense, A. K. Sen coins the term *rational fool* to refer to the classical characterisation of this model of human behaviour that is only motivated by self-interest and socially isolated (Sen, 1995, p. 89). We think it is fair to say that, we can find here one of the roots of the "dissatisfaction" that all of us who move into the area of economics, especially those who are close to it at some point, have felt. It is true that, although we are proud of the theoretical elegance of the models, we are "embarrassed" by their lack of anthropological realism. The reality is that human actions hardly conforms to a set of equations, and, as Chesterton (1910) said, something is lost to science when it enters the human head. Nevertheless, we all agree that any improvement in the understanding of economic reality must attend to a better understanding of man within society.

Situating economic facts in the social fabric has been a long tradition, although it has never been part of the hard core of economic science. There are attempts ranging from the strictest orthodoxy of economic theory to heterodoxy from economics and sociology. What will occupy the present volume is the avenue that has been explored most recently: Social Capital Theory. Frankly, this programme is

DOI: 10.4324/9781003375302-1

promising, to say the least. Economic action is socially situated so that not only can the actions of individuals not be explained by individual motivations alone, but individuals are situated in networks that influence their preferences, decisions, and, above all, the social resources they can mobilise. Likewise, at the macro level, a society will be more efficient in its functioning to the extent that it achieves a good articulation of the networks that make it up.

The network concept is at the heart of this theory, and its usefulness in the sociological analysis of the economy lies in its proximity to concrete empirical reality. How individuals manage to find a job or mobilise any material or immaterial resource is linked to a social support network at the individual level. Simultaneously, how a society solves its coordination problems involves the interaction of multiple networks in an extensive social network.

As we will see in the text, this is not something new; notwithstanding, the number of studies on the subject is growing exponentially. Numerous studies have attempted to take advantage of the benefits offered by this conceptual framework to explain how social functioning affects the economy and vice versa. However, the risk faced by this developing programme, as is often the case with all paradigms under construction, is more than remarkable. As a curiosity, we invite the reader to look at the works that have been published in recent years, and it will surprise them that in the first pages of many of them, a large section is devoted to defining the concepts that will be used. In other words, we can find an apparent lack of terminological convergence. At the same time, we come up against the problem that in an expanding literature, some of the authors remain oblivious to the controversies that arise, which are essential for the progress of the research programme and a large part of the advances that can be considered consolidated.

Not long ago, at a meeting where we were discussing research work on the subject, a famous phrase came to mind, uttered amid those more than productive discussions that took place at the London School in the 1930s. At one point, one of those present stood up and shouted: "I'm fed up; we're all talking about the same thing, and we don't even know what we're talking about". In other words, in a research programme such as this one, it is essential to review, compile, and consolidate what we already consider to be accepted by those who participate in it. This is not at all strange; it is to be expected in a transitional stage. As Kuhn (1962) suggested, in a period of change or reconfiguration of a vision of reality or paradigm, the disorder will likely be a particularly relevant problem, and many will even doubt which paradigm is the most profitable, bearing in mind that the others also generate convincing explanations.

In this panorama of ambitious expectations and relative disorder, it is necessary to stop, look back and take stock of the progress made. This is the purpose of the present work, and we believe it could not be timelier. To set out in a unified and systematised way where we have come from, where we have arrived, and what paths remain to be travelled, that is, as the classics in philosophy used to say, someone has to set out the *status quaestionis* to ensure the first steps of those who approach theory.

What is our aim, then? The study of networks of relationships from the contributions of the various proposals can be integrated under the broad and ambiguous name of Social Capital Theory. The option for this theory allows us to consider this socially situated rationality in which individuals integrate social relations, values, and emotions (dimensions of social capital) in their decisions. In other words, it would make it possible to situate the economy socially. In fact, the study of social capital is one of the few bridges that economics opens up to debate with other social sciences, not only sociology but also political science, anthropology and even psychology.

Throughout the text, we will try to analyse the problem of the social nature of the economy, critically review the foundations of the Social Capital Theory, and, in a final section, propose works that analyse specific areas of this interaction between the social and the economic: subjective well-being, inequality, corruption, etc.

Consequently, our project focuses on a critical review of the concept of social capital, one of the most used and least theorised among those canonised by the economic literature. This review also has a propositional part: restructuring the study from a solid micro or individual social capital perspective and studying the positive and negative effects of the existence of social networks.

What can this work contribute to previous critical work? There is already a body of alternative proposals on social capital, much of which was developed at the turn of the century (Baron, Fine, McClellan, etc.). In light of these, our review seeks to be more comprehensive in that we start by situating and taking stock of what the concept has meant vis-à-vis the general problem of embeddedness. In addition, in terms of propositions, our review aims to resituate the link between the programme's two lines of research, micro and macro, prioritising the microfoundations. Finally, we show the multiple faces this research can present when introducing social reality in economic analysis.

Concerning the method we will follow in developing the work, we aim to be both an open introduction to the problems and the existing or possible lines of research. In this sense, given that we are dealing with one of the subjects that shows an infinite number of connections, we wanted each chapter to introduce a Box in which we address questions that, although they do not form part of the core argument of the chapter, deal with connected problems that merit at least some reflection.

1 The structure of this text

The book is divided into three main blocks. In the first block, **The interrelationship between economy and society**, we seek to raise one of the radical problems of the Economy, its deficient incorporation of the social condition of man and how social capital can constitute a proposal for integration.

In the first chapter, **Bringing the social into the economy**, we review the different approaches that address the social roots of the economy. Our starting point is characterising the apparent absence of anthropological realism within the neoclassical current. Subsequently, we aim to contextualise the contributions offered by disciplines such as Economic Sociology, Sociology of Economics, Neoinstitutional Economics, Socioeconomics, and, notably, the Theory of Social Capital. This review will facilitate an evaluation of the current state of knowledge and position Social Capital Theory as a potentially successful response. The latter endeavours to integrate a fundamental sociological notion emphasising human relationality, albeit revisited through an economic lens.

The second chapter, **Social capital: the controversial trajectory of a concept**, looks at the notion of social capital to explain the divergences and inconsistencies we find today, both in definition and measurement. Starting from the first seminal references found in the classics, passing through the first explicit use in Hanifan's work and the explosion of research after the success of Putnam's work, we arrive at two separate and somewhat confrontational approaches that will be analysed in detail in the following section. The explanation of how we have arrived here aims to understand the paths taken and abandoned and to situate ourselves critically before the present.

The second block, **Two conflicting approaches**, focuses exclusively on the two current research programmes, macro and micro, to propose articulating them. This section consists of three chapters.

In Chapter 3, **Complex consensus: the micro, the meso, and the macro**, we address the main problem with social capital theory: the dissociation of micro, meso, and macro approaches. Simply put, the great controversy at the theoretical level is whether social capital should be considered a collective or an individual good. It can be considered from both points of view; because social relations generate effects both at the general level of society as a whole and at the individual level; what is not clear is the articulation between the two. The introduction of the concept of individual social capital, that is, the personal networks of access to resources that individuals possess, is fundamental to articulate the understanding of the theory. Returning to the traditional "Coleman's Boat", macro-theory needs a solid micro-theory. Thus, the variables traditionally used to measure social capital (trust, associative networks, etc.) must be causally linked to individual behaviours and, therefore, to the personal networks constituted by each social actor. This objective leads us to the need to deconstruct the two main approaches in the following chapters.

In Chapter 4, **What is behind macro-social capital?**, we look at the macro approach to social capital. This term serves as an overarching concept encompassing a wide array of elements such as informal organisations, trust, culture, and social and business networks. Its overly flexible nature, characterised by circular reasoning, positions it as an example of a concept where rhetoric often outweighs logical rigour. The fervent and repetitive utilisation of descriptive statistics frequently supplants a thorough examination of the broader impacts that networks and associations can exert on a macro level, impacts which may not necessarily be positive. Simultaneously, networks can function as constraining mechanisms, restricting access for those external to them. Factors such as race, ethnicity, religion, language, friendship, or mere alignment of economic interests frequently underpin many of these exclusions from both market and non-market spheres in the real world.

A punctual review of each of its characteristics will allow us to distinguish what is salvageable in the concept while at the same time showing how it is an attempt to gain conviction from a bad analogy.

Chapter 5, **Personal networks as capital: individual social capital**, is central to the book and aims to propose the micro approach to network analysis as the starting point to base Social Capital Theory. Our perspective is not a Social Network Analysis but a neocapital approach. Individual social capital is the set of personal attributes and access networks that enable individuals to achieve market and non-market goals resulting from interaction with other individuals. In other words, individual social capital is the network of relationships available to a given individual, and its value lies in the resources that can be extracted from them. As with human or cultural capital, its status as capital lies in analogical reasoning; it is a personal investment and a form of capitalisation. This opens up a new line of research and can provide a solid basis for macro analysis. The centrality of personal networks at the individual level is evident. Not only are they opportunities for advantageous access to resources and privileged information flow channels. They also generate interdependence of utility functions between individuals and selective influence on the preferences and welfare of others, consequently facilitating social trust. Returning to the methodological argument proposed in the "Coleman boat", individual social capital constitutes the micro mechanism underlying the generation of macro social capital.

Once the analytical framework for the study of social networks has been delimited, in the third section, **Constructing from individual social capital**, we propose a set of studies with macro derivations that are based on this micro approach. These chapters address some of the multiple effects, not always positive, that derive from this investment in social networks. Specifically, we will focus on three aspects: social inequality, corruption and, finally, individual well-being.

This section is distinctly forward-looking in its orientation. We put forth a set of research initiatives to scrutinise diverse facets of social capital through a micro-level lens. Contrary to the simplistic macro perspective, these facets may not always yield positive or socially beneficial outcomes. For instance, we will delve into topics such as inequality and corruption. On a more positive note, we suggest exploring the realm of happiness economics by applying the concept of relational goods. Drawing on the authors' prior scholarship, these chapters exemplify the essential methodological recalibration social capital theory requires.

In the sixth chapter, **Inequality, homophily and individual social capital**, this individual endowment of social networks interacts with the social structure and contributes to the reproduction of inequality. Individuals, like classes, are not only distinguished by their level of wealth but also by the social characteristics that facilitate the monopolisation of social opportunities through social networks. However, this is arguably the least studied of the three forms of capital (economic, human, and cultural) despite being vital to understanding class relations. Analysis of this particular form of inequality requires consideration of both the institutional context and individual determinants: inherited inequality, inequality arising from personal investment processes in which expected returns are decisive, and the interrelationship with other expressions of capital. If these factors are linked, inequalities replicate themselves and worsen generation after generation in a kind of Matthew effect.

Within this study of the not-always-positive manifestations of social capital, the analysis of the social backgrounds supporting corruption refers specifically to negative social capital. Chapter 7, **Is there a negative social capital? Social capital and corruption**, is devoted to studying the relationship between some expressions of social capital, which we will call particularistic, and the corruption problem. Although there is convergence on the effects of corruption in terms of growth costs, the controversy over causality persists insofar as this analysis requires an approximation to cultural and institutional variables, factors that reflect a specific prior configuration of society and which are difficult to alter through political actions.

The causality between social capital and corruption is not self-evident. Unlike the institutionalist approach, whose methodology focuses on the cost-benefit calculations for the individual, from a social capital perspective, it is not sufficient to consider corruption as the exclusive result of an inadequate organisational and institutional framework. Institutionalist approaches suffer from a particular weakness as they do not consider the socio-economic contexts in which transactions occur. The culture and values shared by individuals, as well as the social networks in which they are embedded, influence behaviour, the functioning of the economy, and their own institutional and legal foundations. Evidence shows that individuals develop corrupt attitudes and practices conditioned by the broader socio-economic environment and are linked to particularistic forms of social capital or familism, that is, a poor integration between the micro and the macro.

In societies with strong ties to close groups, the expectation that all that is official will be impartial in applying the rule is non-existent, making the Weberian claim of a technical bureaucracy unfeasible.

Finally, to end the book with a distinctly positive consequence, Chapter 8, **Well-being and relational goods. The intrinsic value of social relations**, studies the influence of personal social networks on subjective well-being.

The social essence of humanity necessitates the differentiation between two categories of needs: acquisitive and expressive. Acquisitive needs pertain to purely material aspects and are fulfilled through the consumption of market goods, thus inherently linked to income. Conversely, expressive needs involve the recognition of our identity, requiring communication or interaction with others for fulfilment. Therefore, it is imperative to reassess the conventional classification of economic goods. Traditionally, based on the potential for exclusion, goods are categorised as private, public, and club goods; however, relational goods constitute a distinct category with a unique production function. Relational goods emerge from personal interactions generated through interpersonal connections to satisfy expressive social needs such as belonging, recognition, and personal development. Unlike other types of goods, their valuation necessitates the existence of an interdependent utility function.

In this context, it is essential to highlight that economic literature, in addition to factors such as individual health, family environment, employment status, and age, considers social capital and relational goods as significant socio-economic determinants influencing individuals' happiness. Building upon this foundation, this chapter delves into the impact of individual social capital on individuals' subjective well-being facilitated through relational goods. Specifically, it examines the paradoxes in the relationship between income and subjective well-being and the role played by the stock of personal relations.

Overall, and through an initial presentation, we propose a critical review of the capacity of Social Capital Theory to introduce realism into the social character of the economy. We encourage the reader to enter the debate and, if convinced by the argument, move on to studying the link between networks and micro and macro effects.

Part I

The interrelationship between economy and society

1 Bringing the social into the economy

> She was like everyone else, a congeries of contradictions and inconsistencies, but obedient to the general expectation of what a girl of her position must and must not be.
>
> (Howells, 1890)

This brief quotation, which we came across when we began writing this chapter, seems to be a valuable introduction to the problem we will study. It belongs to a literary work centred on social critique and includes two key ideas: the complexity of human beings, a set of contradictions that are difficult to rationalise, and their essentially social constitution, a society that conditions what we should and should not be, what a person desires or should desire and where they stand in the social fabric. Both realities are pending subjects in economics.

Among the most common criticisms of economics is the accusation of irrelevance regarding "real problems". Usually, when these are intertwined with anthropological, social, and political facts, economics opts for a double alternative: either it analyses them from an individualistic methodological approach, or it qualifies these dimensions as irrelevant from an economic point of view. The consequences of both options are apparent. On the one hand, it will give rise to a notable methodological imperialism in the study of aspects that should be interdisciplinary; on the other hand, it will generate an evident isolationism concerning the other social sciences. In this chapter, we will critically review the economic way of understanding human behaviour and the various proposals for the "integration" of the social condition. We intend to answer three questions: What is the root of the problem of integrating the social dimension of man into economics? How has the mainstream dealt with prosocial behaviour? What attempts have been made to incorporate the social and economic dimensions?

1 The original sin of economics: an unsociable social science

The fact is that economic theory, with honourable exceptions that we will discuss later, does not do justice to the cultural and historical dimensions of its subject matter. In particular, the *mainstream* that we usually identify with neoclassical economics has replaced a study of the complexity of human nature with the analysis

DOI: 10.4324/9781003375302-3

of a simple and powerful imaginary that we call *homo oeconomicus*.[1] This generalised orientation is limited to addressing the functional logic of the market system and presents itself as a pure, value-neutral explanation of the interactions between individuals. However, the anthropological assumptions it is based on are either untested or contradict evidence from other social sciences (Hausman & McPherson, 2007; Aktipis & Kurzban, 2005).

1.1 The individual vis-à-vis society

The ultimate root of the problem lies in adopting a methodological individualism intending to establish a society based on a self-ordered balance of "egoisms". Under these circumstances, actors do not need to be aware of the social and ethical dimensions of human interactions, or at least these are dispensable in the analysis. However, as emphasised by the substantivist orientations (see Box 1.1), mere observation in everyday experience leads us to affirm that the proper object of economics is a complex social practice mediated or preceded by social relations in which values, norms and institutions are involved. In other words, it cannot be understood as context-free or value-neutral. Society sets the goals and establishes the accepted ways of achieving them.

This imaginary that lies at the basis of the deductive construct of economics is related to a particular conception of rationality. As H. Simon (González, 2004) has noted, there is a fascination with the theory of expected utility immune to divergent evidence. If we understand that the intelligent search for appropriate ends primarily characterises rationality, the notion of rationality in economics is limited to instrumental or practical aspects, abandoning the evaluative ones. Instrumental rationality seeks to maximise expected subjective utility, but it is alien to the rationality of ends or evaluative rationality. Open discussions are only from the point of view of means since the ends are considered given. Thus, values such as solidarity, equity, and justice are relegated to optimising choices based on anticipating consequences (pleasure or pain) for the chooser. In other words, an individual will only be altruistic to the extent that they foresee the pleasure or pain of others and is affected by it (Simon, 1993).

Alongside this, there is another problem: the autonomy of individual preferences. All choices concerning oneself and others depend solely and exclusively on maximising personal preferences. However, we encounter many phenomena that lead us to think that preferences are not so free and autonomous but maybe "socially" or "culturally" determined, as our opening quotation suggests. In this way, the contributions of other behavioural disciplines, particularly psychology, sociology, and anthropology, are systematically abandoned to make the explanatory models more consistent. The notion of preferences is integrated from moral opinions to culinary tastes to become the real "deus ex machina" of the theory. We talk about preferences rather than about how they are formed.

Consequently, *homo oeconomicus* could be caricature-like, defined as an optimiser, unthinking in terms of ends and materialistic. From a social point of view, he would be devoid of any group identification and is oblivious to the welfare of others. She or he is a rational being in the instrumental sense, possessing a fully ordered set of preferences, perfect information, immaculate calculative ability, and seeking to maximise utility. This man is defined as a kind of "*bargain hunter*" (Sen, 1985), and society merely provides a framework for individual action.

The defence of this initial methodological option held by economics usually has a twofold orientation. On the one hand, in Friedman's (1953) traditional response, economics considers irrelevant that these assumptions conform to reality as long as they provide plausible explanations. That is, *homo oeconomicus* would be a parsimoniously functional representation that generates a set of testable results. On the other hand, systematically, in the face of any dissonance, ad hoc hypotheses are introduced in the form of specific assumptions about the limits of rationality or information capacity that alter the explanatory capacities of the models (Simon, 2000).

However, this problem of bias is not exclusive to neoclassical economics. The so-called "critical" orientations opt for anthropological simplifications of a different sign (Cason, 1990). Thus, in the Marxist tradition, individuals are determined to act under a social position delimited by the ownership of the means of production, constituting the framework of the class struggle. Institutionalists, on the other hand, deny the existence of real alternatives; the subjects' behaviour is essentially inertial and tends to repeat the previous choices. In both cases, as opposed to a maximisation process from given ends, we would find ourselves with the option for a cultural and social pre-programming of economic behaviour.

To sum up, we could make three statements that call into question the realism of this anthropological simplification.

i. First, the presupposition of "selfishness" is unacceptable. While it may be true that human beings pursue their self-interest, the critical question is to what extent self-interest is their primary concern. From the point of view of cognitive development, established theories in the field of behavioural sciences, such as the Wilber life cycle, the seven stages of moral development of Piaget and Kohlberg, or the better-known Maslow's hierarchy of needs, show the existence of temporal evolution in man's models of practical rationality and his priorities, which go beyond the narrow individualistic view. These theories, which are at the basis of studies on the evolution of value priorities, recognise a process of human development from pre-personal (self-centred) stages, in Wilber's terminology, in which the priority concern is the satisfaction of basic elementary needs (physiological, security, etc.) to transpersonal stages, in which priority is given to recognition and even to transcendent dimensions (Wilber, 1996; Bowles, 2016).

   Even experiments based on game theory show that individuals can behave altruistically in simple or one-shot games. This is the case of the work on the well-known "prisoner's dilemma". In theory, we are in a non-cooperative game, so players cannot make commitments in a pre-game negotiation, nor could they agree that nothing obliges them; however, despite the biased presentation of the game itself when it is proposed experimentally, cooperative results are overwhelmingly in the majority of cases. In these, out of sympathy and without communication, players choose not to harm the opponent even though the game induces them to think in their own interest (Sally, 1995).

   In this sense, Nowak & Highfield (2012) goes so far as to assert that human emotional responses have been shaped by thousands of years of living together in small-scale societies and groups. They argue that our interactions never constitute anonymous interactions. In short, humans cannot be understood apart from their familiar and communal human environment, even in a supposedly "impersonal" marketplace.

ii. Human rationality is far from its supposedly mechanistic character. For example, we should consider the existence of costs and limits to this ability to calculate, psychological and emotional influences, and the inescapable need for social acceptance (Brzezicka & Wisniewski, 2014; Urbina & Ruiz-Villaverde, 2019).

   As highlighted by *Behavioural Decision Theory* (Camerer, 1997; Etzioni, 2011), we can speak of two modes of rationality. There is the experimental, intuitive, automatic, and natural mode, centred on images to which positive or negative feelings are associated through processes of learning or experience. This is an *affective heuristic* in which individuals intuitively make judgements and decisions. This form of reasoning seems to be linked to most common behavioural environments, is intuitive, and is particularly suited to responding to situations where experience enables us to anticipate a particular decision's pleasant or unpleasant outcomes. Logically, this mode of reasoning fails when outcomes cannot be anticipated based on previous experience. This leads us to a second mode of rationality, analytical rationality, which neoclassical economics tries to generalise. This is based on a logical process of decisions and evaluations oriented towards a more delayed action. However, this may be exceptional since most decisions are associated with compliance with rules or the execution of routines (Slovic et al., 2002).

iii. The supposedly unreflective nature of *homo oeconomicus* is easily falsifiable. All forms of socialisation entail a process of internalisation of moral, religious, and social values, which translates into a capacity to interpret the goodness or badness of choices, that is to say, the emergence of evaluative rationality. Moreover, as anthropology has shown, social motivations can be broader than individual interests, and consequently, the production and distribution processes are linked to socially fixed interests. "Man does not act to safeguard his interest in the possession of material goods; he acts to safeguard his social position, his social claims, his social goods" (Polanyi, 1977, p. 6).

In conclusion, in Maslow's words, economics as a science is the skilful, exact, and technological application of a false theory of human needs and values. This theory only recognises material and lower-order needs (Maslow, 1954).

Acknowledging this array of criticisms does not entail disregarding the existence of behaviours where both producer and consumer subjects strive to maximise their interests without considering non-instrumental aspects (Sen, 1977, p. 330). However, it underscores the interconnectedness between the social and institutional context and its economic implications, and vice versa. In any economic interaction, elements such as commitment, ethics, morality, and relationality play pivotal roles; they constitute inherent components of economic relationships, even an *a priori* of these relations. This holds true for scenarios involving public goods, familial obligations, business ethics, community engagement, etc. Moreover, the tendency to generalise this perspective can lead to detrimental effects on the comprehension of society and social institutions, including the market. As pointed out by Etzioni (1988), this viewpoint is deeply entrenched not only within the economic sphere but also in social behaviour and the pursuit of individual interest characteristic of *homo oeconomicus* seemingly entrenched in contemporary lifestyle. The widespread acceptance of this mindset as a guiding principle for doctrine and behaviour undermines the sustainability of the market economy itself.

To specify one of the aspects that will concern us for a large part of the remainder of this text, an immediate question arises: Where are prosocial behaviours to be found? Under this generic denomination, we refer to all those behaviours in which an individual acts to benefit others, not themself, that is, those that build community. Altruism, cooperation, and caring are some examples of prosocial behaviour. These are central to our understanding of morality insofar as interpersonal morality mainly involves giving weight to the interests and desires of others in situations where our interests may conflict (Batson, 2011; Sandel, 2013).

1.2 The general equilibrium versus society

Behind this clear bias in understanding human action lies an ideologised vision embodied in the general equilibrium. This general framework does not emerge from a vacuum. Economics, as a science rooted in the Enlightenment period, participates in the whole movement for individualism and in the defence of the establishment of a body of fundamental and inalienable freedoms. By understanding the universe as an interrelated whole and in equilibrium with opposing forces, the Newtonian revolution laid the foundations of the mechanistic paradigm on which the neoclassical methodology in economics is based. Ultimately, the Smithian "Invisible Hand", reinterpreted through the mathematisation of utilitarianism, is the idea underlying the theoretical construct (Skidelsky, 2009).

With the demonstration of general equilibrium (Arrow & Debreu, 1954), formal logic was strengthened in modelling the economy at the micro and macro levels. It is a parsimonious description of an economy with private property as a system in which rational agents move as atoms beyond any social determinants. Because of the completeness of markets, prices will reflect the information available, and uncertainty is zero.

The theoretical elegance of the concept has some essential flaws. Without going into all those related to rationality and the absence of information, for general equilibrium to be efficient, all coordination must be carried out through markets, which introduces substantial restrictions. When these conditions are not satisfied – for example, in the face of a simple externality problem – the system would not be valid, implying that general equilibrium only applies to private goods, not public goods. Similarly, general equilibrium requires that each individual's utility is only affected by their consumption. If individuals have their utility function affected by that of other individuals, the basic assumptions of the system would be destroyed.

If we introduce the existence of "sociality", "solidarity", or "identity", the whole system is compromised.

Today, 70 years later, after considerable theoretical developments, we speak of stochastic dynamic general equilibrium models. Although considerably more sophisticated, they still rely on the same assumptions. As Colander et al. (2004) points out, the economic model relies on three fundamental pillars: rationality, selfishness, and equilibrium. The assumption of an individual, an asocial agent guided by bounded rationality, which must be provided with perfect information, remains indispensable.

This shortcoming carries over into all areas of conventional economic theory, where the main orientations seek alternatives to general equilibrium models. The most prominent case is development economics, which has a persistent difficulty in explaining inter-regional differences in living standards and growth rates. Income disparities are hardly exclusively a product of factor endowments and technological mastery, as factors such as inequalities, dependencies, culture, ethics, religion, etc., play an equally crucial role (Woolcock & Narayan, 2000) (see Box 3.1).

Without wanting to get bogged down in the broad and endless debates in the philosophy of science, we think we can make a brief foray into the proposal of **Critical Realism**. The fundamental question applicable to the generalisation of this type of model is simple: to what extent can a society be studied like nature or physics? Critical realism opts for a return to ontology to stress that the nature of objects determines cognitive possibilities so that the world of the social cannot be studied like that of physical objects (Lawson, 1997, 2003; Scott & Usher, 2011). This different ontology leads them to propose the distinction between open and closed systems. Like society, the economy is an "open system", but orthodox theory treats it as a "closed" system. Societies are not a mere sum of isolated "atomic" individuals, so methodological individualism makes no sense. Moreover, these individuals are not optimisers but operate on socially generated beliefs or desires. Thus, human behaviour opens up new possibilities by constantly breaking the closed nature of the system. For Lawson (2003), only isolated closed systems, such as those used in physics, admit mathematically expressible nomological regularities, such as "whenever event x then event y". This is an enormous criticism of the construction of economics as a science since not even a progressive introduction of perspectives from other social sciences or a change in some assumptions would be enough to generate socially realistic economics.

Social reality is an undetermined "open system" where events are influenced by multiple mechanisms of different strata, where there are no stable regularities or constant conjunctions of events (Bhaskar, 1998; Lawson 1997, pp. 27–28). Thus, from an ontological point of view, the regularities that economists seek do not exist (Lawson, 1999, p. 221), but only semi-regularities, non-universal tendencies caused by the interplay of multiple layers. Multiple variables interfere with causality and co-determine outcomes (Lawson, 1997, p. 204). Then, the much-ironised predictive failure of economics results from unpredictable structural changes that take place outside the purely economic strata.

Under these circumstances, the researcher, aware of the multiple variables that influence social behaviour, cannot deductively prioritise dimensions to focus his enquiry but resorts to Pearce`s abduction. The interpretation of the data described and the unveiling of causal explanations, where all the socioeconomic conditioning factors that may underlie a semi-regularity come into play (Sayer, 2000).

2 Sympathy and attempts to introduce prosociality in economics

As my old logic professor used to say, "Universal general statements are the martyrdom of communities". The above could be unfair if we do not simultaneously recognise economics's attempts to introduce prosociality into its analysis. We will do so by returning to the origins and retracing the path of the concept of sympathy since this has been the privileged way to solve this initial deficiency.

2.1 Sin does not come from Adam, at least in economics

It may come as a surprise that the early stages of economics as a science were particularly sensitive to the social dimension of economics. The current rethinking of the so-called "Smithian problem" may be illuminating in this respect. It is a controversy with a long tradition in the "confrontation" between ethics and economics. Throughout the 19th century and especially among German authors, the apparent contradiction between Smith's main statements in his moral work ("The Theory of Moral Sentiments") and his economic work ("The Wealth of Nations") was highlighted. A contradiction that Smith had never considered. The controversy has survived to the present day, to the point of being given its name in German, "Das A. Smith problem".

To illustrate the root of the problem, we can take the two most celebrated quotations from both works. At the beginning of the first one, we can read:

> How selfish soever man may be supposed, there are evidently some principles in his nature, which interest him in the fortune of others, and render their happiness necessary to him, though he derives nothing from it except the pleasure of seeing it.
>
> (TMS, I, 1)

At the same time, in the most quoted fragment of The Wealth of Nations, it is stated: "It is not from the benevolence of the butcher, the brewer or the baker that we expect our supper (…) but from their particular interest" (WN, I, 2).

The first quotation seems to affirm the existence of a natural tendency to prosociality in man, which could contradict the essential character given to self-interest in the second. However, for the most recent studies on the Das A. Smith Problem (Pena-López & Sánchez-Santos, 2008), Smithian thought constitutes a perfectly articulated whole between morality and economics. Both works are based on what we could call "moral psychology", an analysis of the determinant motivations for action that encompasses aspects that today would be the subject of sociology, economics, or political science.

The key point lies in the classical concept of moral sentiments. Men are not islands, so individual action is not exclusively influenced by self-interest but by moral judgements, social relations, and institutions. Among these, Smith pays particular attention to sympathy, that is, how the well-being of individuals is affected by the situation of others.

The importance of this concept in his work is crucial, but in its articulation with economics, it gives rise to two interpretations. It could be a limiting framework of self-interest, an environment of proximity for each individual in which relationships are of interdependence or community (the extended family, etc.), which would mean accepting that personal relationships and morality are relegated to the non-market (Nieli, 1986). However, according to the most recent interpretations, Smith does not make this distinction; he considers sympathy a common and universal bond in varying degrees in any relationship mode. From this perspective, self-interest and sympathy bonds operate simultaneously in individual actions.

Important additional implications can be derived from the notion of sympathy, such as, for example, the emergence of feelings of belonging, identity, or community (Sugden, 2002; Anderson, 2001), which could hardly be incorporated into the formal models used in the framework of rational choice. Human social life is articulated through the exchange of feelings of correspondence, which can shape collective reasoning in which individuals operate as if they were a single agent, plural subject or groupthink (we rationality). Moreover, for Smith, individuals are not only economically dependent on the division of labour but also psychologically dependent. Through sympathy, the situation of others impacts the agent's decision-making process since their welfare affects their own.

Thus, Smith considers the role of emotions as evaluative judgements about issues that affect the well-being of individuals, which brings him closer to proposals such as those of M. Nussbaum (2001). Additionally, in strictly economic terms, sympathy contributes to the search for mutually beneficial agreements and enhances the division of labour. In other words, exchanges are based on man's communicative capacity. Consequently, morality constitutes a pre-coordination system or a basis of elementary sociality on which market coordination is based (Young, 1997).

The aforementioned Smithian notion of sympathy makes it possible, on the one hand, to correct the traditional paradigm in economics and, on the other, to interweave ethics and prosocial behaviour with self-interest. Economic behaviour is a complex decision-making process in which cultural, moral, and psychological aspects are intertwined. Like Zelizer's proposal (2007), it is a fluid mixture of elements rather than a restriction of economic processes. The evidence of economic relations, from labour relations to the simple commodity exchange, presupposes the existence of underlying personal relations and, in these, some form of sympathy and commitment, a socioeconomic rationality.

2.2 *Sympathy and neoclassical economics*

The neoclassical tradition has tried to introduce prosocial behaviours into its analysis using the concept of sympathy. The idea is straightforward: Altruism and prosociality, those behaviours that build community (families, clubs, etc.), are reflected as an interaction of utility functions or interdependent utility. The first milestone in this simplification is undoubtedly the work of Edgeworth (1967; Collard, 1975). For this author, a more adjusted expression for individual utility should consider the participation of the other's utility in one's own so that the expression that seeks to be maximised would be like this $P + \lambda\Pi$, where P is individual utility, λ is a coefficient of sympathy and Π is other's or group utility. In two individuals' agreement, for example, by mutually incorporating each other's utility into one's own utility, the contract curve would undergo a shift (shrinking theorem), reducing the range of possible outcomes as the coefficient of sympathy widens. This way, mutual sympathy facilitates a social system of pre-coordination.

This suggests that the analysis of impersonal markets differs from the analysis of exchanges in which there is a relationship of closeness between agents or a sense of community, what Edgeworth calls "domestic contracts". In a way, he anticipates the interrelationship between subjects in a bargain to reduce transaction costs. In short, from his perspective, altruism and any form of prosociality are explained by extended egoism without penetrating the nature and meaning of social relations. From the 1970s onwards, an essential body of work appeared that took advantage of the concept of sympathy to introduce "realism" into the models. We can group these works into three trends within the economic orthodoxy (Khalil, 2004): egocentric, egoistic and altercentric (Table 1.1).

The first is the purest neoclassical approach, in which prosocial behaviour is fully compatible with interdependent utility maximisation. To give a simple example, a donation will only be made if the satisfaction generated by the contemplation of utility in the recipient exceeds at the margin the satisfaction derived from individual consumption (Becker, 1974; Kurz, 1978). Although the theoretical derivations of this approach are not irrelevant, it should at least be qualified as remarkably simplistic since it does not move beyond the assumptions of *homo oeconomicus*. In addition, it cannot explain a considerable number of everyday situations: donations without a direct relationship with others, following a rule without the possibility of punishment, contributing to a public good, and, what is more, what happens when this prosocial act directly entails disutility.

The egoistic or reciprocal altruism approach proposes a way of reasoning that selects optimal behaviour at the group level. For example, we can find it in works such as those of Andreoni (1990) and generally in those linked to Game Theory. Prosociality and altruism, in this case, are the product of a long-term strategy oriented towards future benefits in infinitely repeated games. In this sense, the more accurate term would be "calculative altruism". Agents make donations to build a helpful reputation and induce the *donee* to return the goods received. For example, if we consider the problem of contributions to a public good or the acquisition of some

Table 1.1 Main lines of study of altruism in economics

Egocentric	*Giving and cooperation are based on self-centred feelings.*	*G. Becker, O. Stark*
Egoistic	Donation and cooperation as a means of ensuring cooperative responses.	R. Axelrod, Andreoni
Altercentric	Donation and cooperation are based on respect for moral standards.	A. Etzioni, A. Sen. R. Sugden, S. Zamagni

Source: Own elaboration based on E. L. Khalil (2004).

form of moral or personal satisfaction with a donation, this would be produced by the expectation of future benefits.

In terms of game theory, we can find a natural tendency towards cooperation if we observe repeated interactions in "prisoner's dilemma" type games. Agents seek the satisfaction of feeling in accord with their conscience, but they expect future retribution because of this gained reputation (Sally, 1995). Although the concept is suggestive, there is a problem of *petitio principii* in this type of argumentation. If, as Andreoni assumes, individuals perform acts of donation or carry out moral actions in the search for moral satisfaction, this presupposes the existence of prior value scales in the same sense. Consequently, it is not the warm glow that causes the prosocial action but a prior valuation process.

Both proposals fall within the economic orthodoxy. What is truly ironic about both perspectives on prosociality is that they renounce theories of altruism insofar as they do not consider individuals intrinsically motivated by concern for the welfare of others (Fontaine, 2000). If we stroll outside the neoclassical orthodoxy, we will find other altercentric proposals that bring together some ideas that we will study later.

In socioeconomics, the works that adopt a communitarian approach, such as those of A. Etzioni, recognise the weight of moral imperatives in human behaviour. The peculiarity of this argument lies in the fact that the actual prosocial act is not interested in the other in itself but in respecting a specific ethical model that works with the exact mechanisms of the Kantian categorical imperative. In fact, it is formal altruism and ethics "without the other". In an intermediate line is the position of A. K. Sen (1977), clearly Smithian in terms of incorporating sympathy in his argumentation but emphasising acts of duty or commitment.

Similarly, we can find an entirely altruistic or prosocial approach that recognises the importance of gratuitousness in the so-called "Economy of Communion". This perspective holds that an individual is capable of sympathy by his psychological constitution; he can distance himself from his situation and place himself in that of another without abandoning his individual interest. A subject with these characteristics can share his resources with others, even in single-spot transactions. Among the works along these lines, those of Sacco and Zamagni (2002) on the complexity of human relations as a basis for analysing economic behaviour are noteworthy. Some contributions from experimental economics, especially the psychology of economics, provide support in this sense. Its review of the realism of assumptions about rationality in economics has shown the relevance of aspects not considered, such as group membership (Henrich et al., 2001). Within this field, there is also a line of work on analysing prosocial behaviour and its incidence on the valuation of public goods, etc. In this sense, Kahneman's contributions on sympathy and its implications in contingent valuation (Kahneman & Netsch, 1992) are of enormous importance.

Box 1.1 Formalism versus substantivism, or both

There are various ways of expressing the dialectic that underlies the construction of economics as a science in a simplified way. For instance, one could construct a map to position existing economic stances based on ideological spectrums (such as liberalism vs interventionism) or accepted methodological frameworks (like Austrian deductivism vs neoclassical formalism). Nonetheless, let us delve into the ultimate foundations. The dichotomy between formalism and substantivism delineates the study of economics at its most fundamental level, serving as a primary cause for its divergence from other social sciences.

Formalism, embodied in neoclassical theory, portrays economics as a calculation technique or optimisation of means and ends. In contrast, substantivism, embodied mainly in anthropology, contends that economics deals with a group or community's material aspects, connection to the environment, and provision for subsistence. Transposing these definitions to the social sphere, neoclassical economics conceptualises society as a collection of numerous "Robinson Crusoe" in a market. Substantivism challenges the omnipresence of the market by highlighting it as just one of many relatively recent successful organisational forms.

Distilling the defining characteristics of each proposal, we can approach them akin to the scholastics, discerning what they study (the formal object *quod*) and how they study it (the formal object *quo*).

Considering what they study, the substantive perspective regards the economy not as an isolated entity but as intricately intertwined within socio-cultural contexts, forming a part of a more extensive interconnected web. Conversely, formalism adopts a narrower approach, delineating economics focusing on "rational" decision-making to resolve economic issues or scarcity.

Examining how they are studied, the choice of object conditions the response. Formalism employs a deductive and logical approach, emphasising maximising rationality in making "economic" decisions concerning scarce resources. Substantivism, on the other hand, relies on a descriptive approach grounded in experience, focusing on typifying and studying various interactions among social, environmental, and economic factors in satisfying needs. Undoubtedly, the latter presents a more comprehensive vision, commencing with studying any society to analyse exchange and distribution processes without the preconceived notions inherent in defining a form of rationality.

Both options entail consequences and costs, significantly influencing the understanding of economics as a social science, how humanity is conceived within this realm, and which method is employed.

Formalism relinquishes any holistic or humanistic aspirations of social science to enforce a market society's behavioural norm as universal. As Polanyi argued, it is impossible to grasp human society and history from the formal perspective of neoclassical economics, as "reducing the economic specifically to market phenomena eliminates most of human history from the picture" (Polanyi, 1977, p. 6). By analysing a concrete society without theoretical biases, one finds exchange forms not driven solely by maximisation but somewhat socially motivated (such as within family or community contexts). Moreover, formalism promotes an individualistic view of humanity, positing society as a collection of individuals making choices (Godelier, 1984, p. 113).

In contrast, substantivism asserts that all economic activity is institutional. Thus, individual choice calculations are not solely based on economic profit or loss but encompass social, political, and moral considerations (Plattner, 1991, p. 33). As articulated in *The Great Transformation,*

> The human economy is immersed in social relations. People act not only to safeguard individual interests in material possessions but also social positions, rights, and assets. Material goods are only relevant if they serve this purpose (…) Non-economic motivations govern the economic system.
>
> (Polanyi, 1968 [1944], p. 56)

Formalism's assumptions about humanity are ideological and fail to recognise that human needs emerge within social interaction. However, this theoretical option, which fosters multidisciplinarity and grants culture a central role, results in explanatory proposals that often stagnate at relativistic descriptions. Ultimately, these two approaches stand diametrically apart on epistemological grounds, rendering the problem seemingly irresolvable.

Nonetheless, while rationalisation logic may not be universally present, we can find a way of convergence. Empirical research reveals a general logic of exchange even in the absence of markets. As Marcel Mauss (1977) emphasised, individuals engage in economic activity not solely to exchange goods and wealth but also courtesies, entertainment, rituals, and military assistance, where the market is just one element.

The underlying challenge lies in dichotomising economic praxis into two compartments: socially isolated individual rational calculations and "institutional constraints" (Winthrop, 1991, p. 89; Monteiro & Lima, 2021).

As with all dualisms, the problem is resolved in a dialectic that does not favour either extreme but acknowledges their capacity for mutual transformation. Economic practice involves a constant interplay between social arrangements and individual decisions closely linked to optimising subjective well-being (Graeber, 2001). It will leverage the comprehensive concept of social capital to explore bidirectionally how relational networks and their underlying values influence economic operations (e.g., transaction costs) and, conversely, how the economy shapes the evolution of these networks (e.g., stratification) and society itself (e.g., the commodification of social relations). This concept becomes central to the analysis, albeit with limitations arising from "misuses".

3 The forms of interrelation between economics and sociology

The problem of economics' unsociability that we have been addressing leads us to the problem of the interrelation between economics and sociology. Suppose we start from the assumption that economic interrelations are also social interactions. In that case, we need to delimit the specificity of economics to define what is inside and outside the sphere of economics.

There are many reasons to be suspicious. The commonly addressed argument that market forces acquire self-regulatory autonomy apart from the intentions and actions of agents lacks substance. Ultimately, market forces depend on non-market forms of coordination, and they are social in the broadest sense of the word (Hodgson, 2001; Anderson, 1993; Sayer, 2004). More generally, every economic action is a social action because it cannot be separated from the search for approval, status, sociability, and power (Swedberg & Granovetter, 1992), and every subject is a social and economic agent who interacts with others through socially constructed symbols. Thus, for example, how a subject chooses a particular job, sets his social aspirations, determines his consumption or savings, etc., depends on his environment and the influence he perceives from those who constitute his reference.

Among the pioneers, Durkheim (1984 [1893]) pointed out that pure economic action fails to bind people together beyond a single moment in time. A society is not a myriad of juxtaposed atoms with transitory contacts. Still, the members are bound together by ties that extend beyond the moment of exchange. In the same vein, Weber (1994 [1905]) will precisely describe the problem. The economic behaviour of individuals cannot be analysed in isolation. Each subject takes into consideration the behaviour of others through meanings originating in society (Weber, 1993 [1922]). Moreover, economic action is not comprehensible if we disregard that it is the primary source of social power, and even monetary value is social.

This issue is particularly controversial because as we open the lens, we realise that "everything" social, from customs to social norms, affects the economy and vice versa. To give two examples as food for thought:

i. *Interpersonal relationships within and outside the economic sphere can affect economic performance.* Effective interpersonal relationships among economic agents are crucial in reducing transaction costs and facilitating interactions at both macro and micro levels. At the macro level, cooperative habits contribute to improved resource management within communities (Ostrom, 1990, ch. 6). Strong social networks offer material and emotional support for entrepreneurial initiatives (Allen et al., 2000) while trusting attitudes among citizens can foster accelerated economic growth (Zak & Knack, 2001). On the micro-social level, inadequate management of interpersonal relationships negatively impacts organisational productivity and performance (Anderson & Jap, 2005). Conversely, economic decisions can influence interpersonal relationships (Gibbons, 1998). Working conditions, labour mobility, and consumption patterns significantly shape individuals' development of social networks. For instance, the literature emphasises that the lack of job and residential stability directly hampers the formation of long-term relationships (Folbre & Nelson, 2000).

ii. *Interpersonal relationships within and outside the economic sphere affect subjective well-being* more than the "materialistic" view of economics supposes (Flap & Volker, 2001). Subjects incorporate social, relational, and status variables into their well-being function. In other words, man is a consumer of social relations and participates in their production, even conflicting with economic production (Gui & Sugden, 2005).

Despite the evidence of interrelation, this neglect of relationality has led to a mutual misunderstanding between economics and sociology, parallel to formalisation. However, being objective, this problem extends to sociology itself. What is surprising is that the abandonment of the relational was not exclusive to economics. Thus, during the last decade of the 20th century, we witnessed a relational turn in sociology since the publication of the "Manifesto for Relational Sociology" (Emirbayer, 1997). This argued that the basic unit of analysis in sociology should not be individuals or macro-level institutions but rather the social relations between actors (Dépelteau & Powell, 2013).

To systematise the attitudes of both social sciences towards this problem, we could speak of two large groups of responses: Those who consider that there is no room for any intersection insofar as they are incompatible ways of interpreting the same phenomena and those who consider that there is a point of intersection where there is room for common ground to varying degrees.

For those who consider these separate spheres, we start from the assumption that there are different spheres for rational economic activity and personal relations. The sphere of calculation and efficiency and the sphere of relationality. For these hostile worlds, there is no room for interrelation, nor for the disorder generated by studying the social with methodological individualism or introducing the more qualitative sociological methodology into economic analysis. This view of separate spheres ultimately considers that economic activities follow their laws and the social is, at most, a constraint on economic decision-making processes.

Turning now attention to those who accept the **existence of common ground,** these are not a consolidated group. Zelizer (2007) points out that we can distinguish at least two "attitudes" with different and even opposite outcomes: **extension and context** (see Figure 1.1).

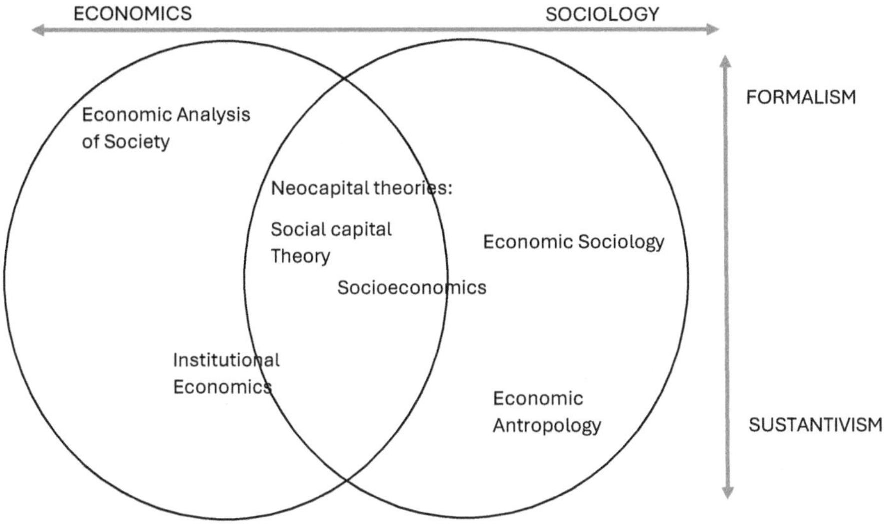

Figure 1.1 The interrelationship between economics and sociology.

Source: Own elaboration.

3.1 Extension: the imperialism of economics and sociology

Here, we mean forms of bilateral imperialism – the extension of the methodology of economics to social facts and the purely sociological analysis of economic facts. Reductionism can occur on both sides:

From the point of view of economics, the social and the relational (personal networks, friendship, solidarity, etc.) would be understandable within the framework of Rational Choice of Neoclassical Economics. This is the case of the *Economic Analysis of Social Facts.* This is the pure expression of what we criticised in the first section: the use of economics methodology in any societal decision-making (Maki, 2000, p. 13; Hechter & Kanazawa, 1997). The first forays in this direction were made when researchers such as Becker (1957) and Downs (1957) argued that society and politics could be analysed based on economic models. Later, in the 1960s, this approach was extended to various disciplines such as history, law and demography and became known as economic imperialism (Swedberg & Granovetter, 1992, p. 1). Becker's 1976 work "The Economic Approach to Human Behaviour" became one of the manifestos of this school of thought.

By way of illustration, from the most mathematical neoclassical approach, economics tackled questions that were theoretically so far removed from its field of study, such as drug addiction, family life, religion, etc. However, by adopting a calculating rationality under the assumption that individuals limit themselves to maximising an individual utility function, it does not consider that choices are also the result of intrinsic, emotional motivations, values, and moral commitments. As Etzioni (1988) writes, when neoclassical economists recognise the significance of moral values, they tend to explain them in terms of costs and benefits. As an example of what it would entail to accept this position in the realm of social relations, Becker (1974, 1981) points out that in the family, everyone will act as if they love each other, even when they are selfish, along the lines of maximising their comfort and income, their consumption, and their opportunities.

The anthropological hole we have already referred to is extreme here, as it reductionistically overlooks relational goods, social norms, and morals, or even the existence of sympathetic bonds that lead to cooperation and altruistic giving.

Similarly, from the opposite side, an extension can be practised. Thus, for reductionists from sociology, such phenomena become expressions of cultural beliefs or political coercion. The economy is seen as materialising political decisions and interests or cultural traditions. This is the case in some expressions of the *Sociology of Economics*. Here, imperialism is not evident because economics is socially situated, so this is reflected mainly in using sociological methods in the study of economics. The sociology of economics starts from the evident influence of social determinants in the economic decision-making process, so variables such as status, sociability, and power become central to the argument (Swedberg & Granovetter, 1992). The classic works of Polanyi (1968 [1944]) and Polanyi et al. (1957) are a reference in arguing that all economic life is intertwined in a cluster through which institutions and social networks flow (Gemici, 2008; Granovetter, 1985). Indeed, without the customs, regulations or economic function of the State, it is not possible to understand the functioning of an economic system (Brinton & Nee, 2001). Despite this, it is also necessary to recognise the existence of an economic logic. Among the classic works from this approach are those of the *New Economic Sociology* and the so-called Harvard group, where markets are studied from a sociological perspective. This is the case of the traditional works on markets; Baker (1984) studied stock markets; Eccles (1981) economic organisations; Granovetter (1985) labour markets; and Zelizer (1983) the motivations of life insurance. Despite their analysis of the social framework, they are still a form of imperialism since they delimit the context but limit the capacity to study the economic fact: the logic of decision-making, efficiency, etc. The results of economics can also call into question those derived from sociology.

3.2 Contextualism and embeddedness

By contrast, contextualists study economic phenomena such as labour markets, firms, and businesses, showing how social organisation as a context shapes the choices of economic agents. This is where we find a more accurate application of Polanyi's classic concept of embeddedness (1968 [1944]). Economic behaviour is embedded in social behaviour and is also explained by it.[2]

Within contextualism, we can find at least three orientations:

Firstly, the broad *Neoinstitutional Economics* is heir to the long tradition of classical institutionalism and seeks to distance itself from the analytical rigidity of neoclassical economics. While the latter conceives of a world without social frictions, more akin to laboratory modelling, neoinstitutionalism points to the legal framework and culture (religion and values, customs, and lifestyles) as mechanisms of social and economic coordination. Its central idea is that any form of economic relationship is always bounded by institutions that shape any interaction. Such formal (legal norms) or informal (agreements, values, codes of conduct…) rules reduce uncertainty, which is ultimately the main problem in social life (Ayala Espino, 2005, p. 38; Conill, 2004) and transaction costs (costs of information, contract monitoring, conflict, intermediation, fraud, opportunism) (North, 1990).

Although this school experienced exponential growth from the 1970s onwards with authors such as Coase (1988), Williamson (1981, 1996), and North (1990), it has its roots in a line of work based on classical economists, German historicism, the Austrian school, and Marxism. Its current version, neoinstitutionalism, is less normative and legal and seeks to be more complementary to the neoclassical paradigm (Conill, 2004, p. 34). It limits itself to emphasising the concept of transaction costs and warns that economics should focus on institutions capable of reducing them (Williamson, 2000). Ultimately, they are more concerned with social efficiency, abandoning part of the analytical side. In short, it could be seen as an extension of economic analysis of social facts that is more benevolent to the use of sociology's concepts.

Socioeconomics represents this same position from the sociological side. It often describes itself as an alternative economic and social paradigm to neoclassical economics, based on the common idea that the economy is a complex social system influenced by social, cultural, and political factors. A paradigm broad enough to recognise that individuals are not "rational" beings in the neoclassical sense, although they can be optimisers in a broad sense influenced by their values, emotions, beliefs, and social relations.

We are dealing with a perspective defined as eclectic, in which diverse sources from sociology to psychology are used to study a broad fact, the socioeconomic fact. For the analysis of the economy, we can use the maximising logic of market economies while simultaneously recognising that preferences are socially fixed. This option has acceptable costs because formal economic methodology can play a role but is not absolute. In this way, the contributions of alternative currents, such as institutionalism and even Marxist thought, can be relevant.

It is not economic sociology, as it seeks to link economic studies with other social sciences (Etzioni, 1988), and, as in the previous case, economics is not a closed, self-contained system. It is more of a multi-contextual (social, psychological, historical, philosophical, ethical, political, and economic) understanding (Pérez-Adán, 1997, p. 19; Etzioni, 1988; Swedberg & Granovetter, 1992, p. 2) or an interdisciplinary bridge linking the fields of market and society. The aim is to provide more realistic arguments about human motivation and institutions that correct the biases we have already discussed in reviewing the neoclassical approach. In contrast to the rational choice model, socioeconomics assumes that people also shape their preferences and make decisions based on emotions and value judgements rooted in a community.

This confluence of diverse perspectives favours a "more enlightened" view of the individual in which there are complex systems of preferences, group-based, cooperative rationality, and not merely individualistic (Etzioni, 1988). Alongside this, *homo socioeconomicus* is part of social structures in which there are different levels of economic and political power, so socioeconomics is also a form of social critique of how neoclassical precepts are rooted in the very lifestyle of the contemporary individual, detracting from the relevance of aspects such as moral education, culture, and community ties (Pérez Adán, 1997; Etzioni, 1988).

However, like all pluri-interdisciplinary projects, it must be recognised that its breadth is its greatest weakness. Everything that is not mainstream could be integrated here. The only proposal that delves into the anthropological roots of the project is that of Etzioni; the others focus on specific aspects not considered by the neoclassical approach without responding to the initial objective. In fact, the last strand we will analyse, *Social Capital Theory*, is integrated within socioeconomics. Considering that it constitutes a whole research programme with various strands, analysing it as a complete orientation makes sense.

Taken together, both contextual approaches are mutually recognisable. Economists apply methodologies to understand market behaviour but disregard the cultural and social framework in which these markets move. Sociologists focus on the context of the activity of these markets without crossing a boundary, which, in many cases, is difficult to delimit. Arguably, separate spheres persist because market transactions remain relatively alien to sociology, despite their dependence on interpersonal relationships. Overall, the assumption that contextualisation solves the problem of the interrelationship between sociology and economics is a statement that opens up many questions.

All these contextualist interpretations underhandedly imply that social processes provide the shell of the economy. Still, the actual content of the egg, the yolk, consists of the exchange systems of the economy. If we think more deeply, economic relations are part of social relations, so social interaction is the yolk, not the shell (Zelizer, 2007). After all, to pick up on Mark Granovetter's (1985, p. 482) point: "Economic behaviour and institutions… are so constrained by ongoing social relations that to interpret them as independent is a serious misunderstanding". Ultimately, our object of work should be economic relations and social relations. This is an *aporia* that is difficult to resolve, although, as we shall see in the following chapters, some conditions can facilitate convergence. This problem is not trivial and will lead us to reflect on the potential of Social Capital Theory.

3.3 Neocapital and the theory of social capital

Social capital theory occupies a central position among the contextual orientations. It seeks to apply an essential notion of sociology that reflects man's relationality but is revised by economics. At the micro level, individuals are situated in networks that influence their preferences, their decisions, and, above all, the social resources they can mobilise. At the macro level, a society will be more efficient in its functioning to the extent that it achieves a good articulation of the networks that make it up.

We have chosen to analyse this perspective last, as it aligns with our ultimate goal of situating it within this debate, a decision the reader will understand. Undoubtedly, it is part of the contextual schools and must be integrated within socio-economics, within the so-called Neocapital Theories.

The Social Capital Theory argues that economic action is situated in the social realm and should never be explained solely by reference to individual motivations. Nevertheless, it presents a series of specificities that open up interesting confluence lines between different social sciences (sociology, political science, and economics). This will undoubtedly be its main advantage, but it will also be a source of many ambiguities and a lack of theoretical concreteness (Adler & Kwon, 2002; Sobel, 2002).

The methodological advantage, in Zelizer's (2007) expression, consists in focusing the object of attention of the various social sciences on the "yolk", the social relations available to an individual or a society, analysing them with their methodologies. A social relationship is multifaceted, ranging from the expressive to the instrumental, and can account for personal well-being, social structure, and economic activity. In order to delimit the object of analysis through the concept of capital, it is crucial to reflect on what we mean by that from the perspective of neocapital.

3.3.1 The analogical use of the notion of capital and social capital

The concept of capital has economic, sociological, and political science roots, allowing it to be understood by all parties (Putnam et al., 1993). Moreover, it can be used by both the orthodox and the heterodox, although it has different meanings. We anticipate that this will be one of the main problems.

The evolution of the use of the concept has been extended and has both sociological and economic theory bases. If we go back to its origins, Smith, Mill and Marx analysed the accumulation processes of "production goods" from very different perspectives. We can interpret the different existing visions from a double construction carried out simultaneously.

On the one hand, capital is a determinant of the social structure. This path is central to sociology and political science and is originally Marxist. Marx is more concerned with the link between accumulation and inequality (Storberg, 2002). For him, capital is not simply a collection of material objects or financial instruments. It is a social relation arising from the production process that facilitates the appropriation of surplus value. Its ultimate foundation is the mastery of the means of production and the reproduction of this mastery (Roemer, 1989). Although he does not introduce it, capital could take various forms by adopting a broad perspective on what constitutes a resource. Thus, leaving aside the exegetical debates on Marx's work, Wright chooses to consider how certain forms of goods not previously considered are both resources and means of appropriation, such as "qualification goods" and "organisational goods" like education or personal relations (Wright, 2015). This position is already in the tradition of Bourdieu's work, in which he analogically (Neveu, 2018) or substantively (Beasley-Murray, 2000) considers capital not only as a resource but also as a social relation legitimising inequality, "an instrument of appropriation of opportunities theoretically offered to all" (Bourdieu, 1991, p. 206).

The development of the theory of capital proposed in "Forms of Capital" (1986) has become canonical in determining the types of resources (symbolic, cultural, and social) that constitute sources of power and their reproduction in a capitalist society. Bourdieu aims to abstract the characteristics of capital that Marx detected in the economic sphere to other social fields. A social relation is expressed through a resource whose function is to facilitate the appropriation of other resources and opportunities (Martínez-García, 2023).

Subsequent developments have emphasised this aspect of resource appropriation. Thus, education is an investment with expected returns, as is the investment in cultural symbols and the personal construction of social networks. Overall, it focuses on capital theory, which comes under the heading of "neocapital" (Waldstrøm & Svendsen, 2008). This shift does not imply a complete break with classical theory; simply, the image of a dichotomised society dissolves, as it does in contemporary societies. Regardless of their belonging class, individuals can invest their surplus value (accumulated labour) in the markets of knowledge, cultural symbols and "social relations" as a differentiation strategy. Differentiated strategies of investment between social classes replace Marxist determinism.

On the other hand, in a second line of work, and almost simultaneously, the "orthodox" study of economics began revising the notion of capital. From the 1960s onwards, the general theory of capital began to analyse those resources that were more difficult to define or delimit. They are not strictly physical but seek to reflect aspects closely linked to human nature. The very evolution of the economy in post-industrial societies towards what has come to be called the "knowledge society" made it increasingly difficult to sustain the limitation of the notion of capital to its traditional approach. Faced with the apparent lack of anthropological realism, studying other forms of capital, such as human and social capital, opened new doors by including human beings' uniqueness and capabilities.

Schultz (1961) is often considered the first author to expand the concept. Specifically, he insisted that human resources should be seen as a form of capital, a means of production, or the product of investment. To abandon this approach is to conceive of labour in a primitive way, a manual capacity without acquired knowledge or skills (Becker, 1964). This capacity is the object of investment with expected returns so that it would be analogically assimilated into the concept of capital. Likewise, the networks of individuals could fall under the same interpretative paradigm, be considered capital and be subject to analysis by Capital Theory (Glaeser et al., 2002).

In this double theoretical confluence, we find a set of theories that try to overcome the limitations of traditional theories focused on the tangible components of capital, such as financial resources or physical assets, when addressing the more "human" dimensions, such as knowledge and sociality. Intangible components are determinants in explaining variables ranging from growth to innovation or competitiveness and social structure and were not incorporated in the models.

From this novel perspective, the emerging forms of capital can be understood as "any reservoir of value that facilitates action" (Light, 2004); they are storable and can be transformed into various other forms. This reservoir has another interpretation from the other side, using Bourdieu's critical lens. Neocapital is regarded as "a general science of the economy of practices", revealing capital in its diverse manifestations rather than solely adhering to the singular form recognised by economic theory (Bourdieu, 1986, p. 242). This perspective encompasses interchangeable material and immaterial forms within specific domains, including the economic, political, legal, artistic, religious, and scientific realms. It diverges from Classical Theory by shifting focus from "exploitative social relations between two classes" (Lin, 1999a, 1999b) towards considering mobility, management strategies, and positive-sum games, wherein individuals and groups can accrue advantages. Culture, symbols and social relations are simply part of the game of classes.

However, this approach risks generating inflated concepts lacking critical evaluation. Concepts like digital capital and religious, cultural, and organisational capital may create a divide between socioeconomic and economic studies. This issue is evident in the concept of social capital as well. As Portes (2000) noted, social capital stands out as one of sociology's most successful "exports" to other social sciences and public discourse. Nevertheless, it leaves unresolved questions regarding conceptual precision, causal relationships, measurement, the absence of a definition for its negative expressions, and the differentiation and articulation between micro and macro levels (Kadushin, 2004, p. 88; Waldstrøm & Svendsen, 2008).

Why does this methodological approach offer advantages in studying the interplay between economics and sociology? By focusing on the form of capital crucial to our inquiry, we observe that the concept of social capital occupies an intermediary position between sociology and economics. It endeavours to illustrate how social relationships, as a reservoir, influence market processes and are, in turn, influenced by them. This research approach acknowledges economic rationality without insisting on its universality, suggesting instead the presence of an economy shaped by social structures that supersede the omnipresence of *homo oeconomicus* (Christoforou, 2011). Relationships are viewed as an economic resource but are also integral to economic strategies and intricate "cultural" games (Waldstrøm & Svendsen, 2008).

In the case of personal relationships, social networks and the norms and values that underlie them are a form of capital insofar as they are the product of a process of individual and social investment of resources, time, and effort. At the individual level, it materialises in the personal agendas of individuals and at the societal level, it is a historical, social, and cultural process that gives birth to norms, values, and relationships, which facilitate the collective action of social groups (Coleman, 1988; Putnam, 1993; Lin, 1999a). The network thus becomes the concept that makes it possible to integrate the economic into the social fabric because it is an elementary truism to admit that our social actions, and economic actions by extension, are mediated by our networks of relationships and the content of norms and values (trust) that underlie them.

These networks are simultaneously the property of the individual, who uses them to extract resources, and the group in which he or she is integrated since all collective members have access to them and perceive the externalities of the network with which they are linked. This dichotomy between individual and social is a key to the concept's success and a source of ambiguity that will be debated in the following chapters.

At this juncture, it is pertinent to highlight a crucial aspect. When asserting that the network serves as the central notion or referent of our analysis, a natural query arises: How does our stance differ from the study of networks, that is, Social Network Analysis? Undoubtedly, analysing social networks constitutes one of the foundations of this perspective's development. Nevertheless, the perspective espoused by neocapital differs significantly.

Social capital studies draw on sociology, economics, and political science theories to elucidate how social connections benefit individuals and societies. Specifically, they concentrate on comprehending the resources embedded within social networks and their contributions to individual and collective outcomes such as status progression, cooperation, and economic development.

Social network analysis, in contrast, is grounded in mathematical and computational methods, focusing on describing and quantifying the structure of social relationships with applications in sociology, anthropology, organisational analysis, or even the spread of diseases. It is a methodology that provides empirical validation to theories related to social networks across various social sciences. It is empirically driven and primarily centres on analysing properties such as density, centrality, and clustering, often without delving deeply into the underlying social processes. The primary concern is mapping and analysing the structure of social networks, including patterns of connections, centrality of nodes, and overall network dynamics.

While the referent may align, diverse methodologies inform the analysis, and Social Capital Theory implies a particular theoretical approach. For instance, as Bourdieu contended, network analysis encounters a quandary when considering the impact of social relations as it risks marginalising the influence of power relations. Moreover, it is asymmetrical since, although it acknowledges the roles of economic and human capital, it disregards networks as a resource that situates individuals within the social network through inheritance and investment. The study of networks constrains analytical capacity by neglecting the examination of the accumulation processes inherent to capital.

While social capital studies and network analysis overlap, they offer complementary viewpoints on social relationships and provide valuable insights into human interaction and behaviour. Network analysis is a quantitative method that concentrates on the structure of social networks, measuring and identifying patterns and properties of connections between individuals (Molina, 2001). This result can offer an empirical contrast to a neocapital analysis like social capital.

In short, we seem to obtain a double result by returning to the advantages of the concept of social capital by two different routes and adopting the perspective of neocapital. Critical socioeconomics is a way of analysing other forms of stratification and reproduction of inequality; "orthodox" socioeconomics, a way to introduce the more specifically human and social resources abandoned by neoclassical economics, as well as a channel for understanding the normative and relational framework that underlies the economy. For both, it is a resource, appropriable and transferable, whether tangible or not. For both, it is a stock of resources that generates an expected return or flow of income.

We face a set of open possibilities and a fundamental problem: the lack of concreteness. Opting to study networks and relationships to wit, converging on a single object, facilitates the application of diverse methodologies but not the homogeneity of results and approaches. Thus, despite the frequent attention given to the notion of social capital, its establishment as a research programme is still far from being consolidated.

In anticipation of what we will see in the following two chapters, the main problem with this orientation is the lack of a coherent conceptual structure. There are no solid contributions on the micro-mechanisms at work in generating this form of capital, even though the main effects are significantly linked to the micro or personal network scale (Yang, 2007). Thus, although it can be labelled as the most balanced and expanding option, it presents a set of outstanding issues that translate into the need to build a good theory on the interrelationship between individual networks and social effects, between the micro and the macro (Häuberer, 2011; Christoforou & Davis, 2014).

4 Recapping

In this first chapter, we have analysed the lack of integration of the social dimension of the human being in the study of economics. The mainstream, associated with the neoclassical school, rejects social behaviour factors as non-economic. This approach isolates economics by excluding fundamental social dimensions such as ethics, reciprocity, altruism, and duty, which are essential aspects of any society and respond to the concept of non-instrumental rationality.

We have identified five proposals for integrating the social dimension into economic analysis: economic analysis of social facts, sociology of economics, neoinstitutional economics, socioeconomics, and social capital theory. However, each of these approaches has certain limitations.

The economic analysis of social facts extends the neoclassical trend to sociology. The sociology of economics, on the other hand, applies sociology's methodologies to economics. Neoinstitutional economics introduces the social context into economic analysis but insufficiently by only considering the frictions that social relations generate in economic activity. Socioeconomics presents a more ambitious perspective of integrating the social dimension, but no unified research proposal exists in this field. Finally, social capital theory adopts the social network concept from sociology and incorporates it into economic analysis. Although, at present, most studies in this field focus on considering the effect of macro-social variables on economic variables, the possibility of studying personal networks and their configuration as a basis for the macro-social opens up an opportunity for the integration of the social into the economic.

In summary, although the proposals for integrating the social dimension into the economy have their limitations, the theory of social capital seems to be the one that offers the most significant possibilities for genuine integration of the social into Economics.

Notes

1 Historically, the origin of the concept of homo oeconomicus goes back to J. S. Mill, who was the first author to opt for the extraction of a series of characteristics of human behaviour to create an abstract construct (Blaug, 1980).

2 The importance of the concept of embeddedness calls for reflection. When Polanyi introduced it in *The Great Transformation* (1968 [1944]), he did so to allude to the changes that the industrial revolution (disembedding) had brought about concerning traditional societies, giving rise to market societies in which the economy is dominant over all other social expressions. In this new situation, the appearance is that society is an adjunct to the market. However, as Granovetter (1985) emphasises, contemporary capitalist processes continue to be enmeshed in the social fabric under the perception that this is an external linkage in such a way that economic and social processes mix and interact in a bidirectional way (Kripper, 2001). It is impossible to approach the economic and the social as separate dimensions, but economics' choice of formalism has constantly sought to make progress in this direction (see Box 1.1). Moving forward in the text, we will see if it is possible to recognise the existence of a form of disembedding by considering the influence that the generalisation of market relations can have on non-market ones.

2 Social capital

The controversial trajectory of a concept

> I refer to the goodwill, companionship, mutual sympathy and social relationship between a group of individuals and families that make up a social unit. If you can get in touch with your neighbour, and your neighbour with other neighbours, (…) there will be an accumulation of social capital (…). The community as a whole will benefit from the cooperation of all its parts, while the individual will find in his associations the advantages of the help, sympathy and companionship of his neighbours.
>
> (Hanifan, 1916)

This text, which serves as a starting point, is credited with being the first work to deal with the notion of social capital. The definition it offers suggests that we are talking about a concept that has been the subject of reflection in various fields for a long time. However, since the 1980s, reference to social capital has grown exponentially in scientific articles, books, theses, citations, etc. (Figure 2.1). With this

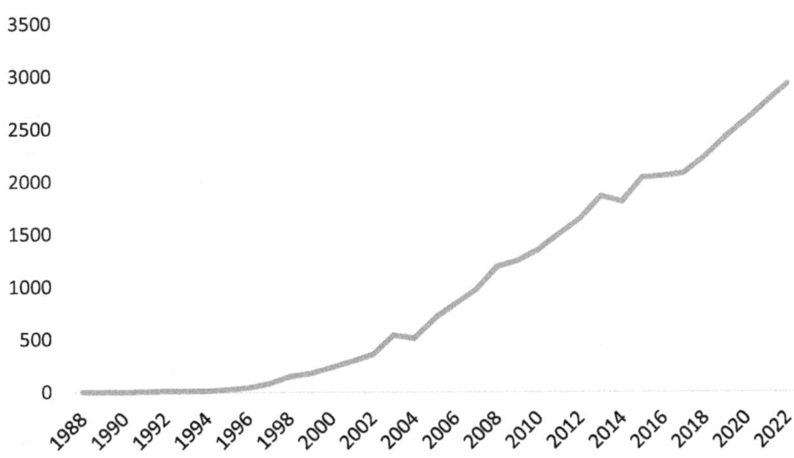

Figure 2.1 Evolution in the number of publications on social capital in the Scopus database.
Source: Own elaboration based on Scopus (2023).

DOI: 10.4324/9781003375302-4

proliferation in usage comes a pressing need to reach a consensus on the definition and conceptualisation of social capital.

As explained at the end of the first chapter, the economic literature has identified different types of capital. These include natural capital (which encompasses the natural resources of a region or country), physical capital (which provides for machinery and industrial infrastructure), financial capital (which is the monetary resources available for investment), and human capital (which includes know-how, experience, and education). These types of capital are present in many economic development and growth models. They can conceptually be considered "precise" because of their ability to be quantified and incorporated into analytical models.

This is not the case for social capital, or at least not so clearly. Most scientific literature describes this variable as complex and multidimensional (Westlund & Larsson, 2021). It is said to mean many things to many people; it is a wonderfully elastic term and ultimately an "umbrella concept" (Dasgupta & Serageldin, 2000, pp. X–XI). It brings together various aspects of a different nature that are related but not identity-related.

Herein lies the main criticism of the concept and theory of social capital. We use "concept" and "theory" because a concept constitutes a building block or fundamental element of the theory (Häuberer, 2011, p. 27), and the latter, for its development, needs to be based on previously defined concepts. According to critics, the definition of social capital is not precise, resulting in a loss of scientific credibility due to the severe problems associated with its measurement (Lin, 2008, p. 50).

This "accusation" is justified because social capital aims to integrate into a single concept the problem of the embeddedness of the economy and the society, and somewhat naively, it is interpreted as a functional asset that can favour economic efficiency, the functioning of society and the performance of institutions (Membiela-Pollán & Pena-López, 2017). On the other hand, it is difficult to find another word with more significant ambiguity than the expression "the social". As a general reference, the term "society" is defined by the Encyclopaedia Britannica (2023) as "people in general thought of as living together in organised communities with shared laws, traditions, and values". We are, therefore, talking about the integration of individuals in a community and, at the same time, about the elements that facilitate this coexistence.

Consensus definitions have been sought over the years. Nevertheless, when one looks at such definitions, one realises that the authors who propose them are somewhat arbitrary and draw their explanation to the approach they follow.

The World Bank, for example, states that social capital refers to the institutions, relationships and norms that shape the quality and quantity of social interactions in a society (World Bank, 2001). Similarly, the World Health Organization (WHO) defines social capital as the degree of social cohesion in communities, processes between individuals that establish networks of relationships, norms and social trust and facilitate coordination and cooperation (Winter, 2001). Leaving aside the shortcomings of focus in these definitions – which we will see in Chapter 4 – both have two components: what social capital is and what social capital does. What it does is a potential contributor to economic, institutional, and social performance. What it "is" is made up of elements of an unequal nature (norms and values, trust, networks) that have to do with the human as a "social animal" in the purest Aristotelian sense (*Politics, I.* 1253a, pp. 2–8) but which present problems of quantification and contrast. Even if we resort to composite indicators, it is difficult to adequately grasp the social aspects and their articulation (Grootaert et al., 2004). We are not talking about a specific asset but about a set of "assets" (Uphoff, 2000) that have the potential to facilitate social coordination at various levels, from the individual, providing material or immaterial resources, to the functioning of society. The returns on these assets are both for individuals and for collectives and can also be public (Dasgupta, 2005).

Based on this general framework, although the research line has only recently taken off, we are not discussing a new object of study. A survey of research traditions on "social coordination and cohesion" as a productive factor can be a good starting point for rooting current work. At the same time, continuing this journey through the research alternatives that have been developed since the "official take-off" of this line of work will help us understand the approaches we will study in the following chapter. This second chapter breaks down the notion of social capital to explain the divergences and inconsistencies we find today. It aims to understand the paths to situate ourselves critically before the present. Here, we intend to answer: What is the trajectory of the concept? Where is the debate? What are the building blocks of this theory?

1 Social capital already was. The background

The concept of social capital is not, in essence, genuine. Its current apparent originality only responds to its systematisation as a construct aspiring to be relevant in the social sciences due to its explanatory capacity (Adam & Roncevic, 2003; Membiela-Pollán, 2016). It is evident that the concern for the effect that norms, values, networks of relationships, and trust have on the individual and the group goes back a long way.

As a broad conceptual framework, social capital finds resonance in the works of thinkers such as Aristotle and Machiavelli, who explored the notion of "civic virtue". Similarly, Locke's ideas on civil society and Tocqueville's assertion regarding the virtuous connection between civic associations, the common good, and democracy align with this perspective. Within the foundational roots of economics, we encounter two divergent traditions (Table 2.1). On the one hand, a functionalist

Table 2.1 Evolution of the concept and theory of social capital

Stage one. Background	*Elements of social capital*
Aristotle. 4th century BC.	Civic virtue
Machiavelli. 16th century	Civic virtue
Locke. 17th century	Civil society
Rousseau. 18th century	Network of human relations
Adam Smith. 18th century	Moral sentiments, empathy, trust, and relationality
Marx. 19th century	Social and class reproduction
Tocqueville. 19th century	Civic partnership and the common good
Tönnies. 19th–20th century	Community value

(*Continued*)

Table 2.1 (Continued)

Stage one. Background	*Elements of social capital*
J. S. Mill. 19th century	Civic engagement
Weber. 19th–20th century	Hierarchy and power
Durkheim. 19th–20th century	Solidarity and group life
Second stage. The emergence of the term	**Elements of social capital**
Lyda J. Hanifan. 1920	The first approach to the concept. Reference to social capital as we know it today. Community and cooperation
Jane Jacobs. 1961	Social capital, social network, social dynamism
Glen Loury. 1977	Social capital, social network, connectivity, and opportunities
Third stage. Configuration of the theoretical body	**Elements of social capital**
Pierre Bourdieu (1980, 1983, 1983, 1984, 1986)	Social capital as resources available in the individual social network. Marxist approach to social reproduction. Micro view
James Coleman (1988, 1990)	Social capital is an element inherent to the social structure that facilitates or inhibits actions benefiting the individual and the structure as a whole. Micro and meso vision
Robert Putnam (1993, 1995, 2000)	Social capital is a feature of social organisation (trust, norms and networks) that can improve the efficiency of society by facilitating coordinated actions. The link between civic participation, trust, and development. Macro vision
Stage four. Consolidation of the perspectives and settlement of the building blocks	**Elements of social capital**
VV. AA. (2000–present)	Three perspectives of social capital: *individualistic or micro-social, community or mesosocial, macro-social, and macro-institutional.* Authors: Burt, Portes, Fukuyama, Dasgupta, Lin, Knack, Ostrom, Glaeser, Woolcock, Uphoff, … Building Blocks of Social Capital Sources of social capital Dimensions of social capital Categories of social capital Criticism of social capital Measuring social capital Functionalities and returns on social capital The dark side of social capital Social capital and the Internet

Source: Own elaboration.

tradition is evident in the writings of Adam Smith, who examined the role of relationality through the fundamental concept of sympathy and emphasised moral sentiments and trust as elementary to the functioning of the economy itself. On the other hand, a more critical approach exists rooted in social dialectics, exemplified by Marx's exploration of reproduction and social structuring.

Within the strictly sociological realm, we discuss one of the central elements of any work. We find parallels in Weber's analysis of issues such as hierarchy and power. Similarly, Durkheim deals with forms of solidarity and emphasises "group life" as an antidote to alienation. Simmel devotes an essential part of his work to the theme of group identity, while Tönnies focuses on the value of community (Bankston & Zhou, 2002; Andriani & Christoforou, 2016).

Of the precedents indicated within economics, Smith's work is of singular interest. Authors such as Winter (2001) and Fukuyama (2001) identify aspects of the theory of social capital with debates opened by Smith's work, particularly *The Theory of Moral Sentiments* ([1997] 1759). Notably, three significant claims stand out: the emphasis on the positive and negative externalities that can result from the activity of a social group, the development of the social virtues of honesty, prudence, and diligence in a commercial society, and the understanding of solidarity as a direct function of the social distance that binds us to other individuals. In other words, "sympathy" has a structuring character for society and economic activity. As we reflected in the first chapter, it is surprising that the "sensitivity" of the father of economics to this issue has not been considered until recently with the revision of the "Smithian problem".

Taken together, these authors constitute what could be our primary antecedents. They all address concepts such as social group, civic virtue, honesty, solidarity, community, or civil society, attributing relevance to them in the functioning of the economy.

1.1 Making the term explicit

At the end of the 19th century, with the work of the Austrian economist Von Böhm-Bawerk (1884), the notion of *capital* became popular. This is not entirely identifiable with the Marxist one but as a set of intermediate products that came into play in the production process. At that time, the concept of capital was mainly physical capital, that is, machinery and industry, and this introduction was very enriching in terms of the ability of economic theory to explain reality. Subsequently, it led to studying a series of "capitals" that operate as productive intermediate goods for various purposes, transcending the realm of economics.

Specifically, the concept of social capital can be found in the economic literature of the 19th and early 20th centuries. However, its use was inconsistent and unevenly meaningful (Wolleb, 2008). These are attempts to capture and concretise the transcendence of the intangible in productive processes. The American rural educator Lyda J. Hanifan will become a classic reference. Since Putnam quoted him (2000, p. 19), he is credited with being the first to allude to social capital as we understand it today. In his work *The Community Center* (Boston, MA: Silver, Burdett & Company, 1920), there is a chapter entitled "social capital", where the author says: "The community as a whole will benefit from the cooperation of all its parts, while the individual will find in his associations the advantages of the help, sympathy and fraternity of his neighbours". Hanifan already sees elements that shape what social capital is and what social capital does. He proposes a micro approach, suggesting that the individual finds support and fraternity in this scenario. Additionally, he points out a meso and macro approach, indicating that the community itself as a whole will benefit from the cooperation of all its parts and will improve its overall living conditions.

Later in the 20th century, in the 1960s and 1970s, the neocapital agenda exploded with the emergence of the concept of human capital. The latter can be defined as the competencies, skills, and knowledge of the labour force accumulated due to schooling, lifelong learning, and experience (Cameron & Neal, 2005). Schultz is often mentioned as the introducer in 1962 when he argued that investment in human capital provides answers to questions such as economic growth, the structure of wages, or the distribution of personal income. Many authors have contributed to this line of inquiry following Schultz's initial contribution. The work of Lucas, Becker, Murphy, and Tamura, or Romer, Barro, and Mankiw, has shown the influence of human capital on economic growth and development (Savvides & Stengos, 2009).

The introduction of human capital is a decisive step in including the uniqueness of human beings and their capabilities in economic analysis. At this point, it is worth noting that elements have been identified in human capital that cross the line of technical knowledge and experience and that interact with social capital in a somewhat blurred boundary. For example, the values and moral attributes that the subject carries are also an essential part of this factor because they can favour the productivity of individual and group work (Becker, 1981; Gui, 2001). In any case, both variables complete the analysis of factor endowments (Membiela-Pollán et al., 2019b).

During the era when human capital gained prominence, Jane Jacobs (1961) and Glen Loury (1977) emerged as pioneers in explicitly discussing social capital, laying the groundwork for subsequent researchers. Nonetheless, the concept appeared to require further systematic elaboration. For instance, Jacobs briefly mentions "social capital" in her book *The Life and Death of Great American Cities* (New York: Random House, 1961), stating, "[N]etworks are a city's irreplaceable social capital. Whenever the capital is lost, from whatever cause, its income disappears, never to return until and unless new capital is slowly and chancily accumulated". As noted by Sobel (2002), Jacobs' work is replete with examples demonstrating how a city's vitality hinges on the social bonds forged among its residents. Similar to Hanifan, the author equates social capital with social networks. In this instance, the connection between the micro-level (networks) and the macro-level (city) is inferred from the excerpt above. Social capital at a small scale yields repercussions for collective dynamism. Here lies one of the fundamental challenges of social capital theory that persists today: Elucidating the interconnection between its various operating levels.

For his part, Loury (1977) studies how racial and socioeconomic conditioning affects young people's educational and occupational achievements. He argues that orthodox economic theories are too individualistic, focusing exclusively on human capital (Portes, 1998). In contrast, social capital favours access to opportunities through social networks and can be conceived as a set of resources that help accumulate human capital. Interestingly, both approaches are micro and structural

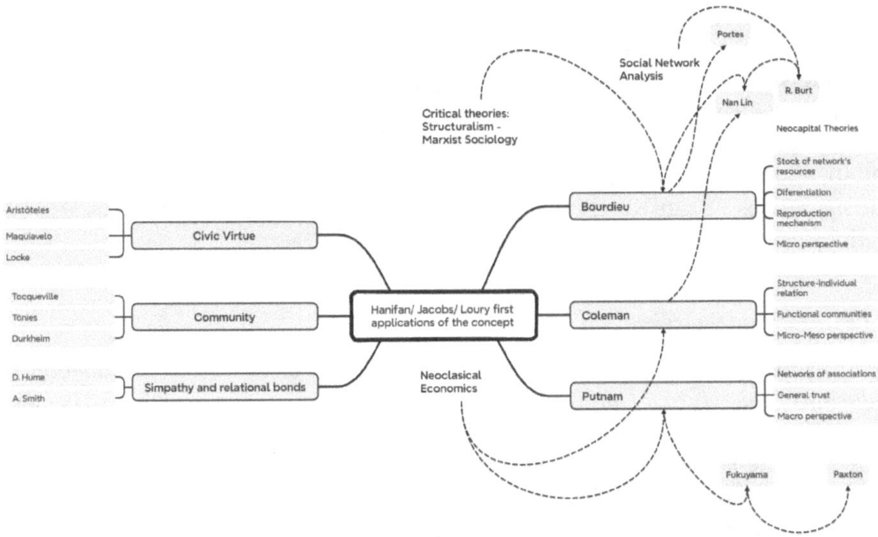

Figure 2.2 The trajectory of the concept of social capital.

Source: Own elaboration.

in their starting point and draw macro consequences by focusing on the social network's functionality available to each individual (Figure 2.2).

At this juncture, it is crucial to delineate a distinction: social capital emerges concomitantly with the advancement of social network research, sharing many commonalities. Network research exhibits an empiricist and methodological bias, leading to a theoretical gap, as Flap (2004) acknowledged. Studies on networks influence social capital research, exemplified by Granovetter's seminal work on the impact of weak ties (1973). Nevertheless, the assertion that networks dictate actions extends beyond the scope of social network theory alone. Institutions shape social networks; thus, the social network concept necessitates a broader understanding that encompasses the resources accessible through the network itself, along with their cognitive and relational implications, not solely focusing on structural aspects (Flap, 2002, 2004).

2 The configuration of a theoretical body: Bourdieu, Coleman, and Putnam

So far, the concept's background and first uses have been presented. The systematic study of social capital, the deployment of the theory with the significant growth in the number of articles and references in the literature, and even its political consideration took place from the eighties of the 20th century at the hands of three sociologists. In the analysis of their approaches, which are, in some cases, wildly divergent, we can appreciate the issues already mentioned, their different approaches and dimensions, and the different returns. The theoretical starting points range from rational choice utilitarianism to neo-Weberian functionalism and post-structuralist Marxism. Choosing this trilogy of authors will serve as a basis for understanding what we propose because each adopts a different approach that generates a diverse line of work, even in the method.

The authors alluded to are Pierre Bourdieu (1986), James Coleman (1988, 1990), and Robert Putnam (1993, 1995, 2000). We will focus on them as they set the main lines of subsequent work. In the following chapters, we will discuss the various perspectives of each approach.

2.1 Pierre Bourdieu

Bourdieu (together with Passeron) speaks of "social capital" in *Reproduction in Education, Society and Culture* (1970) and in a short article entitled "Social capital, provisional Notes" published in *Proceedings of Social Science Research* (1980). However, the landmark text in the literature is "The Forms of Capital" (Bourdieu, 1986). This short work, which we will revisit repeatedly, is the founding act of any theory that emerges under the umbrella of neocapital. The study of those immaterial factors that constitute a stock and a form of investment and that are integrated into social and economic processes (human, cultural, social capital…). In this work, in addition to economic and cultural capital, the French sociologist places social capital as the resources available to the subject and a function of his or her belonging to a group.

Precisely, he states that social capital is

> the aggregate of the actual or potential resources which are linked to possession of a durable network of more or less institutionalised relationships of mutual acquaintance and recognition – in other words, to membership in a group – which provides each of its members with the backing of the collectivity-owned capital, a credential which entitles them to credit, in the various senses of the word.
>
> (Bourdieu, 1986, pp. 248–249)

From a Marxist perspective, but also close to structuralism (although he refuses to integrate himself into both currents), he tries to outline a general theory of social reproduction in which the forms of capital are determinant. His perspective on the management of these "factor endowments" is instrumental. Thus, for example, social capital as a stock of relations is the product of "social investment strategies, individual or collective, consciously or unconsciously oriented towards the institution or reproduction of directly usable social relations in the short or long term" (Bourdieu, 1986, p. 249). In other words, individuals receive and invest in networks of relations that are functionally useful in the reproduction of social status, so that social capital is an instrument of the dominant class that engages in mutual recognition to preserve its position (Pena-López et al., 2021, p. 680).

For Bourdieu, like economic or cultural capital, relationships are functional and facilitate "material and symbolic resources. Thus, the social capital possessed by the agent depends on the network of connections he can mobilise and the volume of capital (economic, cultural, or symbolic) held by those to whom he is connected" (Bourdieu, 1986, p. 250). As we shall see, this way of analysing the problem is the paradigm of the micro approach, its starting point being the individual in the structure and the interactions of both.

From this basic definition, three significant implications can be derived:

a. On the one hand, Bourdieu alludes to the solidarity and material support that derives from social capital and the mutual recognition and status that group membership offers its members. These aspects become material or immaterial resources that can be useful for security, individual well-being, and the projection of the individual (Häuberer, 2011, p. 38).
b. It also outlines an identity, or at least an analogy, with any form of capital, which will be further developed in the work of Nan Lin (1999a, 1999b, 2000, 2008). Social capital is capital in terms of endowment and returns. The connections that the individual can access and mobilise are configured in a stock that provides resources of a different nature, and, as such, those resources are a return on that stock. In other words, the extension and the "quality" or structure and composition of the network become relevant, and with it, the closure, that is, who can or cannot participate in these networks. Bourdieu (1986, p. 249) writes:

> The volume of the social capital possessed by a given agent thus depends on the size of the network of connections he can effectively mobilise and on the volume of the capital (economic, cultural or symbolic) possessed in his own right by each of those to whom he is connected.

c. Bourdieu also highlights the negative externalities of social capital, the dark side of social capital, and even what *a posteriori* is called bad social capital (Warren, 2008, pp. 121–123). This is because, according to Bourdieu, solidarity and the relationship of influence is intragroup; there is a social investment in the group to reproduce those relationships that will be useful only for the network members. Solidarity, equality, and social mobility can be compromised (Vorhaus, 2014).

Nevertheless, Bourdieu's analysis also gives rise to possible objections.

a. Bourdieu's theory presents an instrumentalist bias in the network's vision and the use of social capital to the extent that intrinsic motivations and moral commitments do not seem to play a relevant role. The personal network seems to be the product of an intentional investment whose only objective is to produce and reproduce the internal links that will bring a profit. Somehow, what we will call relational goods seem to be absent.

> The existence of a network of connections is not a given natural or even social fact. It is the product of an incessant effort to produce and

> reproduce lasting and useful relationships that can secure material or symbolic gains. In other words, the network of relations is the product of investment.
>
> (Bourdieu, 1986, p. 248)

For this sociologist, economic capital is at the root of the other types of capital (Bourdieu, 1986, p. 250), which, in a way, expels the presence of backward motivations in social construction.

b. On the other hand, in his definition – as Lin (2008) and Burt (1992) will do later on – he identifies social capital with the resources linked to the social network and potentially mobilisable by the individual. As we shall see below, other researchers identify social capital with the social network in which such accessible and potentially mobilisable resources are embedded. This point is controversial because it is worth asking whether the origin of the resources and the functionality of social capital do not come from the social element itself, which is the network or relational structure (Membiela-Pollán, 2016, p. 50; Membiela-Pollán & Pena-López, 2017, p. 154). Consequently, there is a risk of focusing on resources rather than the structure when the latter is what conditions the extent and stock of those resources that are useful to the individual. This is not a minor issue, as it entails the loss of analytical potential. For example, concerning the sources of social capital, these are not only providers.
c. Bourdieu's perspective of social capital is micro but ignores the effects derived at the meso and macro levels. As will be explored in the following chapters, these derivations, the interrelationship between the micro and the macro, are crucial and constitute one of the central objects of the study of social capital (Cockburn & Cockburn-Wootten, 2022).

2.2 *James Coleman*

The next milestone in the evolution of the concept and theory of social capital is the work of the American sociologist James Coleman (1988, 1990, 1995). He places social capital in the context of the methodological individualism of rational choice. As a background, we have individuals who make optimisation decisions, an approach that, at the outset, seems opposed to the previous proposal but which will end up finding notable points of convergence. The social relationship is produced by the individual's interest in the resources available to other agents to maximise his own utility (Häuberer, 2011, p. 39). However, some meso and macro derivations must be considered. In this case, the author will enter into the problem.

For Coleman, "social capital corresponds to a variety of functions of social structures, information channels, obligations, expectations, sets of norms, and sanction systems that facilitate or inhibit the actions of actors" (Coleman, 1988, p. 98). In his most cited work, he applies this definition to the field of education to study the effects of social capital on human capital.

Social capital is inherent to the social structure that facilitates the exchanges and actions of the individuals within it. Coleman remarks:

> Social capital is defined by its function. It is not a single entity but a variety of entities having two characteristics in common: They all consist of some aspect of social infrastructure and facilitate specific actions of individuals within the structure.
>
> (Coleman, 1990, p. 302)

Thus, while Bourdieu makes social capital consist of the material and symbolic resources provided by the network, accessible, and potentially mobilisable, Coleman states that social capital resides in the infrastructure itself, which enables actions that ultimately potentially maximise the individual's utility through the achievement of goals (Coleman, 1988, p. S98, 1995, p. 392). This focus on structure allows us to understand social capital as a private and public good (Coleman, *1988*, pp. 116–118). Since its elements (e.g. norms of reciprocity) are not the property of a single subject but also of the rest of the individuals that make up the community or group, social capital is not only a private good but also a public good. For this reason, despite the methodological individualism, it can be affirmed that social capital is a resource of the organisation and is productive and beneficial for it (Coleman, 1995, p. 410), beyond the fact that any subject makes use of social capital to maximise its utility. Then, Coleman's approach can be described as "sociocentric", while Pierre Bourdieu's approach is more "egocentric" (Halstead & Deller, 2015).

Coleman calls "forms of social capital" inherent features of the structure that can facilitate certain actions of individuals: trust, information, norms, and social organisation.

Mutual trust is based on expectations of reciprocity, where the obligations undertaken become a kind of insurance policy (Coleman, 1995, p. 402). Trustworthiness progresses when social structures have closure property, as far as internal relations are concerned. This element induces possible "collective sanction" and an individual's exposure to reputational damage within the structure if internal norms are broken (Coleman, 1988, pp. 107–108). Potential information, another form of social capital, is contained or provided from social relations and helps maximise individual utility, facilitating members' actions (Coleman, 1995, p. 402). Practical norms (internalised or enforced) also constitute a form because they facilitate some actions and constrain others, being important in the operation of the community, preventing the actor from behaving in pursuit of mere self-interest, reducing negative externalities, and encouraging positive ones (Coleman, 1988, pp. 104–106). Regarding "appropriable social organisation", Coleman states that organisations formed for specific issues can be helpful for other purposes and can benefit their members and even non-participating actors in different ways (Coleman, 1995, pp. 406–407).

This study of the attributes that networks possess has essential effects on what social capital is and what social capital does. The outcomes here can be diverse regarding returns and at the collective level, as they do not necessarily have to be positive at the societal level. Education, security, health, job search, physical and economic support, or collective action towards various goals can be approached from the point of view of the mechanisms, the "forms of social capital" that underlie the social structure. For this reason, Coleman's studies facilitate the analysis of social capital's cognitive and relational dimensions (norms and trust) and the leap from the individual or micro to the meso and macro.

In his classic 1988 work, we find a set of cases that highlight the multiple dimensions and approaches to social capital. For example, he studies how forms of social capital within the social structure (family and community) are an explanatory factor for educational outcomes. He also discusses the case of the New York diamond market, where the danger of product theft is reduced or eliminated because of the collective sanctions that the individual who commits such an act would receive from a community that is endowed with high closure because of high interaction and ethnic and familial ties. It also expands on the underground study circles in South Korea, an example of an association that derives from relationships within the school or a church and that serves to carry out collective protests.

As with Bourdieu, Coleman's approach is also subject to criticism.

a. Coleman pays excessive attention to strong ties and closure relations, the family, the personal environment, the company, etc. He loses sight of the importance of weak ties outside the more direct social structure, where closure is almost irrelevant (Portes, 1998, p. 5). The development of the theory has shown how these weak ties play a relevant role in providing information, knowledge, and opportunities as resources that may be lacking in the primary social structure centred on strong and redundant ties (Granovetter, 1973; Lin, 1999a, 2001).
b. He identifies social capital as a public good (Coleman, 1988, pp. 116–118). Qualifying it as a collective and individual-private good would be more correct. This author focuses on the micro level - as Bourdieu does- and on the meso level, not the macro level. His analysis needs to include the study of social capital at the macro level (where it could be categorised as a public good). At most, from his perspective, we can speak of the good of a given community.
c. He does not allude to negative returns to social capital (Häuberer, 2011, p. 49) or the possible existence of so-called bad social capital. Social capital can be negative or contain negative externalities. For example, when the closure of a social group excludes those in dire need of specific resources. In addition, closure may make it difficult for a group member to interact with individuals outside the group or from whom he or she could draw valuable resources. Finally, closure may occur in a group whose nature is not prosocial (Membiela-Pollán et al., 2023, p. 15), making it difficult for the individual to leave the group.

2.3 Robert Putnam

Although the initial theoretical groundwork on social capital can be attributed to Bourdieu and Coleman, it was the works of Robert Putnam, particularly *Making Democracy Work* (1993) and *Bowling Alone* (2000), that brought social capital into the public discourse (Castiglione et al., 2008a, 2008b). These works sparked significant interest among scholars and led to a publication surge. However, it is essential to highlight that Putnam's approach differs significantly from those of Bourdieu and Coleman. In contrast to the earlier individualistic and class reproduction perspectives of Bourdieu or Coleman's micro-meso viewpoints, Putnam develops a more culturalist and macroscopic outlook on social capital (Tarrow, 1996, p. 340).

In his first mentioned work, which examines inequalities among Italian regions, Putnam emphasises the significance of social capital in fostering democratic institutions. Specifically, Putnam (1993) defines social capital as "...features of social organisation, such as trust, norms, and networks that can enhance society's efficiency by facilitating coordinated actions". He highlights that varying levels of civic engagement between northern and southern regions of Italy played a crucial role in the north's superior economic and institutional success compared to the south. A vibrant associational life stands out as a distinguishing factor, as associations instil in their members habits of cooperation, solidarity, and civic-mindedness (Putnam, 1993).

A second work, *Bowling Alone* (2000), addresses the causes that have given rise to what it diagnoses as a loss of social capital in the case of the United States, paying attention to the characteristics of social organisations that facilitate cooperation for mutual benefit (Sánchez-Santos & Pena-López, 2005, p. 139). Trust and norms of reciprocity are promoted by horizontal networks of civic engagement, recalling Tocqueville's classical ideas (Putnam, 1993, p. 171). Democratic development depends on these networks, as they facilitate the generalisation of virtues such as solidarity, reciprocity, participation, and socialisation and reduce opportunistic behaviour (Putnam, 1993, 2000). Beyond reciprocity related to exchanging goods of equal value, what Putnam calls generalised reciprocity assumes that the individual will behave prosocially and help the other without expecting an immediate return. This will lead to the generation of trustworthiness, reduce transaction costs, and improve the efficiency of economic and social functioning.

In essence, Putnam presents a macro perspective of social capital, focused on social and institutional trust, that differs from the two previous authors. He systematises (albeit little) the study of social capital limited to norms and values and addresses the meso and micro only when he studies the extension of associative networks (Putnam, 2000).

Previous authors assumed that the subject behaves prosocially with his group because this favours him in reproducing relationships valuable to him and his group or in maximising his own utility. In other words, there is clear support for individual mechanisms to explain this behaviour. Putnam turns the study of Social Capital into "civic virtue" and the generalisation of prosocial behaviours that he links to the extension of associationism (Putnam, 2000, pp. 18–19). Consequently and a priori, the individual does not make such a premeditated calculation as is posited under the rational choice or social reproduction approach.

Extending this type of behaviour always produces positive results, either macro or for society as a whole. For example, it improves the functioning of the state and the market (Putnam & Goss, 2001; Putnam, 1993) or, of a micro nature, for the individual himself in terms of welfare and social insurance. Thus, regarding effects, social capital is both a private and a public good.

Putnam's work opens two key questions that are not always well answered: the link between the micro and the macro and the effects of macro-social capital. On the one hand, the different levels of social capital cannot be interpreted as isolated cells but are subject to interdependencies (Pena-López & Sánchez-Santos, 2013; Membiela-Pollán, 2016). On the other hand, concerning the effects, the externalities of social capital, as the author acknowledges, are not always positive. In fact, he will propose as examples amoral familism, the mafia, corruption, the Ku Klux Klan, urban gangs, and power elites that exploit social capital for antisocial purposes or the mere exclusion of people from outside one's group (Putnam, 1993, 2000). This point is left aside to focus on the positive side.

In short, Putnam's perspective is that civic norms and trust emerge as a by-product of social networks, particularly associationism. This collective good benefits society and the economy through political stability and economic development.

There are several objections to Putnam's theory.

a. His definition of social capital mixes very different elements without explaining the interrelations. Putnam's conceptualisation is broad and diffuse, given that it encompasses the positive attributes that the bulk of theory describes as constituting social capital. There is a lack of concreteness; he mixes elements of the social life of different natures (norms, networks, trust), which do not constitute a single dimension (Häuberer, 2011, p. 59). This problem will hinder its subsequent empirical study. We are discussing a proposal that seems to want to unify all the positive aspects of social functioning in a single concept but does not explain it. The result is that any research becomes obvious with generalist statements, such as "greater general trust is good for social functioning".
b. The link between the meso, associationism, and the macro is unclear, and the link between the micro, individual networks, and the macro is non-existent. For Putnam, it is an associative activity that promotes civic norms and social trust. However, this link is not evident to many authors (Knack, 2002, p. 778). It will depend on the nature of the association, the level of interaction within the association, the degree of connection with other associations, or the role of associationism in one country versus another.
c. Putnam pays excessive attention to formal associationism, as opposed to informal networks of relationships such as friends or family (Häuberer, 2011, pp. 60–61). Similarly, although he alludes to the resources available in the individual social network and numbers them more than his predecessors, his analysis lacks the depth of Bourdieu and Coleman. It is a mere enumeration.

3 Consolidating the main lines of research; establishing the "Building Blocks" of social capital

The above can be seen as the first part of the evolution of social capital theory, implying the construction of the theoretical body.

The antecedents are classified into two types: those that speak of the dimensions of the concept of social capital (networks, norms, values, and trust) without referring to the term itself and those that outline the first profile of social capital – Hanifan, Loury, or Jacobs.

Pierre Bourdieu, James Coleman, and Robert Putnam conducted a wide-ranging and far-reaching theoretical development. These three authors inaugurated approaches to mark the lines of subsequent work (individualistic, communitarian, and macro-social).

After the construction of the fundamental body, consolidation begins. This is the second part of the evolution of the theory of social capital, which involves consolidating these perspectives and establishing the main building blocks (Figure 2.2), the latter being understood as the entities on which any research in this field pivots.

3.1 Consolidating the prospects for social capital

Although it may be oversimplifying, it can be argued that Bourdieu, Coleman, or Putnam established all the possibilities of conceptualisation. Subsequent work can be assigned to any of these three strands.[1] For example, studies by Ronald Burt (1992, 2001) and Nan Lin (1999a, 2001) follow a micro and social network-centred view, clearly rooted in Bourdieu and Coleman. Fukuyama (1995a, 1995b) and Uslaner (2008) refer to macro-social issues such as civil society, civic participation, trust, or development, as does Putnam. Others, such as Uphoff (2000) and Bowles and Gintis (2002), focus on the community from a perspective close to Coleman as the domain that best captures the idea of social capital.

All researchers working in the field recognise this diversity of approaches, even if they opt for different classifications. For example, Herreros (2002) distinguishes between the "network" approach and the "culturalist" approach. Robison et al. (2002), on the other hand, choose to classify works by their object of study, distinguishing between those that focus on "what is social capital", others on the "sources of social capital", and others on its "effects or consequences". Häuberer (2011) further develops the typology and distinguishes the rational choice approach (Bourdieu and Coleman), the civic perspective (Robert Putnam), the network perspective (Ronald Burt) and the resource perspective (Nan Lin).

The proposal of an "optimal" classification of the conceptual currents must be simplified, integrating a specification of "what social capital is" and "what it is capable of doing" and a methodology of measurement and contrast. Taking this into account, we can integrate the previous classifications into a triple division, which, as we have already pointed out, is related to the three authors on whom we have focused.

a. Bourdieu introduced the individualist or micro perspective. It conceptualises social capital as an "individual resource", comprising the networks of relationships surrounding the focal individual and their associated instrumental and expressive resources. This is part of an ampler mechanism of social reproduction and differentiation.

b. The communitarian or meso perspective, pioneered by Coleman, views social capital as a "community resource" or a collection of attributes and properties inherent in the social structure (such as shared norms and values, particular trust, and closure). These facilitate community functioning and collective action. This perspective pays attention to the characteristics of communities but does not abandon an individualistic approach.
c. Putnam's macro-social or culturalist perspective regards social capital as a macro-social and macro-institutional resource. It emphasises aspects like civic-mindedness, general trust, and social cohesion that contribute to the functioning of the economy and society.

3.2 The building blocks we must manage

Today, the construction of a theory of social capital requires articulating a set of building blocks (Figure 2.3). These include issues that have been underdeveloped in theory and are essential to its construction. We say developing because, as we shall see, there is no established consensus; nevertheless, any proposal will need to articulate these elements.

3.2.1 The three categories of social capital: cognitive, structural, and relational

The unfolding of the theory from its background makes clear that what we are dealing with is under the concept of capital. Whatever the approach, it mixes very different dimensions. An individual's social resources involve ties, contents, and perceptions. We are talking about networks and structures, as well as cognitive constructs such as trust and formal and informal norms embedded in the behaviour of individuals that generate expected behaviours. Although there is a relationship between them, this is not identity.

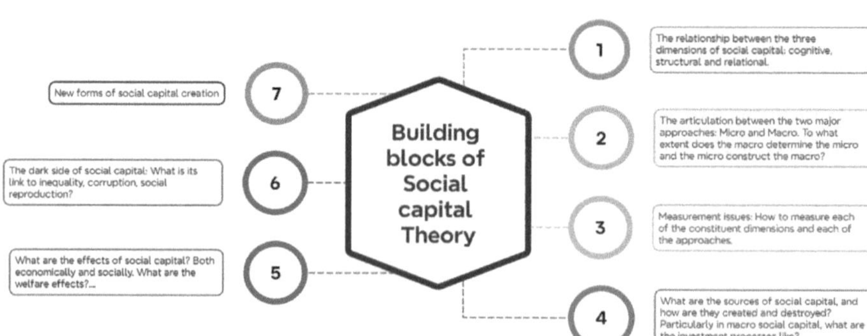

Figure 2.3 The building blocks of social capital.

Source: Own elaboration.

We are implicitly considering the social network (structural dimension), internalised norms and values (cognitive dimension), and trust (relational dimension). As we shall see, the weight attributed to each of these dimensions will depend on the approach adopted. While some authors identify social capital as trust and macro-public functioning, others identify it with the social network that provides resources for the individual, and others place it on prosocial norms and values that favour meso-collective functioning.

The problem is compounded by the simple fact that definitions of concepts such as trust or norms may not converge either. For example, the structuralist approach focuses on the social network, referring to "norms" as intragroup cooperative norms and trust as particular trust. Instead, a macro approach such as Knack and Keefer (1997) broadens the concept of a norm to a "civic norm" and understands trust as "general trust" beyond a particular group.

In any case, all authors are clear about the complementarity of the dimensions, whether at the micro or macro level. For this reason, social capital can be understood as an accumulation of cognitive, structural, and relational assets that foster cooperation and mutually beneficial collective behaviours (Uphoff, 2000). This definition is helpful because it can be applied to different levels of social capital and is open to possible externalities that emerge in the micro-macro relationship.

In any case, theory must continue to explore the content of the three dimensions and the link between them. Particularly the endogeneity problems because, in some research, shared norms and values build social networks (Fukuyama, 1997) and, in others, it is pointed out that associative activity promotes civic norms and social trust (Putnam, 1993).

3.2.2 Articulating the micro and macro dimensions of social capital

As we will see in the next chapter, we can simplify the ways of dealing with the problem to two. The existence of two approaches to social capital, micro and macro, traces back to the theoretical origins of the concept: "individual social capital" and "general social capital".

Individual social capital refers to the micro dimension. It is the network of relationships a given individual possesses, whose value lies in the tangible and intangible resources he or she can extract from them (Pena-López & Sánchez-Santos, 2013). General social capital, on the other hand, focuses on macro-social aspects. It abandons the study of individual networks and the resources imbricated in them, accentuating the public good character.

This breakdown is relevant because it points to the two main approaches to social capital (Portes, 2000). This is probably the great controversy because while the micro approach operates on the relational structure and on the resources that an individual accesses and mobilises through his network (Bourdieu, 1986; Lin, 1999a), the macro approach has a marked culturalist character, where some attributes that favour the good functioning of the economy and society are highlighted (Putnam, 1993; Serageldin, 1996).

This is a significant gap in the theory, which we will analyse in the following chapters. It is essential to distinguish between them and establish a causal sequence between the dimensions. As Lin (1999b) reminds us, the operationalisation of social capital must be analysed primarily at the micro level, that is, in the individual's social network and its associated resources, to approach the vehicular process with the macro-social aspects from there.

3.2.3 *Measuring social capital*

Over the years, many methods have been developed to measure social capital. The specific choice depends on the perspective and the study's intention (Van Deth, 2008). The problematic complexity of the concept influences a heterogeneous range of measurement systems (Gannon & Roberts, 2020), the vast majority of which rely on the development of surveys. These can be used to obtain information on civic norms, values, trust and behaviours (the macro) or to explore the social networks, ties, and resources that people have at their disposal (the micro) with methods such as the "name generator", or the "position generator".

Macro surveys focus on opinions, attitudes, and personal characteristics. This is the case with the World Values Survey, the European Social Survey, the General Social Survey, and the Eurobarometer (Guiso et al., 2011). Similarly, official statistics measure social capital concerning different collective aspects, from associative participation and blood donations to political and religious participation. Some "inverse indicators" also reflect the lack of social capital, such as crime rates or low voter turnout (Fukuyama, 1995a).

The experimental side also has obvious utility. For instance, the experiment of "lost" wallets in different cities aims to measure civic capital and trust. Experiments are often conducted to analyse values, beliefs, and levels of trust and trustworthiness (e.g., sharing money with strangers) (Guiso et al., 2011; Van Deth, 2008, p. 165).

This lack of convergence in an accepted measurement leads to difficulties in testing the theory itself. There is a proliferation of studies whose results are conditioned by data extracted "ad hoc" and not replicated in other cases.

3.2.4 *The sources of macro-social capital*

The issue of "the sources of social capital" is a crucial block that has not been fully addressed in the literature. The question is how social capital is generated, and studies' answers seem ambiguous and insufficient. Social capital is created and a product of social interaction. Again, we depend on our starting definitions.

In any case, there are two types of sources of social capital: internal and external (Membiela-Pollán, 2016).

The internal or endogenous ones are the dimensions of social capital to which we referred earlier (cognitive, structural, and relational) (Uphoff, 2000). These are three distinct but mutually dependent assets. For example, trust is a relational asset that lubricates the socioeconomic exchange system and promotes the extension of the social network. Norms and values are cognitive assets that facilitate social coordination and reduce economic transaction costs while raising individual or social trust. Finally, the social network is a structural asset in which cooperation and collective goals are established. Still, it can also serve the transmission of moral values and civic norms of behaviour.

External or exogenous factors are contextual or cultural factors which can be precursors or determinants of social capital (Lin, 1999a; Deller et al., 2018). These factors can potentially modify cognitive, structural (social networks) and relational dimensions, ranging from greater or lesser social homogeneity to establishing a stable legal system. Their understanding seems more straightforward than in the case of endogenous sources. Putnam indirectly addresses his study in his work *Bowling Alone* (2000), in which he discusses the reasons for the decline of social capital in America. He cites cultural identity, geographical conditions, the legal and political system, economic conditions, religion, the media, and lifestyles, among others. We are then talking about a broad set of factors that contextually and culturally condition interactions and favour or hinder the development of networks, norms, and trust.

At the micro level, investments are both conscious and unconscious. Some are inherited, and some are the subject of an intentional action, which includes membership in a particular group or collective. Pure social interaction, social support, and investment behaviour are constantly mixed. Moreover, they are mixed with the implications of other forms of capital, such as human capital.

The creation of micro-social capital has macro-social precursors, which constitute the context in which networks of relationships are generated. Cultural, institutional, and social structure can condition the endowment. However, everyone also develops an investment process conditioned by expected returns, which are also influenced by contextual factors and an endowment in other forms of capital (Lin, 2000; Pena-López & Sánchez-Santos, 2017).

3.2.5 *The functionality, returns, and contributions of social capital*

If we take into account the breadth and ambiguity of the definition, it is foreseeable that the effects of social capital will be in the most diverse order according to approaches and dimensions. The support function has been studied: physical, economic, and emotional. It has also a function of socialisation and education, closure and social control, the flow of information and opportunities, cooperation and collective action, and cohesion.

The theory refers to economic development, social welfare, and institutional performance. In other words, three effects have been investigated from the outset: economics, politics, and welfare. Looking at its broader context, social capital is one of the many variables that try to explain the "Solow residual" or the 50% of growth that economic variables do not explain (see Box 3.1). The link between social capital and education, insofar as it favours the generation of human capital, has also been studied since the beginning. Over the years, research has consecutively delved into other areas, such as family, health, delinquency and crime, happiness, organisational theory, marketing and business, or technological research and innovation (Tsai & Ghoshal, 1998; Woolcock & Radin, 2008; Dufur et al., 2015; Wong, 2023).

In any case, most of the research focuses on social trust at the macro level as a dimension that facilitates economic interaction and reduces transaction costs. At the micro level, it focuses on the role that social capital plays in the job search and promotion process, as well as the role it plays in the performance and productivity of the business organisation.

One problem is a lack of broadening the research agenda and sharp and novel exploration. An example of the latter could be Alesina and Giuliano (2010), who express that the economic support function in informal networks not only benefits the principal agent but is also a remarkable buffer against the fall in consumption, thus becoming a kind of "automatic stabiliser" of the economy.

In a different sense, the study of the relationship of social capital with other types of capital (human capital, cultural capital, physical capital, natural capital, financial capital) is not fully satisfied. Social capital acts by altering the returns of the other forms of capital with which the interaction is crucial, to the point of being considered as a multiplier of these other forms of capital (Eloire, 2017).

Box 2.1 The new strands: social capital in the online world

It is evident that the "online world" has disruptive features in how networks of social relations are built at all levels: strong ties, weak ties or governance and identity. Its rapid development, including social media, has reached a point where it grasps the daily reality of citizens and organisations. This entails positive effects identified in areas such as business, marketing, health, education, social relations, collective action, social participation, or well-being (Akram & Kumar, 2017; Membiela-Pollán et al., 2020). Nevertheless, it also involves ambiguities and risks.

The academic literature's most studied topic is social media's effect on social capital at the individual or organisational level (bonding and bridging social capital). In terms of dimensions, it affects the structure as well as the cognitive and relational level, how relationships are perceived, and trust in them. By extension, its effect reaches subjective well-being and institutional functioning.

Specifically, the effect of the Internet, digital media, and social media on issues such as individual and generalised trust, social cohesion, social norms, mental processes, perception, attitudes and beliefs, civic behaviour, lifestyles, identity, political preferences, ideology, and public opinion have been studied (Castells, 2008, p. 6; Antoci et al., 2019; Miu, 2019, p. 62; Pang, 2022). This "socialising" and multifaceted influence is not surprising considering that globally, the average daily internet connection today is 6.37 hours (Digital 2023: Global Overview Report).

From a micro perspective, examining individual social capital necessitates considering its influence on existing social capital and its capacity to generate new capital that extends beyond the virtual realm. Moreover, assessing whether they are "comparable" in their ability to generate expressive and instrumental resources is essential. It is noteworthy that amassing a large array of expressive and instrumental resources often requires physical presence, whereas some resources may be attainable in virtual contexts. Similarly, the impact of social media on individual or organisational social capital, particularly on bonding and bridging social capital, varies depending on the specific tool or platform (Spottswood & Wohn, 2020).

Defining our analysis framework, from an ample point of view, the digital network encompasses various platforms and tools, including social network sites (such as Facebook, QQ, Instagram, and YouTube), professional network sites (like LinkedIn and IBM's Beehive), chat boards, discussion fora, social/casual games like Fortnite, Wiki "talk" pages, online dating applications like Tinder, and other tools such as Wanelo, Yik Yak, Twitter, WeChat, Reddit, and Tumblr (Membiela-Pollán et al., 2021). Let us consider some of the results that have been already proposed.

Effects on bonding social capital or strong ties

Bonding social capital pertains to an individual's network of close ties, primarily family and intimate social circles. Social media's impact on this type of capital is somewhat paradoxical. On the one hand, it aids in maintaining and fostering relationships, facilitating interaction, emotional support, and even practical assistance, particularly for individuals separated by distance (e.g., migrants, non-cohabitating relatives, and childhood friends) or experiencing loneliness and isolation (Hämmerle et al., 2020; Suzuki, 2021). Nevertheless, adverse effects have also been observed among individuals living in close proximity (such as married couples, parents and children, and siblings). The increased reliance on social media for communication can lead to a diminished quality of face-to-face interaction, resulting in issues like a loss of empathy (Lanier, 2018) and an inability to appreciate relational experiences fully. Additionally, negative consequences have been noted, including ideological feedback and the potential radicalisation of closed groups with antisocial aims, as social networks tend to reinforce group closure by filtering information and contacts tailored to individual preferences. Common tools and platforms utilised in bonding social capital interactions include WhatsApp, WeChat (in China), and, to a lesser extent, Facebook (Sheer & Rice, 2017; Shane-Simpson et al., 2018).

The effects on subjective well-being are mixed. Social media can have positive outcomes by facilitating more frequent interaction, enhancing trust, fostering a sense of connectedness with close ties, and providing support and assistance (Lee et al., 2018; Bae, 2019). However, negative effects may arise when excessive internet use displaces face-to-face interaction, potentially diminishing the quality of interpersonal relationships.

Effects on bridging social capital or weak ties

In the realm of weak ties, which encompass acquaintances, colleagues, and contacts, also known as bridging social capital, studies consistently demonstrate the positive influence of social media. It maintains, strengthens, and cultivates social capital while functioning as a resource conduit with lower interaction costs (Spottswood & Wohn, 2020). It is crucial to recognise that these ties specialise in instrumental resources, including information dissemination, opportunities, fostering cooperation, and offering expert advice across various domains such as labour, healthcare, finance, education, and professional advice. Social media has demonstrated its efficacy in formal and informal educational settings, business transactions, customer relations, marketing endeavours, civic and political engagement, job searches, personal promotion, and interactions with individuals sharing similar or diverse interests (Carr & Hayes, 2015).

Bridging social capital is mediated through a diverse array of network platforms and services, each serving distinct purposes and exerting varied effects on individual social networks, the types of contacts maintained or generated, and the resources they facilitate. In addition to instant messaging services like WhatsApp or WeChat, platforms such as Twitter, Instagram, or LinkedIn play significant roles in bridging social capital (Shane-Simpson et al., 2018).

Regarding subjective well-being, the impact of social media is generally positive, as it provides valuable resources and alternative avenues for entertainment and communication. However, it also carries risks, including potentially dehumanising personal relationships due to excessive reliance on online social networking (Chen & Li, 2017). At the same time, digital interaction platforms may foster curiosity and social comparison (Mayol & Pénard, 2017) and also pose risks such as bullying, cyber aggression, cyber harassment, sexting, and isolation, which detrimentally affect not only the well-being of individuals but also their surrounding environment (O'Keeffe & Clarke-Pearson, 2011; Membiela-Pollán et al., 2021).

In conclusion, social media positively affects bonding and bridging social capital (Bian & Leung, 2015; Carbonell & Oberst, 2015; Chan, 2015; Karapanos et al., 2016). It facilitates the expansion of contacts, sustains them through online media, and fosters opportunities for face-to-face interactions. Notwithstanding, it is imperative to acknowledge the nuances surrounding its usage:

a. While the use of social media is relevant, it is noteworthy that online communication prioritises some less significant forms of social capital. Activities such as searching for information, browsing, and excessive time spent on social networks often prove counterproductive in fostering meaningful social connections. Such behaviour can detrimentally affect subjective well-being and diminish the time allocated for face-to-face interaction (Meshi & Ellithorpe, 2021).

b. The crowding-out effect, sometimes induced by the Internet, digital media, and social media, can impede individuals' ability to engage in face-to-face communication – a crucial component for developing moral sensibilities. Within these face-to-face interactions, individuals perceive social approval or disapproval of their actions, thus influencing their moral growth (Gui & Sugden, 2005; Karapanos et al., 2016).
c. Despite the possibilities offered by virtual interaction, it cannot fully substitute for social capital derived from face-to-face communication. Various socioeconomic functions of social capital necessitate the physical presence of individuals. Moreover, the effects on subjective well-being differ between virtual and in-person interactions, as the enjoyment of relational experiences is more profound and productive when experienced firsthand (Meshi & Ellithorpe, 2021).

3.2.6 The risks associated with equality and bad social capital

Most of the work developed from the macro approach "a la Putnam" considers social capital as a generator of always positive effects, leaving aside the possibility of negative externalities.

This bias does not exist in the micro approach. While shedding light on the utility of the social network, Bourdieu's approach speaks of the relational structure as an instrumental element that serves for social reproduction and the perpetuation of systems of privilege. Similarly, the different forms of social capital identified by Coleman (obligations and expectations, practical norms and sanctions, potential information, authority relations, closure, appropriability, and trust) could have negative effects beyond the group. As Portes (1998) points out, the exact mechanisms that operate in good social capital can work in the opposite direction, leading to negative consequences. Social capital present in the social structure may favour goals at the "intragroup" level and be negative to aggregate social capital (Paldam, 2000; Durlauf, 2008; Villalonga-Olives et al., 2020).

The curious thing is that Putnam himself already pointed out in *Bowling Alone* (2000) that networks and the associated norms of reciprocity are generally good for those who belong to the network. Notwithstanding, the external effects of social capital are not always good in themselves. To illustrate this problem, he proposed the example of urban gangs and power elites exploiting social capital for antisocial purposes from an aggregate perspective. Another example mentioned is rent-seekers, understood as groups that acquire rents by manipulating their political environment (Pena-López & Sánchez-Santos, 2005, p. 144). Thus, we can speak of "bad social capital" (Warren, 2008, pp. 122–123) for the simple reason that organisations such as the mafia, terrorism, clientelism and corruption, ethnic rivalry, and unfair distribution of resources are also derivations of forms of social capital.

These issues involve forms of intentional or expressed exclusion or closure, as in the case of racism or gender discrimination; however, they may be notably subtler mechanisms that have effects within the social structure. This is the case of homophily (Lin, 2008, p. 60), based on preferential interaction with network members with whom one shares a particular affinity, ranging from a geographical background to following a particular sports club. This effect will be particularly evident in inequality when homophilic networks are linked to high social strata and situations of privilege (Pena-López et al., 2021).

3.2.7 Criticisms of social capital

Given the contentious construction of the concept, criticism from both sides has been a constant. Nevertheless, it should be borne in mind that criticism is part of the take-off of any new theory and can be considered a sign of health when it is accompanied by the relevant response (Ahn & Ostrom, 2008). In the case of social capital, theoretical disagreements are no more or less frequent than in any other field of social science, particularly when it comes to establishing abstract and new concepts (Castiglione, 2008). We can point out a quick overview of the open debates that we will examine in depth later.

Social capital is an "umbrella concept" (Sobel, 2002, p. 145). This label is due to its complex and multidimensional nature, encompassing norms, values, rules, social networks, and trust. This breadth makes it difficult to delimit, and some criticise it as too elastic, vague, and imprecise (Roche, 2004, p. 107).

The definitions are circular or tautological. This context makes it difficult to determine their causal direction (Sánchez-Santos & Pena-López, 2005, p. 142). We find that what, for some, is social capital, for others are products or manifestations of social capital (Kliksberg et al., 2000). Thus, social capital can be both a cause and an effect of social relations.

The "micro" and the "macro" lack a clear and precise link. Social capital's individual and collective dimensions are dissociated, making it challenging to analyse the construct. For some, social capital focuses on the individual and the resources they can draw from their social networks, making it a "private good". For others, social capital points to issues such as civic-mindedness and social trust and is thus a "public good".

Lack of empirical rigour. The problem of conceptual delimitation raises a new difficulty: its scientific rigour is undermined (Lin, 2008, p. 50). Because definitions are so varied, it is not fully known what should be measured and how it should be operationalised (Dasgupta, 2005).

It is unclear whether it can be qualified as capital (Fine, 1999; Arrow, 2000). It is also unclear whether it fulfils specific properties found in other types of capital (initial investment, transferability, depreciation).

Regarding *the concept's functionality*, some critics point out that its effects are ambiguous, given that it can imply negative individual and collective consequences (Sánchez-Santos & Pena-López, 2005). Others have questioned the concept of social capital, considering it "a fad" or relating it to economic imperialism (Woolcock, 2001, pp. 72–76).

3.2.8 Social capital, social change, and the Internet

Changes in modes of interaction and how these affect social capital are noticeable lines of research. At the time of the publication of *Bowling Alone*, the significance of the digital world was incipient in a way that Putnam likens to the costs of social links or networks brought about by television. The subsequent reality turned out to be very different. Over the years, especially with the emergence of online social networks (Facebook, Twitter, Instagram, WhatsApp, etc.), an essential body of scientific research has emerged that analyses at length the consequences of the Internet and social media on network social capital (Field, 2016). This social capital-Internet causality, now the subject of debate, will not be as simple as Putnam's initial intuition. The extension of a network is not necessarily linked with social trust (see Box 2.1).

In their current state, the evidence shows that social networks have a remarkable capacity to influence norms and values as well as social perceptions and attitudes. Likewise, there are also relevant effects on trust in all its forms: individual, social, and institutional. Above all, the critical point is how they affect ways of relating in both weak and strong ties. The Internet and social media's role in social capital can be positive (it can even be born digital) or negative (a trade-off with valuable relationships) (Membiela-Pollán et al., 2020).

4 Recapping

In this chapter, we have set out to take a quick look at the trajectory of the concept to explain its current situation.

Although we are talking about a relatively recent and expanding line of research, its object of analysis is by no means new. The "social" as an asset has been continuously approached using concepts that can be assimilated in some way to that of social capital and be its precedents (civil society, civic virtue…). However, its analysis as a form of capital is a product of the last quarter of the 20th century. In the 1980s and 1990s, the configuration of the theoretical body was established by three crucial authors (Bourdieu, Coleman, and Putnam). They set the potential approaches to the problem. Norms, values, trust, and networks of interpersonal relations impact the individual, the group, and society. Nevertheless, the approach to definition, mechanisms, and outcomes will be disparate.

One aspect that is still relevant today is that social capital is multidimensional and complex to define. Nonetheless, this does not prevent us from attributing a high degree of importance to it because, in some way, it is necessary to capture that which comes from the social dimension and which generates consequences in all areas, from economic growth to individual well-being. After the theoretical body had been established, the consolidation phase began, which has lasted until now. Three perspectives are established, derived from the studies of Bourdieu, Coleman, and Putnam, and they can be called individualistic or micro-social, communitarian or meso-social, and macro-social or macro-institutional. Social capital scholars will align themselves to a greater or lesser degree with one of these three distinct approaches.

Now that we are in the present, we can systematise the state of the question based on a series of building blocks, which gather the central points to be studied and construct the theory simultaneously.

Briefly, the building blocks on which the theory is built and which are the subject of debate are:

Firstly, the micro and macro approaches to the analysis of social capital, and especially the study of their causal interrelationship. Also, at a more theoretical level, the analysis of the internal dimensions of social capital, that is, the cognitive, relational, and structural categories. Thirdly, it is essential to solve and thus reach a certain degree of convergence about the problem of measuring social capital. Fourthly, and now entering the field of causes and effects, the study of the basis of the development of social networks (micro) and general social capital (macro), as well as the conditioning factors, is critical. We need a general model that explains the process of capitalisation. Simultaneously, on the output side, we need to clarify its functionalities and returns and what social capital generates at the micro and macro levels. In this field, possible negative externalities (corruption, inequality, etc.) are an object of study. Finally, the criticisms of the concept and the need for a relevant response are also made explicit.

Note

1 In the following chapter we will see how, given the construction of the theory, these three approaches can really be reduced to two broad perspectives: micro and macro.

Part II

Two conflicting approaches

3 Complex consensus

The micro, the meso, and the macro

A seductive but exasperating concept.

(Li et al., 2003)

The expansion of divergent trajectories from the last quarter of the 20th century onwards that we have observed in Chapter 2 is evidence of the danger that Portes (1998, p. 2) warned us about. Social capital applies to so many facts and contexts that it can mean something different in each case. Moreover, one can get the impression that it is applied according to the convenience of the research object and the researcher's ideological orientation. An apparent uncontrolled "success" may be the prelude to a resounding failure (Woolcock, 2010 and 2021; Ferragina & Arrigoni, 2017).

The previous chapter also shows that the concept lacks a common reference point. To put it simply, many authors concerned about the lack of realism in economics, or the lack of attention to its social framework, have introduced into the concept a set of elements that are difficult to quantify, associated with a prestigious notion in economics, such as capital.

As we showed in the first chapter, this concept's success is associated mainly with its presumed capacity to situate economic facts within the social fabric. It allows us to address the question of the economy's embeddedness in a way that allows economists, sociologists, and political scientists to converge on the same object of analysis.

The concept initially appears enticing, but upon closer examination and beyond the first seduction, we encounter numerous perspectives that render the construct ambiguous and challenging to define (Dasgupta, 2005). Amidst the multitude of qualifications, it has been described as "a wonderfully elastic term" (Adler & Kwon, 2002, p. 18), "a notion that means many things to many people", and a term lacking clear boundaries (Dasgupta & Serageldin, 2000, p. XI), characterised as ambiguous, if not incoherent, and serving as an all-encompassing concept (Fine, 1999). As Ahn and Ostrom (2008) suggest in the form of a disclaimer, it is essential to acknowledge that critique is inherent to the advancement of every theory and paradigm, mainly when dealing with novel and abstract concepts.

Beginning with the most elementary from the previous journey, we must at least recognise the coexistence of three definitions and three research strategies, which

DOI: 10.4324/9781003375302-6

we will later see that can be integrated into two and require a unifying theory (Portes, 2000). For a large group of researchers, probably the largest and perhaps the most affected by the problem of lack of concreteness, social capital is, by definition, a collective rather than an individual property. Consequently, their research strategy is to study communities and associations, not individuals. The rationale seems obvious: if social capital is built on social relations, these are not alienable individual property but depend on and are an attribute of a community. Underlying this is tautological evidence. Well-functioning societies generate positive effects on their economies. Thus, in contrast to unstructured societies or lacking a unifying bond, stable networks of social relations with shared values and identities improve social and economic functioning (Andriani & Christoforou, 2016).

However, statements of the type that a "well-functioning society" is something that necessarily refers us to this construct's "multidimensional" nature. It is clear that what we mean by "social" is a broad and complex entity. Alongside this, the mechanics in which networks of social relations, shared norms and values, and trust affect economic activity are not self-evident. Each study or research may focus on a particular characteristic that gives advantages to a specific social group.

At this point, the researcher faces two dilemmas: First, which is the critical dimension: structural, cognitive, or relational? That is, which is the starting point: social networks, values, or trust (Portes, 2000)? Second, and even more important, we must start from the individual or society, the micro or the macro?.

The historical overview in the previous chapter leads us to consider a current cross-section that reflects the ways of answering previous questions. In this chapter, our objectives are twofold: to arrive at a consensus definition of social capital and to construct its geography. This simplified diagram will help us advance along each of the proposed lines. We will leave the bulk of the criticisms of each approach for later chapters. Alongside this, and following the aspiration of any self-respecting theory, we will seek to integrate both approaches into a single "causal" explanatory model, that is, we will finally seek to propose an overall view that integrates both perspectives. This chapter addresses the main problem of social capital theory: the dissociation of micro, meso, and macro approaches. We will address the following questions: What are the main approaches? What are the interrelations, and what is the main structural flaw of this model?

1 Dimensions and approaches to the concept

In traditional economic discourse, three forms of capital are typically distinguished, representing the diverse array of resources available to a community. Among these, two are commonly recognised: natural capital, encompassing the environment's natural resources, and productive capital, which pertains to the generated physical assets commonly referred to as physical capital. However, the emergence of neocapital approaches, as previously discussed, has underscored the inadequacy of these classifications in encapsulating human beings' unique attributes and capabilities (Bourdieu, 2001). Therefore, the taxonomy has been augmented to include the concept of human capital, denoting the skills and knowledge acquired by individuals, and the concept of social capital, aimed at integrating the relational underpinnings of economic activity. This relational foundation stems from personal and social investment, constituting a stock akin to any other form of capital.

When seeking a common referent for what may constitute this stock, three concepts are always mentioned: norms and values, social networks, and trust (Sobel, 2002, p. 145; Sánchez-Santos & Pena-López, 2005, p. 142). These three components are presented as three dimensions of the same referent to the extent that the definitions we will analyse later include them, although not with identical weight. This will be one of the crucial problems in the study, and it will have significant consequences for the lines of research open to us.

1.1 The three dimensions of social capital: structural, relational, and cognitive

Suppose we penetrate the nature of social capital with an analytical will. In that case, we must recognise that whatever definition we adopt, three dimensions or elements of a different nature are interrelated and must be explained. The first and most apparent is that social capital comprises "tangible and intangible" elements.

What we could call tangible falls under the structural dimension, that is, networks of individuals who recognise each other and play a certain role. The intangible are perceptions and values that condition behaviours. This intangible part can also be divided into two: the cognitive and the relational (Krishna & Shrader, 1999). The distinction between the two subjective dimensions is linked to the weight given to the trust variable in social analysis (Nahapiet & Ghoshal, 1998). The cognitive relates to subjective interpretations of shared understandings, common values, and identities. The relational (also cognitive) is the feeling of trust shared by the many actors within the social context (group, organisation, community) (Claridge, 2018b).

The study of the interrelationship between the dimensions is critical to understanding what social capital is because the dimensions are obviously intertwined (Claridge, 2023; Lefebvre et al., 2016).

1.1.1 The structural dimension

Structural social capital indicates the presence of a network of access to people and resources, a network of connections between actors or a structure of actors engaged in social exchange. Network ties facilitate social interaction, stimulating the development of social capital's cognitive and relational dimensions. Similarly, the cognitive and relational dimensions reinforce and foster the development of these networks by providing the inclination to interact and form new relationships, roles, rules, and procedures. Thus, causality is bidirectional and results in a mutually reinforcing cycle. Nevertheless, we can establish a principle in this circularity: the precondition for developing and maintaining social capital's relational and cognitive dimensions is sustained social interaction to prioritise networks (Gooderham, 2007).

As we will see, this reference point exhibits a distinct micro "bias", delineating the configuration of ties among individuals or units. Structural social capital refers to the network of individuals known to an individual and upon whom they can rely for benefits such as information and assistance. Consequently, compared to the cognitive and relational dimensions, it manifests as tangible, observable, and quantifiable. For instance, one can gauge the number and structure of an individual's connections or assess the network's density, connectivity, hierarchy, and appropriability within an organisation. However, it is imperative to clarify that our discussion pertains to the network and access to people and resources rather than the quality and content of these relationships, as both aspects fall within the purview of the relational and cognitive dimensions.

1.1.2 Cognitive and relational dimensions

Organising this subjective domain, the cognitive dimension is an antecedent to the relational one. This is because shared goals and narratives can lead to shared norms and obligations and enhanced feelings of trust and identity. Although one could speak of a certain bidirectionality since trust and identity can lead to a homogenisation of values and representations (Uhlaner et al., 2015), the priority is on the cognitive side.

The cognitive dimension captures the shared representations, interpretations, and systems of meaning between the parties reflected in common values and narratives (Gooderham, 2007). We are discussing an open category that could include concepts such as Habermas' Theories of the World or Bourdieu's Habitus (1986). Dispositions, representations, hierarchies of values and accepted or unaccepted forms of behaviour that subjects acquire through complex socialisation processes. Their manifestations are manifold, from forms of language to codes of conduct, from clothing to the predictability of behaviour.

Without leaving this subjective realm, the relational dimension is expressed in the characteristics and qualities of personal relationships, such as trust, obligations, respect and even friendship (Gooderham, 2007; Nahapiet & Ghoshal, 1998). Objectively speaking, their specificity is the only reason for dividing the two dimensions. The relational dimension only relates to the perception of social relationships, whereas the cognitive dimension captures a broader social framework, a global view of social functioning. The two dimensions are overlapped; one could even argue that there is only one cognitive dimension since everything is within the framework of the subject's mental representations (Uphoff, 2000).

If we accept this specificity, the relational dimension of social capital is an attribute of the bond established, its reliability (Lefebvre et al., 2016; Davenport & Daellenbach, 2011). Granting it an entity vis-à-vis the cognitive in general also has to do with the complexity involved in perceiving relationships within the cognitive. Thus, this same relational sphere includes the affective (relational goods and evils) and even personal and collective identity. At the same time, it includes the complex world of ethics, prosociality, and associationism (Lazarova & Taylor, 2009; Ramos-Pinto, 2012).

Once we have discerned the dimensions of the object of study, we must ask ourselves: What should be our starting point and our natural object of study? This question, which may seem absurd, is by no means so. We can propose three approaches to analysing social capital based on these dimensions.

Researchers examining social capital at the individual level may prioritise the structural dimension, particularly if they conceptualise it as a private good generated and owned by the individual. This preference stems from the fact that individuals often have agency over their investment in social relationships but possess limited control over the broader social environment that underpins them. Conversely, researchers may also direct their attention towards the cognitive and relational dimensions, thereby relegating the study of networks to a secondary position. In this scenario, the emphasis would shift towards variables such as trust, norms, identities, and collective representations. Consequently, the focus naturally extends to macro-level entities such as organisations, communities, societies, and cultural factors.

1.2 The three approaches to social capital: macro, meso, and micro

From the previous section, it can be deduced that we must consider which unit of study should be our starting point: individuals, groups, or society as a whole. Social capital can be considered from these three points of view. Social relations generate effects both at the general level of the whole society (macro), as well as at the level of social organisations (meso) and individuals (micro) and the effects at each level are related. In other words, we must answer whether social capital should be considered a public good, a collective good or an individual good. As we have seen, some authors treat social capital as a private good, some as a public good, and others as having both private and public good characteristics. It is private if we focus on the social relations available to an individual (micro), and it is public if we consider the whole social framework and the social structures it generates (macro) and its effects of solidarity and trust. However, we could interpose an intermediate level (meso), a kind of local or group public good, the world of associations and their interrelations. This intermediate level links the previous two (Jackson, 2020; Gannon & Roberts, 2020).

The answer to these questions is crucial insofar as what we will analyse in each of these dimensions will be different; we will use different methods, and what is more, focusing our attention on any of these three levels implies a series of "biases" about social functioning.

Given the considerations above, we propose a classification grounded in regarding social capital as follows: firstly, as an "individual resource", encompassing the networks of relationships of the focal subject that provide tangible or intangible resources; secondly, as a "community resource", denoting a set of attributes and properties inherent in a social structure that facilitate collective action; and finally, as a "macro-social and macro-institutional resource", relying on factors such as civic-mindedness, social cohesion, and general trust, which contribute to the functioning of the economy and society at large (Membiela-Pollán & Pena-López, 2017; Engbers et al., 2017) (Figure 3.1).

Each approach focuses on a different dimension, leading to different measurement methodologies (Figure 3.2) ranging from the structural in the micro approach to assessments of subjective variables such as general trust with a clear cognitive component.

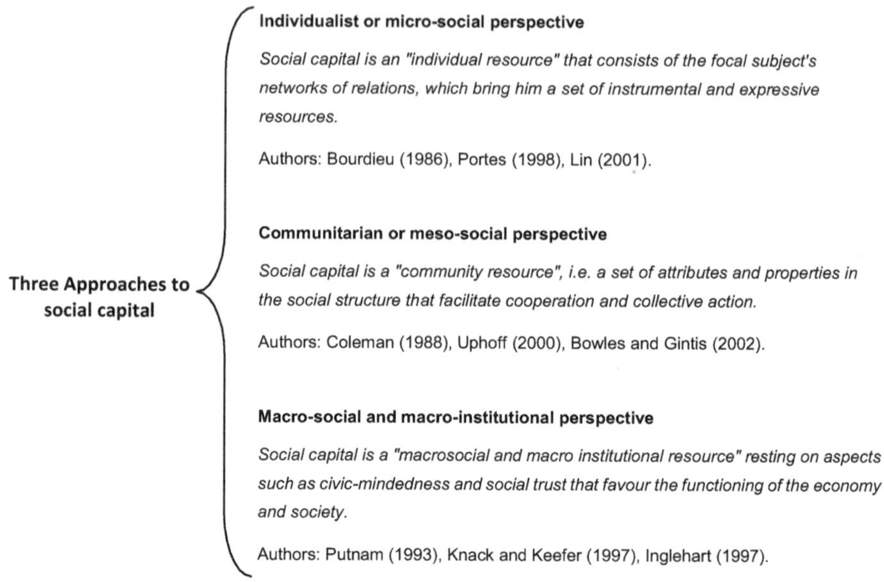

Figure 3.1 Approaches to social capital.

Source: Own elaboration.

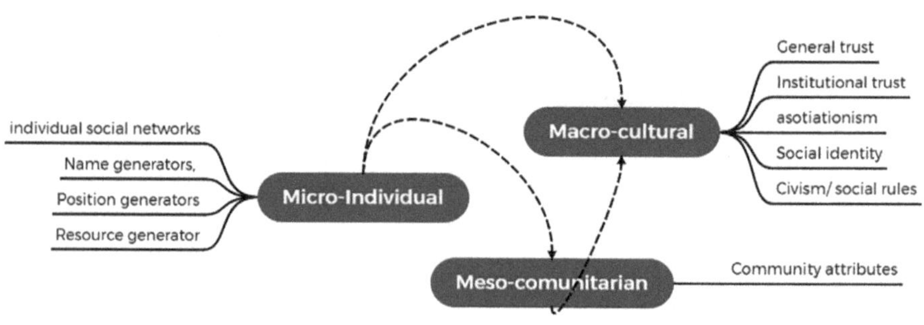

Figure 3.2 Micro, meso and macro measurements of social capital.

Source: Own elaboration.

In what follows, we will examine each of the approaches and the interrelationship between them, one of the main problems of social capital.

1.2.1 The micro and personal networks as stock. The primacy of the individual

The "micro" perspective, also referred to as the "network approach" or "ego-network approach", is widely recognised and centres on analysing social capital as an individual resource. Within this framework, actors utilise their networks of relationships to pursue personal objectives, encompassing both instrumental goals (such as income, status, and power) and expressive aims (including well-being, health, recognition, and mutual assistance). This perspective emphasises the pivotal role of an individual's network to the extent that the concept of network capital becomes salient.

Nan Lin (2001) is a prominent figure in this line of inquiry. However, Pierre Bourdieu, one of the progenitors of social capital theory, articulated a seminal definition of social capital in his foundational work "The Forms of Capital" (1986, p. 248). Drawing from a Marxist perspective closely aligned with structuralism, Bourdieu characterises social capital as "the aggregate of actual or potential resources linked to the possession of a durable network of more or less institutionalised relations of mutual knowledge and recognition". From this standpoint, Bourdieu posits that an individual's cultivation and maintenance of networks can be construed as an instrumental endeavour aimed at safeguarding one's class position. He asserts that "the network of relations is the product of investment strategies, individual or collective, consciously or unconsciously aimed at establishing or reproducing social relations that are directly usable in the short or long term" (Bourdieu, 1986, p. 249).

Essentially, relationships serve as a means to acquire material and symbolic resources. Consequently, an agent's social capital is contingent upon the network of connections they can activate and the magnitude of capital (economic, cultural, or symbolic) encapsulated within these networks. Starting from this foundational definition centred on the instrumentality of networks, we can find a wide range of analogous proposals (Table 3.1). They all have two elements in common: the individual as the focal subject and the social network as the entity from which a return is extracted. The divergences focus on what constitutes the actual capital, the network, or those resources accessible, and thus the real object of the investment.

Table 3.1 Definitions of social capital in the individualistic perspective

Authors	*Individualistic perspective*
Pierre Bordieu (1986)	"The aggregate of the actual or potential resources linked to possession of a durable network of more or less institutionalised relationships of mutual acquaintance or recognition".
Nan Lin (2001, chap. 2, 2008, p. 51)	"Resources embedded in one's social networks, resources that can be accessed or mobilised through ties in the networks".
Baker (1990, p. 619)	"A resource that actors derive from specific social structures and then use to pursue their interests; it is created by exchanges in the relationship among actors".
Burt (1992, p. 9)	"Friends, colleagues, and more general contacts through whom you receive opportunities to use your financial and human capital".
Nahapiet and Goshal (1998, p. 243)	"The sum of the actual and potential resources embedded within, available through, and Ghoshal derived from the network of relationships possessed by an individual or social unit. Social capital thus comprises both the network and the assets that may be mobilised through that network".

(*Continued*)

Table 3.1 (Continued)

Authors	*Individualistic perspective*
Portes (1998, p. 6)	"The ability of actors to secure benefits by membership in social networks or other social structures".
Knoke (1999, p. 18)	"The process by which social actors create and mobilise their network connections within and between organisations to gain access to other social actors' resources".
Boxman et al. (1991, p. 52)	"The number of people who can be expected to provide support and the resources those people have at their disposal".
Belliveau et al. (1996, p. 1572)	"An individual's network and elite institutional affiliations".

Source: Own elaboration.

Focusing the object on the network may be the most acceptable from a sociological point of view, as the centre is on the networks and their attributes, that is, the "social fact" from which the resources available to the leading actor emerge *a posteriori*. Likewise, these are the real object of the investment insofar as individuals seek to have an endowment of social networks that provide them with resources. However, these networks may not be defined in terms of concrete resources. They constitute an endowment that is transformable into still indeterminate resources, a system of social support and identity that acts as insurance. In this sense, networks are instrumental and polymorphic, allowing many resources to be obtained. What is defining is the ability to access these people and the possibility of exchanging material or immaterial resources with them, from a favour, a resource, an encounter that impacts well-being or simple recognition. This will be discussed at length in chapter 5.

Nonetheless, if one opts for a specific definition, Lin's (1999b, 2008) perspective effectively integrates both proposals. According to Lin, social capital encompasses the resources embedded within social networks, which can be accessed or mobilised through network ties. In essence, this perspective acknowledges the amalgamation of both material and immaterial resources within networks, as well as their accessibility and mobilisation. While networks facilitate access to and utilisation of embedded resources, mobilisation implies their effective use. Although equating the two notions is erroneous, they are interrelated (Lin, 2008, pp. 58–59). Lin (1999b) also posits that individuals perceive their network, comprising both strong and weak ties, as a platform for exchange where interests or preferences can naturally coordinate and generate mutual benefits. Individuals invest in social relations with the expectation of reciprocation, interacting with others and assuming that responses will yield rewards or returns. This investment in relationships fosters the flow of information and opportunities, enabling access to diverse resources, both instrumental and expressive.

Grounded in this conceptualisation of personal networks as investments, it becomes imperative to recognise that a network serves as a structure that orchestrates the distribution of material and immaterial resources while determining individuals' strategic positions within it. Moreover, this underscores that social interaction is a conduit for accessing these resources and fostering alignment between positions (Millán & Gordon, 2004, p. 741).

We will address measurement in another chapter. However, we can outline some peculiarities to specify the referents alluded to in the definitions. Firstly, by integrating the various definitions, we can measure both the network's dimension (accessible) and the resources (mobilisable) through it. The breadth of resources accessible through a network will lead us to introduce the need to consider the orientation of the various links (instrumental or expressive) and the social composition of the networks by considering stratification.

The critical question at this level of analysis is the extent to which the micro approach considers our trilogy of social capital. If we return to the three dimensions that we identified as constitutive, we can review this approach's advantages and biases.

From a structural perspective, it is clear that networks of social relations at the micro level are a crucial component of the concept, the central element. Networks shape social interactions, which determine everything from economic activity to subjective well-being. The micro approach has a radical advantage; the referent is clearly defined, objectifiable and quantifiable, including qualitative aspects. The latter is crucial since not all types of relationships involve similar links. It is important to distinguish between strong or proximity relationships, which can be assimilated to bonding in macro relationships within the same group or network, and weak relationships, which link individuals with members of different groups, which can be assimilated into bridging.

With the relational dimension within the micro, we are referring to the existence of trust between the network members (Table 3.2). As a result of repeated interactions, the strength and, in some cases, the closure of that network, individuals can rely on the compliance of certain behaviours by the other members. Here, the distinction from the cognitive dimension is somewhat subtle. However, it is essential to differentiate between strong and weak ties. Trust in networks of strong ties is called particular trust, and trust in society as a whole, not embedded in a particular set of social relations, is general trust. The two can both be related to each other and show clear trade-offs. At this point, it is advisable to focus mainly on some caveats. We should not disregard the general context in order to analyse the micro.

Table 3.2 Dimensions of social capital from the micro approach

Level	*Structural dimension*	*Relational dimension*	*Cognitive dimension*
Micro Provision of personal networks and resources accessible through them.	Social structure Strong and weak links between individuals *Similar to connectivity*	Individual and general trust: Systems of norms and behavioural expectations	Code sharing: Values, attitudes, and beliefs that make behaviour predictable

Source: Own elaboration from T. Claridge (2020).

The network interactions that constitute the micro do not take place in isolation from social organisations and the characteristics of society as a whole. More generalised trust will influence the relationships established in any personal network. Nevertheless, particular trust in personal networks may not necessarily be linked to general trust, as in the case of criminal organisations and so on.

The cognitive dimension derives from trust but relates to shared understandings that provide systems of meaning that make behaviours predictable. Membership in networks hinges upon the potential for communication and adherence to a code of shared values. Consequently, these dimensions are less tangible than structural factors, residing within individuals' mental constructs – hence the term cognitive. This dimension resembles sociological concepts, such as habitus, lifeworld, and worldview, about the social construction of reality (see, for instance, Berger & Luckmann, 1966; Bolton, 2006; Bourdieu, 1986). Within this realm, distinctions between particularist and universalist values and codes can be drawn, with significant implications for subsequent chapters. These cognitive and relational dimensions distinguish the micro approach from mere network analysis. While the emphasis remains on networks, they exhibit emergent properties with individual and social repercussions, from personal identity and well-being to comprehension of social dynamics.

1.2.2 The communitarian or mesosocial perspective. The primacy of the "we"

The second of the approaches we have mentioned considers social capital as a "community resource". It focuses on what constitutes a community or any form of non-generalist grouping. Unlike the individual perspective, where the starting point is the subject as an investor in social networks with material or immaterial returns, we now find ourselves with the "we" approach and the study of relationships as a local or community public good. Its axis of study is consequently the "social organisation", which contains a set of resources that, in addition to serving the individual subject, favours cooperation and the functioning of this "group with advantages" (Aldrich, 2017).

The change in approach also implies a change in the understanding of what we can call a resource in this context. In the previous approach, resources had value from an individual point of view. Now, more focused on the group, resources become an attribute of the collective that facilitates its functioning. Thus, a rule or a sanction constitutes a resource for the subject and the collective.

The most immediate reference for this approach is the functionalist definition of social capital proposed by Coleman (1988, p. 98, 1990, p. 302), combining social capital's individual and group character. In his approach, social capital resides in a structure and its characteristics, and it has the property of facilitating individual actions. Resources are the features of the structure that facilitate repeated interactions and the achievement of individual and group goals: expectations, potential information, effective norms and sanctions, authority relations and closure (Coleman, 1998, p. 98). In sum, we focus on group and community, where the structural is mixed with the cognitive.

Among the characteristics of these networks, closure and appropriability are essential. Closure refers to the presence of sufficient connections among a certain number of individuals to ensure adherence to norms (Portes, 1998). Coleman (1988), for instance, highlights that establishing and enforcing norms rely not only on the negative external repercussions of "punishable" actions but also on the degree of closure or openness within the structure. The concept of appropriability within organisations indicates that social ties of one nature (e.g., friendship) often serve multiple purposes (e.g., providing moral and material support and offering job counselling) (Adler & Kwon, 2002, p. 18). These characteristics of networks are pivotal for grasping the "social" or "prosocial" nature inherent in all forms of community or association.

Other scholars adopting a community or mesosocial perspective underscore the significance of cognitive and structural assets (Uphoff, 2000) facilitating collective action (see Table 3.3). Francis Fukuyama (1997) defines social capital as shared norms and values within the organisation that foster cooperation. Woolcock (1998) and Bowles and Gintis (2002) emphasise that it comprises information, trust, and norms of reciprocity embedded within the social network, while Brehm and Rahn (1997) speak of a "network of cooperative relationships". Membership in these entities serves as a resource for individuals, enabling them to pursue specific interests or fulfil particular needs (Millán & Gordon, 2004). Simultaneously, each member contributes to the overall functioning of the structure.

Table 3.3 Definitions of social capital in the communitarian perspective

Authors	*Communitarian perspective*
M. Schiff (1992)	"The set of elements of the social structure that affects relations among people and are inputs or arguments of the production and utility function".
Fukuyama (1995a, 1995b)	"The ability of people to work together for common purposes in groups and organisations".
Brehm and Rahn (1997)	"The web of cooperative relationships between citizens that facilitate resolution of collective action problems".
Fukuyama (1997)	"Social capital can be defined simply as the existence of a certain set of informal values or norms shared among group members that permits cooperation among them".
Woolcock (1998)	"The information, trust, and norms of reciprocity inherent in one's social networks".
Nahapiet and Goshal (1998)	"The sum of the current and potential resources embedded within, available through, and derived from the network of relationships possessed by an individual or social unit. Social capital thus comprises both the network and the assets that may be mobilised through that network".
Bowles and Gintis (2002)	"Social capital generally refers to trust, concern for one´s associates, a willingness to live by the norms of one´s community and to punish those who do not".

Source: Own elaboration.

Based on the above definitions, we can refer to any intermediate social organisation, regardless of its objectives and values, from a company to a neighbourhood association or a cycling club, and any organisation dedicated to capturing income by illicit means. The development of intra-group relations and closure can lead to the creation of a specific "group capital" that favours both the productivity of the group and the promotion of its members through relationships of trust and reciprocity (Gui, 2001; Kaiser et al., 2020). A community of neighbours could be such a case, as could the well-studied case of the diamond market linked to the Jewish community in New York and its closure (Coleman, 1988, pp. 98–99). However, this definition is perfectly adaptable to organisations such as the mafia or any structure of corruption and kleptocracy (Portes, 1998; Durlauf, 2008). Ultimately, the values inspiring the organisation are not indifferent, especially if they are particularist or universalist.

If we look at the dimensions from this approach (Table 3.4), any human grouping has structures, trust, and norms. We are embedded in various forms of community that shape social life, from the family to a company to a sports club. These structures shape social relations and simultaneously create meaning by creating obligations and expectations and removing uncertainties by placing the individual in a normative framework that presupposes a particular role. Although it might be thought that this aspect is no different from the micro level, it should be borne in mind that a role arises from the organisation's structure and is entirely distinct from an individual's set of relationships. The organisations and institutions where individuals are situated create norms and roles that persist for those who occupy them.

If we place ourselves in the structural dimension, we speak of functionally oriented and closed structures of relations that make up each organisation. A community is constituted of a set of organisationally and functionally situated individuals.

From the cognitive and relational dimensions, the community in which individuals are situated, its norms and the trust are now the central objects of analysis. Thus, we cannot speak of relational trust but particularistic trust in the organisation itself. This way of conceiving trust is complex. As Coleman (1990) argues, care must be taken to transition to the macro. The characteristics of individual

Table 3.4 Dimensions of social capital from the meso approach

Level	*Structural dimension*	*Relational dimension*	*Cognitive Dimension*
Meso Factors applicable in the context of a social grouping.	Group roles Organisational structures in which each member is assigned a specific role.	Functional and social relationships between the members of a given organisation or community.	Shared norms and values are integrated through socialisation, which creates an identity.

Source: Own elaboration from T. Claridge (2020).

relationships may not necessarily align with those of the group to which individuals belong. For instance, while most individuals within a social group may share trusting relationships with one another, they might not exhibit the same propensity to trust within the group context. Trust is a multifaceted phenomenon that is contingent upon context. Different social groups cultivate distinct norms and behaviours, which significantly influence actions. Therefore, the inclination to trust within a social context is shaped by factors associated with the social grouping, not solely by the nature of individual relationships. Specific forms of trust within local or close-knit communities or organisations cannot be automatically generalised to encompass social trust. In essence, trust within a particular context may diverge from broader social trust and even naturally conflict with it. While relational, particular, and general trust are interconnected, their relationship is not one of identity or aggregation. Summing up, the jump from particularistic forms of trust (relational or organisational) to general is not evident and may even be conflictual.

In essence, trust, norms, and identity operating at higher levels entail shared understandings that are not necessarily tied to specific relationships but exert influence nonetheless. Conversely, trust, values, and norms within a relationship may have organisational and community implications, although numerous intermediate factors, including homogeneity and social identity, play roles in this process.

When discussing trust, we also consider elements of the cognitive dimension, such as shared values and norms, along with socialisation processes. Individuals develop a socially constructed understanding of reality that shapes their actions and interactions within the social network. These shared understandings help alleviate uncertainty in interactions and exchanges, thereby facilitating collective action. Such shared values foster a sense of belonging that motivates cooperation and collaboration, giving rise to a group culture.

Overall, and anticipating what we will see in the macro approach, we could, after reviewing the dimensions of this approach, speak of an overload of the cognitive with a lack of concrete referents that will be reflected in the measurement problems.

1.2.3 The general social capital or macro approach. The primacy of the society

This generalist approach is probably the one that has had the most resonance in both economics and sociology, becoming the mainstream approach. Following the logical sequence of the previous cases, this approach leaps to society as a whole and adopts what we might call a "culturalist" perspective (Woolcock, 2001, p. 70; Castiglione et al., 2008a, 2008b).

This macro reference aims to create a single variable that captures "social functioning", acting as an input for the entire economy and democratic system. In this sense, this approach argues that social capital, understood as a series of characteristics that can be integrated under the heading of generalised trust, is vital for the functioning of democracy, for institutional performance, for the articulation of the market and economic development, and social cohesion (Josten, 2013).

Robert Putnam's *Making democracy work: Civic Traditions in Modern Italy* (1993) is the traditional exponent of this approach. This author offers one of the most "accepted" and, above all, "generalist" definitions of social capital, identifying it with those "characteristics of social organisation, such as trust, norms and networks that can improve the efficiency of society by facilitating coordinated actions" (Putnam, 1993, p. 167). We will leave the criticisms related to the problems of definition for a specific section in chapter four, simply pointing out that the lack of a common referent or the fact that it is an umbrella concept is evident.

Putnam's classic definition (Table 3.5), Knack and Keefer (1997) and Knack (2002) equate social capital with the level of civic-mindedness within a society. Similarly, Serageldin (1996) and the emerging perspective within the

Table 3.5 Definitions of social capital in the macro-social perspective

Authors	*Macro-social perspective*
Putnam (1993, p. 167)	"Features of social organisation, such as trust, norms and networks, which can improve the efficiency of society by facilitating coordinated actions".
Serageldin (1996)	"The glue that holds societies together".
Inglehart (1997, p. 188)	"A culture of trust and tolerance, in which extensive networks of voluntary associations emerge".
Thomas (1996, p. 11)	"Those voluntary means and processes developed within civil society which promote development for the collective whole".
Turner (2000)	"Those forces that increase the potential economic development of a society by creating and maintaining relationships and patterns of social organisation".
Grootaert and Van Banstelaer (2002)	"The social capital of a society includes the institutions, the relationships, the attitudes and values that govern interactions among people and contribute to economic and social development".
Sánchez-Santos and Pena-López (2005, p. 137)	"Social capital represents the idea that trust and the internalisation of rules conducive to cooperative and prosocial behaviour are the basis for the better functioning of the economy and society in general".
The World Bank (2001)	"Social capital refers to the institutions, relationships and norms that make up the quality and quantity of the interactions of society. Numerous studies show that social cohesion is a critical factor for societies to thrive economically and for development to be sustainable. Social capital is not only the sum of the institutions that make up a society but also the stuff that holds them together".

Source: Own elaboration.

Table 3.6 Dimensions of social capital from the macro approach

Level	*Structural dimension*	*Relational dimension*	*Cognitive dimension*
Macro: Factors that are generally relevant and broadly applicable to a community or society	Associative networks. Stable social institutions. Collaborative behaviours at the institutional level. Institutional and cultural environment.	General trust and institutional trust.	Trust, identity and belonging, perceptions of security, shared understandings, culture and customs.

Source: Own elaboration from T. Claridge (2020).

World Bank liken social capital to "social cohesion". In broader terms, social capital is associated with diverse cultural and attitudinal dimensions, including civic engagement, social trust, reciprocal relationships, cooperative norms, and civic-mindedness, all of which contribute to the effective functioning of social, economic, and institutional systems. As summarised by Sánchez-Santos and Pena-López (2005, p. 137), all these definitions underscore the significance of trust, cooperation, and prosocial behaviour in facilitating the smooth operation of both the economy and society, a point that becomes immediately evident.

However, having recognised the obvious, researchers differ in the relevance attributed to the dimensions and how they are articulated (Table 3.6).

The variable of general trust and the relational dimension stand out prominently among these defining elements. Not only Putnam but also a wide range of others, including Fukuyama (1995a, 1995b), La Porta et al. (2000), Dasgupta (2005), and Paldam (2000, pp. 629–630), emphasise the significance of "trust" as a central component of social capital. Trust acts as a lubricant in the functioning of society and serves as a mediator in any relationship or exchange, with its economic manifestation evident in the reduction of transaction costs (Wolleb, 2008, p. 378). Here, the cognitive and relational dimensions assume a determinant role, while there may be disagreements regarding structural causality. Putnam perceives associational networks as a preliminary step towards fostering civic-mindedness and social trust. In contrast, his critics argue that trust and associationism have no significant correlation (Caïs et al., 2021).

In the structural dimension, the accepted referent is remarkably multiform, ranging from associationism to institutions. Associationism, which forms the basis of the social fabric and channels individual actions into collective action, is the most immediate structural referent. A complex society implies a multitude of groupings of individuals who translate communities of values and norms and create a certain value consensus. Associations and their interactions are the first point of reference, but we must also add the social institutions themselves (laws and political structures) that channel individual actions. These macro-social structures help to reduce uncertainty by forming a common and relatively stable understanding of social reality. This "institutional framework" creates expectations and obligations and the confidence that non-compliance is formally (judicial) or informally (social) sanctionable.

In the relational dimension, the web is not limited to individual relationships but also incorporates relationships with organisations and even with an identity (region or country). There are many different forms of trust, which even entail the perception of a collective identity (Frederiksen, 2019).

At this point, the reader may think that we are lumping institutional arrangements, identities, perceptions of security and shared values under the same umbrella. All the desirable requirements of a society are bonding together without first clarifying the internal causalities.

Although we will address this problem in more detail later, the logic implicit under this approach, or indeed the last two approaches, rests on the assumption that the frequency of interaction, typical of dense social networks, favours the emergence and diffusion of norms of reciprocity, fosters trust and contributes to cooperation. Thus, we could assume in the purest Tocquevillian sense[1] that horizontal networks of civic engagement (from neighbourhood to football clubs…) favour such generalised reciprocity and extend a cooperative agreement beyond the particularist group. Accepting this somewhat idealised presupposition of the organisational movement, greater associational participation should be linked to greater generalised trust (Putnam, 1993, p. 172; Uslaner, 2008, p. 116). Associations thus play a "didactic" role in shaping the cultural landscape of the population and serve as a catalyst for social involvement by nurturing internal values such as cooperation, solidarity, and civic engagement and contributing to general trust.

In essence, according to this perspective, trust and civic cooperation are interconnected facets of the same phenomenon (Knack & Keefer, 1997, p. 1258). However, as we have already stated, establishing causality and determining which aspect takes precedence over the other presents considerable challenges.

While we will defer discussions on measurement issues to subsequent chapters, it is worth contemplating a reflection applicable to both meso and macro perspectives. Given the lack of a definitive definition and shared understanding of the concept, one might, following Putnam's approach, consider using the density of voluntary organisations or levels of participation and civic engagement within the population as metrics. This could involve assessing the *per capita* involvement in various groups and associations (such as religious congregations, labour unions, sports clubs, academic or professional societies, political parties, and fraternal organisations) in each region or state (Kawachi et al., 1997, p. 1493). Alternatively, to gauge cognitive aspects tied to established identities, one could directly inquire about the general level of trust among members of a social group or society as a whole. Regardless of the approach chosen, empirical testing faces significant challenges.

Box 3.1 The capital stock and the Solow residual

Neocapital studies have found a propitious framework to develop from economics' shortcomings when explaining problems at the very core of their research, such as growth. The famous "Solow residual" refers to the inadequacy of classical models centred on traditional productive factors to explain the growth of some economies instead of the stagnation of others.

The concept of the "Solow residual" emerged in the 1950s, at the height of the expansion of the study of growth models by neoclassical economists such as Robert M. Solow (1957, 1957). The conventional explanatory model is simple and centred on markedly economic variables Y = A-F (K, L). The factors considered are capital accumulation K and the increase in the labour factor L; however, it is noted that the observed growth differs from that predicted and explained by these two factors. Solow (1963) recognised that his results were insufficient and lacked explanatory power, pointing out that half of the growth is outside the proposed model. This is probably the most obvious example of the inadequacy of conventional economics and the need to incorporate other variables that introduce socioeconomic realism into the models.

In this case, and taking a swift look at the proposals for reducing the unexplained part, we have to talk about a series of attempts from different fields to penetrate the black box of growth (Mata & Louçã, 2009).

Some works have focused on the role played by, for example, natural resources, innovation, investment in R&D, advances in technology and knowledge, human capital, the role of foreign investment, demographic factors, or institutional and political factors (Mata & Louçã, 2009). Social capital is also situated within this body of works, questioning the realism of the mainstream approach. Arrow (1972, p. 345) already argued that virtues such as trust play a crucial role in the operation of economic systems. These virtues form the foundation or, at the very least, facilitate the process of exchange, which is indispensable for any economy to function. This argument stems from the assumption that economic activities are embedded within social contexts and governed by a society's norms, regulations, and ethical obligations.

Similarly, Sen asserts that cultivating and relying on trust in the words and commitments of others can be a pivotal factor for success in the marketplace (Sen, 1999, p. 262), emphasising that no society could be sustainable without certain norms and codes of conduct.

The stock of norms and values, trust and networks of relationships influence the degree of cooperation and social coordination, logically conditioning productivity. As Coleman (1988, p. 98) points out, social capital is productive like other capitals, such as physical or human capital, making it possible to achieve different ends (Putnam, 2002, p. 14).

We can identify several direct mechanisms through which social capital operates.

First, trust has a direct effect on transaction costs and these, in turn, on economic growth. Transaction costs occur in all areas (see Box 4.1), making any exchange and the possibilities of division of labour and specialisation more expensive, to the point of preventing them. Thus, financial sectors, investments, and commercial activity are susceptible. Trust also facilitates any form of cooperation to achieve collective goals by eliminating incentives for opportunism. At the micro level, greater trust reduces the relevance of principal-agent problems, facilitating both the reduction of costs and the simplification of contractual procedures.

However, there are also other indirect mechanisms through their impact on other forms of capital: more investment in physical and human capital, higher levels of innovation and entrepreneurship, etc. (Whiteley, 2000, p. 451). In this sense, its explanatory role has been studied through the impact on total factor productivity and human capital efficiency (Argentiero et al., 2021; Iyer et al., 2005). The role of social capital in economic growth has been pointed to through its positive influence on entrepreneurship (Neira et al., 2009). Similarly, the impact of key elements of general social capital (trust, civic associations, civic-mindedness) on economic development has been shown (Doh & McNeely, 2012; Argentiero et al., 2021; Roth, 2022).

As far as empirical tests are concerned, there is important work to be done. At the micro level, the results are evident and highly robust. For example, there is compelling evidence regarding the influence of social capital on firm performance. Nevertheless, as the focus shifts from individual agents to spatial units comprising numerous anonymous actors, the findings become less definitive due to inadequate measures of the two primary components of social capital: social networks and the norms and values. Developing metrics for values, norms, and attitudes associated with creativity, tolerance, entrepreneurship, and knowledge sharing, alongside identifying more robust measures for social networks, pose significant challenges for future research on the economic ramifications of social capital. Hence, its correlation with the Solow residual warrants further exploration (Westlund & Frane, 2010). For example, little research has been done on the leading role of social networks of strong ties (family and community) in the so-called non-monetary economy based on reciprocity relations. This fact has micro- and macroeconomic effects, given that the family network performs functions of all kinds, from care to education, which would otherwise have to be assumed by the market or the state (Membiela-Pollán et al., 2023). Nor is the relationship between the existing stock of social capital and defensive expenditure usually captured. That is, an absence of social capital (e.g., in the form of civility) leads to an increase in necessary but unproductive public and private expenditures to respond to social problems such as crime and anomie.

2 Summing up the three approaches: *Entia non sunt multiplicanda sine necessitate*

Our sequence leads us to propose a joint vision that integrates the three approaches. Our reflection on the inconsistencies anticipates the need for crucial critical work and for the construction of a causal model that integrates and gives logic to the three approaches (Cockburn & Cockburn-Wooten, 2022).

Summarising some essential characteristics that we have evidenced in our previous journey, social capital is a form of capital, at least from an analogical point of view, since it is the product of a process of individual and social investment of resources, time and effort. At the individual level, it materialises in the personal agendas of individuals, hence the term "rolodex" capital. At the societal level, it is a historical, social, and cultural process that gives birth to norms, values, and relationships, facilitating collective action networks. As capital, it is incorporated into productive processes at both the micro and macro levels. At the micro level, it is the provision of material or immaterial resources through a network of relationships; at the macro level, it is the development of any social action and the reduction of transaction costs.

It is capital by analogy; however, as in any other analogical use (Bankston & Zhou, 2002), it is not free of singularities. We can highlight three: It is a capital with a particular asymmetrical process of capitalisation and depreciation. Its constitution entails a long process of individual and group investment that conflicts, dissensions, etc., can quickly destroy. On the other hand, this form of capital does not experience obsolescence with its use, but on the contrary, with its abandonment and the consequent loss of the networks generated.

Its prominent uniqueness lies in what we could call appropriation, and this is where the justification for the various approaches we have mentioned lies. Social capital is both the property of the individual, which he or she uses to extract resources from the network he or she owns and the property of the group he or she is part of, since all members of the collective have access to it and, therefore perceive externalities from this network to which they are only indirectly linked. To a certain extent, it is also a form of public good. To be more precise, since certain groups can control access, it is more accurately described as a club good or interest group good.

As we have seen, work on social capital forces us to distinguish between micro, meso and macro approaches. That is, we could focus on individual networks, social organisations, or society. After the review we have carried out, it is worth considering the possibility of a simplification. We are only considering two approaches: the individual or micro and the macro. The reasons for integrating meso and macro lie in that, although meso gives greater prominence to the study of specific social organisations, the general approach is the same from a methodological point of view and presents the same problems. The study of the set of networks and network systems, as opposed to the individual and his or her particular endowment of networks. In short, following Portes' proposal (2000, 2018), there are only two meanings of the concept of social capital, and the logical priority falls on the micro approach.

2.1 *What would be a consensus definition?*

The dominant definitions in social capital research have been the culturalist "Putnam-style" ones. Nevertheless, both mechanisms and effects move in a micro-environment, even if they have a macro translation (Yang, 2007). The priority is personal ties, and these are determinant for three reasons (Lin, 1999a, 2001).

- Personal networks generate interdependence of utility functions between individuals and selective influence on preferences (individuals are affected by the welfare and preferences of others in the decision-making process), norms and valuations.
- Personal networks affect expectations about the behaviour of other agents (they allow us to predict the outcomes of an agreement) and consequently facilitate social trust.
- Personal networks are opportunities for advantageous access to resources and privileged information flow channels, affecting output, income, and welfare.

In other words, personal networks serve as both a personal investment yielding returns in material and immaterial resources and a mechanism for community building and directing social action (such as trust and consensus on values). Central to the macro perspective, this community-building aspect can be understood as both an externality and a broader context for individual investment.

Summarising this perspective in a consensus definition: *Social capital is the set of social networks that enable individuals to achieve market and non-market objectives (income, status… recognition, mutual aid…) and, at the same time, the social result of the interactions of these networks.* In other words, its value lies in the resources an individual can extract from them and in the prosocial externalities derived from their extension.

Thus, according to this primarily individual viewpoint, social capital is determined by the number of networks they have through their past relational experiences, granting access to a pool of resources. This "past relational history", interpreted as capital, is shaped by contextual and familial influences, including status, cultural background, and personal investment. Our ultimate referent is the individual, which affects the macro-social scale or the formation of associations in the broader social space, trust in the relational and shared values and identity in the cognitive.

Similarly, the broader social framework, its greater or lesser stability, the frequency of interactions, etc., affect personal networks' form, extent, and character. However, this macro-level social capital can extend beyond simple aggregation of the individual social capitals of those who make up a given social group; it is a function of the latter in which the externalities derived from interpersonal relationships are incorporated. The effects generated by the social relationship (positive or negative) inscribed within a given network cannot be limited to those directly involved; they reach society as a whole. In other words, the aggregation problem is evident given the difficulty of determining the value of the externalities generated, which are not always positive, as in the case of corruption or kleptocracy.

3 From macro to micro and back to macro. Coleman's boat and the Theory of Social Capital

In the realm of social sciences, the primary object of study is, obviously, social phenomena, which also include economic phenomena. While economics and sociology, along with social psychology, share an interest in elucidating the properties and behaviours of individuals, their primary challenge lies in comprehending collective phenomena – actions involving groups of individuals, social norms, structures, and so forth – that cannot be defined solely by reference to any individual member of the community (Hedström, 2005, p. 67). Instead, these collective phenomena are elucidated by the actions of intentional human agents and their relationships.

The concept of the Coleman's boat serves as a particularly illustrative example of the micro-macro articulation problem (see Figure 3.3). Explanations that merely link macro properties to one another without delving into the causal mechanisms operating at the micro level (arrow 4) prove inadequate because they fail to address the underlying micro causality. In this regard, social capital, particularly within the macro approach that has become predominant in the field, is one of the most emblematic cases. Achieving a comprehensive understanding necessitates opening the black box of micro-level mechanisms that give rise to macro-level observations.

In our case, it is necessary to go beyond macro-level statements by studying a general model which, starting from a given macro context (culture and social structures) that constrains the action of individuals (arrow 1), explains the individual mechanisms of action (arrow 2) and then the mechanisms of transformation by which, through their actions and interactions, they generate intended and unintended social outcomes that are again reflected in macro transformations (arrow 3). Coleman reiterates that we can only make sense of macro-level relationships by understanding the whole chain of situational, action-forming and transformational mechanisms (Coleman, 1990; Hedström & Swedberg, 1998).

The background to this critique, which aligns with what we have been discussing, is that the macro or aggregate must have a micro-causal foundation. That is, observations at the level of collectives must be connected to a logic derived from individual observations to construct social scientific explanations. Rather than

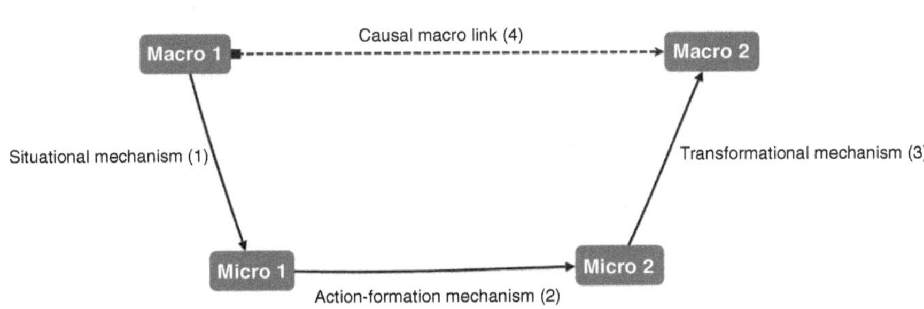

Figure 3.3 Coleman's boat on social methodology.

Source: Own elaboration adapted from Hedstöm and Ylikoski, 2010, p.59.

establishing relationships between macro variables of the development of associationism – social trust type – our concern should focus on the discussion around causal mechanisms at work in individual agents or the micro-foundations and detailed explanations of individual-level processes (Little, 1998).

Nonetheless, it is worth introducing a caveat: this process of investigating causality does not imply assuming, following Rational Choice, that we operate with the atomistic individuals characterising methodological individualism. It is about individual actions that are socially situated, and that result in macro-level interactions and outcomes. In this sense, to categorise this approach in some way, we would be dealing with a structural individualism that emphasises the explanatory weight of the individual, their relationships, and relational structures. The mechanisms we explain with arrow 3 imply a protagonism of the individual and the structures of individuals while simultaneously being conditioned (arrow 1) by the institutional rules, formal or informal and the context in which they operate. It is not a simple aggregation of actions of autonomous individuals but an interaction of intentional subjects operating "according to" a given theory of action. The social context, habits, routines, and cognitive processes can be essential to explanations going from the macro to the micro and again to the macro (Hedström, 2005). It is a mechanistic proposal in its structure, but it is open to explanations that can come from the most diverse fields of social science.

3.1 Coleman's boat and social capital

Applying the "Coleman boat" (Figure 3.4) directly to the problem of social capital, community ties are the general framework in which personal networks develop. For example, an environment of security and trust facilitates the development of these individual networks or associationism (Coleman, 1990). However, since the work of Putnam (1993) and the incorporation of other disciplines (political science and economics), there has been a subtle transition towards a macro perspective in such a way that social capital has become an essentially communal attribute, a stock possessed by communities and even nations, separated from individual networks. Social capital as an attribute of a community is distinct from its individual version, so the two perspectives diverged without a theorisation between them.

As we have discussed in the second and third chapters, any scholar of social capital finds it perplexing that in one work, social capital is studied as personal networks; in another, it is the stock of networks an organisation has, and in the vast majority it is good governance and general trust, autonomously. In particular, the risk of the latter macro view is evident because it tends to become synonymous with everything positive in social life and to establish relationships between macro variables without a study of causality.

Anyone who has delved into the study of general social capital has noticed the profusion of circular reasoning (Smith et al., 2016). In this case, social capital is a community property facilitating better social functioning and governance.

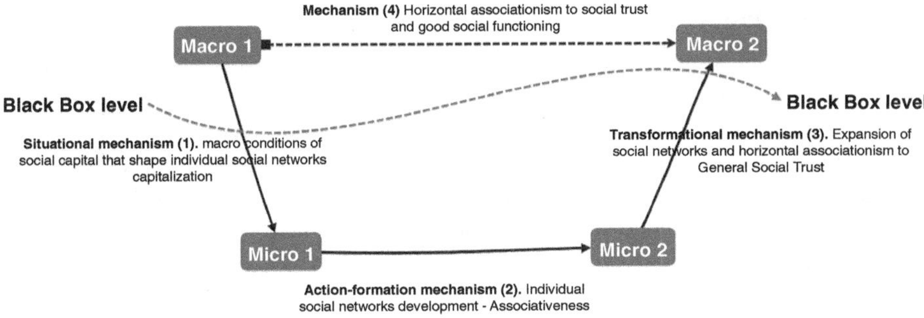

Figure 3.4 A typology of social mechanisms.

Source: Own elaboration.

In contrast, good social functioning leads to the generation of social capital. What is curious about the situation is that this problem of lack of causality has been compensated for by a profusion of proxy measures that are logically interrelated: associationism, safety, trust, respect for norms, etc. Measures of social capital are the same as governance measures, so endogeneity is assured. As Porter reminds us, they claim that widespread "civic-mindedness" leads to better political outcomes, leaving any study of causality out of the question (Porter, 1998). In this case, following Coleman, we are only applying incomplete (arrow 4) mechanism.

This problem does not exist in studies developed under the micro approach since causality can be defined. At this level, the sources of social capital were associated with an individual's social network, inherited and the product of an investment, goal-oriented and with effects on material or immaterial resources. In our view, this is one of the cases where the application of Coleman's proposal is necessary to shed some light on the black box of causality between the micro and macro dimensions (Figure 3.4).

Correct structuring of the explanatory mechanisms should start (1) from the study of the macro as situational mechanisms that restrict individual decisions. In a second step, penetrating the black box of explanatory mechanisms, the study of the process of generating networks of individual agents based on macro conditioning factors (2) should facilitate a series of micro conclusions on the characteristics and functioning of these networks to derive (3) a series of consequences or effects both at the individual level and on the general functioning of society. Ultimately, the macro link (4), which in previous studies was completely tautological, would now have a set of causal mechanisms that could provide a rationale or logic for social operation.

In short, the problems presented by the lack of definition of macro-level social capital require penetration into the black box of the mechanisms operating at the micro-level. Consequently, we need a general model that links social capital's micro and macro levels.

In following chapters, we will try to make some proposals.

4 Recapping

A clear need in social capital studies is the articulation between micro and macro dimensions. In this chapter, we have proposed a critical review of the various approaches used within this research programme based on the study of the dimensions involved in the study of social capital. From our perspective, the micro approach allows us to establish the working reference point more solidly: the study of the configuration of individual networks and their functionality with derivations in the functioning of society as a whole. In other words, the micro-foundation of macro variables.

As a consensus definition, we understand that social capital from this micro perspective is the set of access networks that facilitate individuals to achieve market and non-market objectives (income, status… recognition, mutual aid…) as a result of the interaction with other individuals, as well as the social interactions of these networks and the prosocial externalities derived from them.

Thus, personal networks are both a personal investment with a return in material and immaterial resources and a means of community building and channelling social action (trust and value consensus). This community building, which is the focus of the macro perspective, is both an externality and a general context of the investment.

As H. Flap and Volker (2001) point out, the core of this research programme is that social networks are functionally goal-oriented and that individuals will invest in them because of the perceived future value of the associated resources.

The essential problem in Social Capital Theory is the lack of a general model that integrates the various approaches, more specifically, the macro and micro approaches. Drawing on Coleman's proposal on explanatory mechanisms in the social sphere, in contrast to the tautologies that often characterise macro work, the study of causal mechanisms that explain the links between macro and micro variables should play a predominant role.

Note

1 In Tocqueville (1987 [1835–1840]) there is a virtuous link between civic associations, the common good and democracy. In this sense, the author writes: "If men are not solidly and permanently linked, it is difficult for them to act in common" (1987, p. 477). "Political parties may be considered as great free schools, where all citizens come to learn the general theory of associations" (1987, p. 481 [1835, 1840]). "In all countries where political associations are forbidden, civil associations are rare […]" (Tocqueville, 1987; taken from Millán and Gordon, 2004, pp. 731–732).

4 What is behind macro-social capital?

> The glue that holds societies together.
>
> (Serageldin, 1996)

Despite the continuous growth in publications on social capital, there has recently been a certain stagnation and a reduction in the number of relevant contributions. Theoretical discussion is more significant when a term is born, especially when it is complex, as in the case of social capital. Nevertheless, this complexity and the multidimensionality call for greater depth. What can be observed is that social capital has achieved a considerable international presence within the social sciences (Woolcock, 2010; Field, 2016); it has become a successful concept, a fashionable term, and even, although not desirable, a cool reference. Its interest has crossed the academic sphere and has established itself in the political, organisational, and institutional spectrum, but with serious flaws that call into question a vital part of the contributions.

The success of this approach lies in its capacity for synthesis and its provision of a conceptual framework that integrates various research streams from sociology, political science, and economics (Adler & Kwon, 2002). Furthermore, politically, it enables the alignment of individuals advocating for the defence of traditional social institutions with those supporting participatory third ways; bridging perspectives from those opposing regulatory interventions and advocating for a free social organisation to those uneasy with the unfettered operation of market forces (Sobel, 2002). Social capital emerges as a valuable tool due to its potential influence on significant variables such as growth, income distribution, and quality of life. Entities ranging from governments, the WHO, multinationals, and the World Bank to NGOs and the "2030 Agenda" all engage in discussions surrounding this concept. Nevertheless, the indiscriminate use of the term at times evokes a clichéd response akin to the frequent occurrences with sustainability and corporate social responsibility.

Given what has been seen in the previous chapter, the reader will anticipate that this supposed success is associated with the pre-eminence of the macro perspective in a way that establishes an identity with social trust and simultaneously with civic participation. This conceptual reductionism of "soft generalities" is far removed

DOI: 10.4324/9781003375302-7

from the work of Pierre Bourdieu and James Coleman in the initial construction of the concept. In addition to impoverishing research, these simplifications bring an epistemic and empirical problem: no one can establish causality beyond circular arguments.

Social capital thus becomes a rhetorical concept that is neither descriptive nor predictive (Pena-López & Sánchez-Santos, 2013), where contradictions and unfalsifiable arguments abound. An example of this is the average valuation of the contribution of social capital to growth in the OECD, which, according to some reports, stands at only 0.07 percentage points for the period 1970–2003 (Fundación BBVA, 2007). These same studies indicate that social capital, and by inference its contribution to growth, has increased in recent years when the measurement of the variable beyond the "trust" factor says otherwise; for example, if one takes into account the level of associationism in Western countries.

This chapter is deconstructive, we will review the macro-social capital concept and its causes and effects, focusing mainly on criticisms. This will allow us to refer to the structural holes in the theory and to the general macro-micro articulation that we will see again in the following chapter. We will answer the questions: What is inside the macro-social capital umbrella? What is the last reference point? Moreover, what causes social trust?

1 Macro-social capital: integrating an ample semantic field

In the previous chapter, we discussed the existence of two main approaches to the study of social capital: "micro-social capital" and "macro-social capital", the individual or collective approach (Portes, 2000).

Macro or general social capital focuses on macro-social and macro-institutional aspects and abandons the study of individual networks and the resources they imbricate (Membiela-Pollán & Pena-López, 2017). In this approach, the usual analysis fields are generalised trust, social integration, civic-mindedness, cohesion, solidarity, and social participation. These variables are usually encompassed within the so-called formal social capital (Pichler & Wallace, 2007, p. 22).

This approach leads us to favour a characterisation of social capital as public, whose economic and social effects go beyond the individual (micro) and even the group (micro-meso) to encompass society as a whole. This linkage to society favours ambiguous expressions such as "culture of trust and tolerance", "glue that holds societies together", "social cohesion that makes societies prosper economically and sustainably", "cooperative norms", "widespread reciprocity", "persistent and shared beliefs and values that help overcome the free rider problem".

As we saw in the previous chapter, macro-social capital mixes cognitive-relational and structural elements that influence cooperation and social coordination. What is not clear is their relevance and the fact that they are both causes and effects, that is, endogenous (Durlauf, 2002; Sánchez-Santos & Pena-López, 2005). For example, civic participation is social capital, but in turn, it generates trust and norms of reciprocity, identifiable as social capital. In parallel, civic behaviour (social capital) generates social cohesion and trust (social capital). Relationships are bidirectional, full of feedback loops.

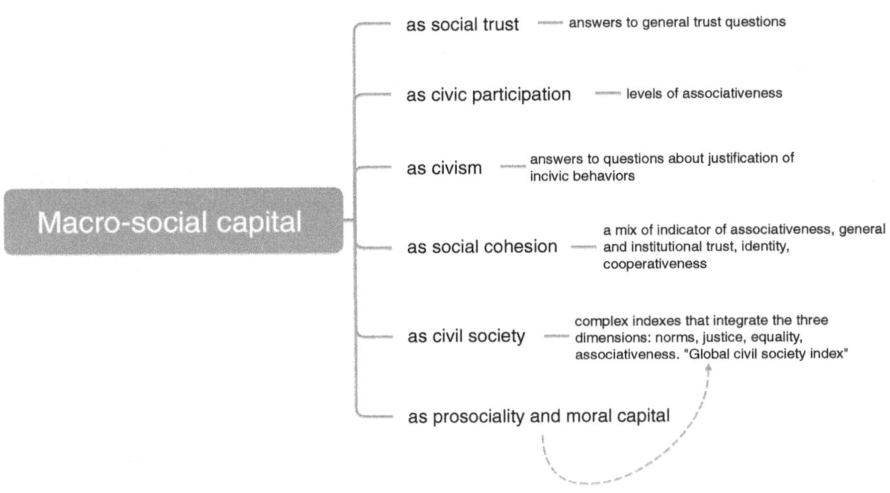

Figure 4.1 The macro-social capital semantic field and measurement.

Source: Own elaboration.

In what follows, we set out the most prominent conceptual trends within the macro perspective to propose a final consensus (Figure 4.1). All of them attempt to find a concrete definition of social capital.

1.1 Social capital as social trust

Almost all authors emphasise this relational dimension because of the importance of trust for social sustainability (Simmel, 1950; Paxton, 2007), and for many, trust is an element identifiable with the notion of social capital (Engbers et al., 2017).

Trust encourages cooperation and social cohesion, mitigates collective action problems, and favours institutional functioning (Fukuyama, 1995a, 1995b; Welch et al., 2005). In sum, an atmosphere of high trustworthiness reduces the transaction costs (see Box 4.1) associated with economic activity. At this point, clarification is needed. Trust operates at various levels, from family and neighbourhood relationships to intra-group and inter-group ties, formal and informal social networks, in any economic-business relationship and between strangers (Narayan & Cassidy, 2001, p. 67; Lins et al., 2017).

In a simple definition, trust is the belief that the consequences of someone's intended action will be appropriate from one's point of view (Misztal, 1996). However, trust's conditionalities and functionality vary depending on the domain in which it operates. Thus, we can distinguish between individual, political, institutional, and social trust (Stone, 2001).

Social or generalised trust is defined as trust in strangers, in those about whom there is a lack of information (Herreros, 2004, p. 605). It is, therefore, a general attitude or expectation about the behaviour of individuals or the social system in which they are embedded, a belief about the correct intentions of others and their commitment to fulfil their obligations (Luhmann, 1988; Gheorghiu et al., 2009). The critical problem here lies in the mechanisms that promote this belief. Some will favour the "associationism theory", whose primary reference is Robert Putnam (1993, 1995), which links generalised trust with rich associative activity. On the other hand, some critics deny, partially or totally, that this is linked to a society's level of civic commitment, pointing out other determining factors, as we shall see below (Rahn & Transue, 1998, p. 548).

1.2 Social capital as civic-mindedness

As noted above, the macro approach suffers from hypercognitivism. Hence, alongside the weight of the trust variable, other research emphasises civic and cooperative norms, or more specifically, civic-mindedness (Edyvane, 2017). For example, seminal work by Knack and Keefer (1997), using World Values Survey (WVS) indicators on civic norms and trust, finds that both dimensions are significant in countries with higher and equal incomes, strong institutions, higher educational attainment, and more ethnically homogeneous populations. Civic cooperation is central, and trust would be one of its expressions (Knack and Keefer 1997, p. 1258). This civic atmosphere of high trustworthiness reduces the costs linked to economic activity, in general, all transaction costs, and creates less society's dependence on formal institutions, less bureaucracy and corruption. Civic norms thus promote cooperative solutions to numerous collective action problems. They solve "prisoner's dilemmas" without imposing external costs while increasing allocative efficiency (Knack & Keefer, 1997, pp. 1252–1254).

Similarly, Guiso et al. (2011) equate social capital with "civic capital", defining it as those beliefs – including trust – and shared values that help a community overcome its problems of opportunistic behaviour in the pursuit of socially valuable activities. These authors go back to civic culture, referring to the set of beliefs, attitudes, norms, and perceptions underpinning participation (Almond & Verba, 1963). Hence, it is only linked to positive externalities.

1.3 Social capital as social cohesion

Social cohesion is a complex and multidimensional concept with considerable definitional problems. Some authors establish a bidirectional relationship with social capital and verge on identity (Jenson, 2010, p. 9). In this sense, it is striking that the WHO and the World Bank use both constructs interchangeably. For example, the World Bank states,

> Social capital refers to the institutions, relationships, and norms that shape the quality and quantity of a society's social interactions… Social capital is not just the sum of the institutions which underpin a society – it is the glue that holds them together.
>
> (The World Bank, 2001)

We call this surprising because it defines something fuzzy with something equally fuzzy.

Among the works on social capital that focus on cohesion, Botterman et al. (2012) practically replicate Putnam's definition:

> Social cohesion refers to the presence of structural and attitudinal mechanisms of solidarity, cooperation and exchange among the citizens of a society. These constituent networks can be material or structural (exchange of goods, economic interactions) or immaterial (informal relationships, shared identities).

Likewise, Schiefer and Van der Noll (2017, p. 592) posit that social cohesion represents a characteristic of a collective and reflects the quality of its unity. Consequently, a cohesive society is distinguished by intimate social ties, a pervasive sense of emotional attachment, and a resolute commitment to the common good.

In general, all the traits attributed to cohesion are also expressions of social capital in a kind of tautology. This way, social capital and cohesion are observable attributes in social groupings that express good social functioning, but none explains more than the other.

Such a definition also makes it impossible to find a concrete reference point and leads us to expressions such as that of Festinger et al. (1950): "The total field of forces which act on members to remain in the group". We speak of an aggregate of interrelated structural and cognitive-relational factors, ranging from a close relational connection (structural dimension) to shared values, attitudes, and behaviours for the common good (cognitive dimension), and finally, identification, emotional connection, and trust (relational dimension). This is extensible to another similar concept found in the literature, belonging social capital, which refers to the identity that emanates from communities, the "feeling of belonging" (Lin, 2008, p. 60).

In sum, when we speak of social capital as cohesion, we describe the desirable traits in a human community. There is no causality, but rather, it integrates causes and effects: social stability, economic development, participation, and individual and collective well-being (Van Staveren & Pervaiz, 2017). Social capital is always deployed positively, a condition that, let us recall, is stated for social capital to be considered a form of capital, but without considering the characteristics of the association.

1.4 Social capital as civil society

Among the looser identifications, some authors go so far as to propose that the referent of social capital is civil society (Paterson, 2000; Kotzé & du Toit, 2005). Like the previous proposal, this is a flight from the complex to the more complex (Anheier, 2014). From the outset, we are talking about two different categories: social capital, which is a variable, and stock, while the latter describes, in a more "static" way, a space of social life.

This proposal avoids hypercognitivism by focusing on a structural and aggregate perspective. From a general point of view, civil society is understood as the set of intermediate associations and organisations that stand between the individual and the state (Bobbio & García, 2001) or as a sphere of social relations not regulated by the state. So, it is true that there is a clear link between the two, and we can even say that social capital expresses the formal and informal relations that make up "civil society" (Heinrich, 2005; Sánchez-Santos & Pena-López, 2005). Moreover, civil society cannot be understood without civic-cooperative norms and trust as they are a prerequisite for adequate cooperation and collective action (Ramos-Pinto, 2012).

Nevertheless, it is worth clarifying that understanding. "What is" civil society must go beyond the superficial and generalised idea of equating it terminologically with the associations of the Third Sector. For example, let us take NGOs, neighbourhood associations, trade unions, non-profit organisations, religious groups, charitable associations, voluntary work, and citizens' associations. This approach would be a limitation because "social relations not regulated by the state" must, by definition, include the community and the family – intermediate groups between the individual and the state and a transcendent part of bonding social capital. In particular, the family or "Fourth Sector" (Donati & Prandini, 2007) is an informal social network that generates a wide range of instrumental and expressive resources valuable to the individual and society, as we will see in the next chapter on micro-social capital.

The concept of civil society must encompass all relational networks and include the cognitive components (trust, value consensus, etc.). Only in this case would it be equivalent to the concept of macro-social capital. This identity does not simplify the problem but better assesses its overall socioeconomic impact. It goes beyond concepts such as trust and civic-mindedness and integrates aspects of the micro approach (personal networks).

1.5 Social capital as prosociality and moral capital

Social capital, understood as prosociality and moral capital (see Box 7.1), obeys a denser and more agglutinative approach than notions like "civic capital". It is a thick conception – a more detailed definition, with more information, which allows a more complete understanding – rather than a thin conception – a more fundamental description.

Prosociality refers to behaviours and attitudes oriented towards the benefit and well-being of others and society at large (Dakin et al., 2022). This behaviour assists the construction of social groupings, develops under the prism of public interest, and promotes the common good (Zamagni, 1995, pp. 15–16; Membiela-Pollán, 2013). Under this fundamental concept, any individual and collective action can be evaluated, so we do not presuppose the value neutrality of social capital.

This way, moral capital can be delineated as the network of sympathetic relationships – comprehended as the interconnection of individuals' utility functions – existing between individuals or a group of individuals towards others (Sánchez-Santos & Pena-López, 2005, p. 145). It is about integration into a group and their reference to society at large as a "prosocial" being (Membiela-Pollan, 2013). Indicators such as paying taxes, returning money found at random, reporting damage caused by an accident to a parked vehicle, littering in public space, or not accepting bribes express a contribution to a good general climate and trust within a society. Moral capital includes these aspects but goes further.

Prosociality and moral capital offer an advantage over civic capital as they impact social capital's cognitive-relational and structural dimensions. On the one hand, its cognitive dimension expresses the degree to which values, norms, attitudes, dispositions, and trustworthiness affect social construction. On the other hand, it emphasises the coordination of social groupings, thus linking with the structural dimension. Both concepts offer the possibility of assessing the "norms of reciprocity" and "cooperative norms" associated with social capital. In this case, as opposed to particular or group norms, the social norm must be universal for a community or general society (Jon, 1989).

This context provides another advantage: the link between the macro and micro levels or the incorporation of the general into the particular. Universal norms and values affect not only what is expected of citizens' civic behaviour but also the vision of culture, social structures, and networks of interpersonal relations (micro-social capital) and their functions. That is, what is appropriate to obtain through a network?

Reducing the notion of social capital to sympathy and moral capital would eliminate some problems surrounding the definition and facilitate its identification as a type of capital comparable to physical capital (Robison et al., 2002; Sánchez-Santos & Pena-López, 2005).

1.6 What are we putting under this umbrella?

One question that immediately arises from this broad set of umbrella definitions is what relationships we consider under macro-social capital (Figure 4.2). The works focusing on this approach point to three types of relationships: Strong or proximity relationships, bonding social capital, and weak relationships beyond the narrow framework or bridging social capital (Granovetter, 1973). We must add that global emotional connection, common purpose and identity play a relevant role in giving meaning to globality, linking social capital (Portes & Vickstrom, 2015, pp. 50–53). Under this typology, we are considering the strength of ties, homophily-heterophily and the formality of relationships (González Heras, 2023), which can be helpful as a classification and disconcerting in terms of causality.

Bonding social capital is a micro-level relational network characterised by closeness and frequency of interpersonal interaction. It is related to "strong ties" and "primary groups", namely, family, friendship, and close social circle ties. In general, social bonding capital is a dense network of relatively homogeneous individuals that reinforce horizontal ties within the structure (Durlauf, 2008).

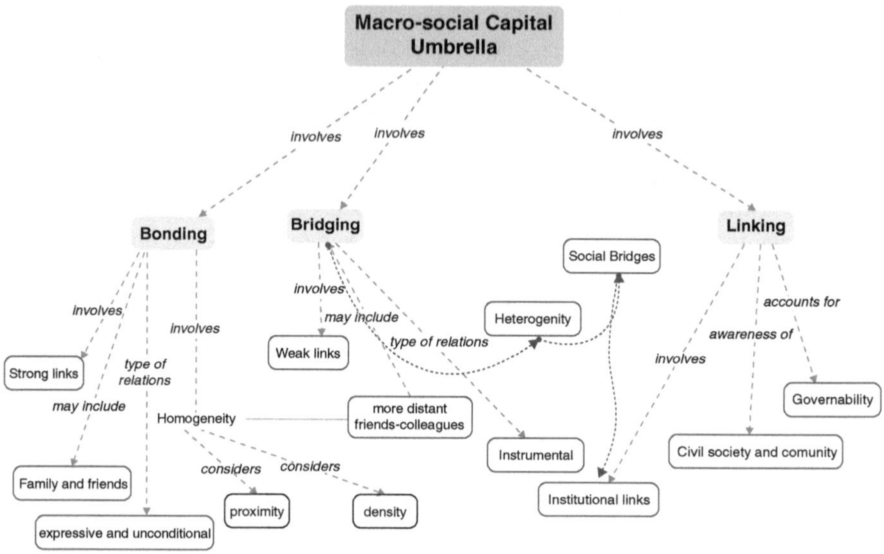

Figure 4.2 Levels under the macro-social umbrella.

Source: Own elaboration.

These ties are fundamental to individuals' emotional well-being and social support (Lawndes & Pratchett, 2008). For example, in communities with strong bonding social capital, members have a greater sense of belonging and solidarity. This type of social capital also plays a crucial role in crises, where mutual help and support are indispensable for survival and community resilience (Membiela-Pollán, 2016).

Bridging social capital builds "social bridges". It encompasses relationships with distant friends, acquaintances, and colleagues and links with people from different groups with unequal socioeconomic and ethnic characteristics (Castiglione, 2008). These relationships allow for the exchange of differentiated resources, information, and opportunities with a scope beyond the primary group (Lin, 2008). Individuals or organisations have access to a wide range of perspectives and experiences, which can lead to greater social mobility, creativity, knowledge transmission, innovation, and social adaptability while also having the capacity to generate trust and social cohesion (Granovetter, 1973; Malecki, 2012).

Linking social capital refers to the connection to institutions, authority, and the general notion of identity (Woolcock, 2001, p. 71; Wolleb, 2008, pp. 380–382). These relationships are critical in facilitating collaboration between civil society and governmental and private institutions (Guribye, 2018).

This typification of the various and unconnected types of relationships that can be integrated under the heading of general social capital reveals the deficient integration between the micro and macro levels we have been discussing. The first two are micro forms of social capital, while the third is properly macro.

Box 4.1 Transaction costs, ethics, and trust

It is commonplace to recognise that many economic development problems are associated with a lack of trust (Arrow, 1972). To quote D.C. North (1990, p. 54): "The inability of societies to develop effective contract enforcement is the most important source of stagnation and underdevelopment".

The expansion of an economy's efficiency and activity implies an exponential increase in interdependence between its members so that everyone depends on the receipt of inputs and the placement of outputs in an ever-widening circle – or, in other words, an increase in the division of labour. In multiplying exchanges and agency relations dominated by information asymmetry, neither the law nor the state is sufficient to regulate them, so a basis of trust is critical for both business and the economy (La Porta, 1997).

In these agency relationships, a principal must rely on an agent to carry out an activity under conditions it cannot fully control. If the principal had to repeatedly face the costs of information, communication, negotiation, and resolution of transactions between the parties involved, any economic activity would be impracticable. This problem is captured in the concept of transaction cost popularised by Coase (1937) to allude to the need to establish costly forms of control over contract performance that prevent opportunistic behaviour. This control includes information costs (knowledge of the market, price/quality checks, etc.), bargaining costs (drafting a suitable contract as completely as possible and reaching an agreement) and monitoring and enforcement costs (ensuring that the agent is complying with the terms of the contract) (Dahlman, 1979). Consequently, the explicit costs of a transaction may not (in fact, never do) coincide with the actual costs the subject faces. This obvious fact slows down the growth of the market and activity and may even endanger the whole system. Consider, for example, a case of generalised distrust in the legal system. The increase in transaction costs could be incalculable.

An alternative for raising the efficiency of the economic system involves finding an effective way of solving this type of problem. In this sense, some authors describe the existence of a specific endowment of social capital in an economy as an advantage analogous to the competitive advantage of nations. Specifically, Donaldson (2001) argues that those nations that have better governance, a higher degree of social cooperation and citizens who have internalised their economic duties, which range from respect for intellectual property, free competition, meritocracies, attention to the environment to the renunciation of favoured relationships with policymakers, etc., have an economic advantage.

This advantage can be expressed in reduced transaction costs, especially those linked to reinforcing compliance with social and contractual norms (Etzioni, 1988). Shared norms, general trust and networks of relationships, and dimensions of macro-social capital constitute a system of pre-coordination of individual decisions before those implied by the market that can effectively eliminate such costs.

Ultimately, the successes of capitalism could not be explained without taking into account this mode of coordination, which presupposes the existence of shared and internalised codes of behaviour, that is, the existence of moral resources that we could consider a form of community capital. Individuals assume a greater or lesser extent a core of ethical norms through socialisation and are influenced by different cultural, social, and religious contexts. As we pointed out in the previous section, this could be attributed to a concept such as moral capital or the extension of morality among the individuals who make up a community. As Habermas points out, "morality entitles the members of a group to expect certain actions from one another in given situations and obliges them to comply with the behavioural expectations justified by others" (1986, p. 51). The ethical somehow enters into every contract, just as there is a trust component behind every transaction, and it is inappropriate to argue that there are legal and police enforcement mechanisms since these are themselves the subject of the contract (Williamson, 1985).

However, it is worth distinguishing: Particularist trust is also a system for reducing transaction costs for particular groups (interest groups, lobbies, mafia, etc.), perhaps even more effective than generalist trust through closure. Thus, we would have to recognise that particular social capital, the existence of social groups defined in society by culture, religion, and language, can lead to two consequences: a reduction of transaction costs internal to the group so that transactions will preferentially take place within the group, with high efficiency; and an ambivalent result as far as society and the economy. Everything will depend on the universalism of internal morals. As we will see in a following digression, we will be confronted with a paradox that can occur in any society. The universal character that must characterise any moral system is a precondition for it to lead to positive outcomes for the economy.

2 Measuring macro-social capital. Trying to put numbers

As we have seen, the lack of consensus and ambiguity about the precise meaning of social capital naturally affect the agreement on its measurement system (Bjørnskov & Svendsen, 2003). Different methods are used to quantify social capital, and the choice of method depends on the study's definition and intention (Van Deth, 2008). Thus, we will find as many attempts at delimitation as the ones analysed in the previous section.

2.1 Measuring as civic participation

This is undoubtedly the most popular, and the classic reference is Robert Putnam (1993, 1995). For him, associative activity and civic engagement favour institutional performance and economic development by promoting civic cooperation and social trust norms. Consequently, the density of voluntary organisations is the key indicator (Paldam, 2000). The level of civic engagement is measured by the number of associations *per capita* to which citizens in each region or state belong. These include religious groups, trade unions, sports associations, and academic, professional, political, school, and fraternal associations (Kawachi et al., 1997, p. 1493).

This option is criticised for three reasons: the diffuse concept of voluntary organisation, the diversity of the intensity of contacts, and the "benign" objectives of the associations (not all of them have prosocial objectives) (Paldam, 2000; Glaeser et al., 2002).

2.2 Measuring as social trust

Given the identity assumed by this approach between trust and social capital, this is the natural second route. Simplistic recourse to this variable is almost universal. Specifically, much of the work focuses on the use of the answers to the question from the WVS – similar to the European Social Survey, the General Social Survey, or the Eurobarometer – "Do you think that most people would take advantage of you if they had the opportunity?" (item for the study of the perceived probability of opportunism) and "Would you say that most people can be trusted?" (item for the study of social trust-distrust). Thus, the percentage of respondents who say that "most people can be trusted" indicates social capital in a given society (Kawachi et al., 1997, p. 1492).

What is criticisable in this case is not the variable, which is undoubtedly one of the indicators of the cognitive components of social capital, but its exclusivity and the fact that the formulation of the question is imprecise and asymmetrical (Torpe & Lolle, 2011, p. 484).

2.3 Measuring as civic-mindedness and norms of civic cooperation

Trust is linked to other indicators that can be integrated under civic-mindedness or compliance with the rules of civic cooperation within a society.

For instance, Guiso et al. (2011, p. 430) advocate for an emphasis on values and beliefs that foster cooperative behaviour. This is exemplified through inquiries concerning tax compliance, misuse of public resources, and uncivil conduct such as queue-jumping and littering streets; responses are rated on a scale from 1 = never justifiable to 10 = always justifiable. Collectively, these inquiries serve as reliable indicators of the prevalence of moral conduct and the prioritisation of the common good.

Similarly, Knack and Keefer (1997, p. 1256) observe that the strength of norms and civic cooperation can be gauged by assessing the extent of justification (fully justified, never justified, or somewhat justified) attributed to various actions: (a) claiming government benefits undeservedly, (b) evading public transport fares, (c) falsifying tax declarations, (d) retaining found money, and (e) concealing damage to parked vehicles. This categorisation of justification facilitates the aggregation of responses for analysis.

Moreover, this assessment can be experimental, as evidenced by the "wallet test" (Paldam, 2000), which examines the proportion of returned wallets out of a set lost in public spaces. Knack and Keefer (1997, p. 1257) highlight that, in their research, the rate of returned wallets correlates with the level of social trust by 0.67.

In any case, these measures are not without contradictions and notable biases. For example, in surveys, respondents are more likely to be reluctant to admit their failures. Respondents try to adjust to moral standards, particularly in the case of objective noncompliance.

2.4 Measuring as social cohesion

The ambiguity of the concept of social cohesion has consequences for its empirical measurement. Those who are guided by this definition choose to mix all the indicators mentioned (Klein, 2013, p. 897; Kaiser et al., 2020): social contacts; membership of formal and informal groups, including the third sector; social and institutional trust; willingness to cooperate; or the sense of belonging and identity.

Depending on the study, micro and macro indicators are chosen. For example, Eurostat and the OECD tend to emphasise macro-social indicators. Other research addresses micro-social indicators at the community or individual level (Dickes et al., 2010; Acket et al., 2011).

In any case, some *ad hoc* indicators do not have an obvious parallel with social capital. This is the case of those describing the economic dimension (levels of material well-being, economic equality, or labour market inclusion), which can be interpreted as a source or result of social capital.

2.5 Measuring as a civil society

Here, we must consider various composite indices that capture structural and cognitive dimensions (Van Deth, 2008, p. 162). Regarding structural attributes, the extent (quantity) and quality or depth of associationism, which are more and less formal, and social infrastructure in the form of networks and cooperation are of interest. Concerning cognitive attributes, the norms and values of social justice, equity, transparency, sustainability, respect for the law, or prosocial public attitudes are fundamental. These methods are complex, as they often draw on primary and secondary, quantitative and qualitative, objective and subjective information, and collect multilevel information (Newton, 2001, p. 201; Payne et al., 2011; Anheier, 2014).

Examples of such composite indices are Anheier and Stares's (2002) "Global Civil Society Index", which covers many aspects of the concept of social capital, the "CIVICUS Index on Civil Society", and the overviews of "Indicators of a Healthy Civil Society" (Heinrich, 2005).

Notwithstanding, they have a shortcoming: they often do not consider family and community ties. This issue restricts their understanding of the interaction between micro, meso and macro levels. Excluding social bonding capital (strong ties) leaves an essential level uncovered.

3 Is macro-social capital really capital?

Given that our perspective is from neocapital, it is crucial to determine whether we are using the analogy correctly or whether this is a forced interpretation. Accepting that it can be considered capital entails fulfilling certain assumptions closely linked to what can be described as "physical capital".

As Dasgupta (2000, p. 398) points out, attributing a form of capital to it can only make sense insofar as it focuses our attention on stable features of a given society and with apparent economic and social effects.

These "conditions" to be considered capital also require the identification of a temporal dimension, a "present sacrifice" for the sake of a future benefit, a form of investment, and the possibility of its transmission. These aspects are evident in physical capital. Nevertheless, in its macro version, social capital does not necessarily entail a material sacrifice and is, in many cases, non-transferable (Quibria, 2003).

Arrow (2000, p. 4) and Solow (2000) also add that, in order to be considered as such, social capital could not have negative economic returns; it should be perfectly distinguishable from other types of capital, such as human capital, and it is necessary to clarify the mechanisms by which it is accumulated. Then, we need to specify a process of capitalisation and depreciation. For these authors, even considering social relations, trust and the ability to cooperate as necessary for economic activity, it is not clear that social capital can be considered durable, productive, accumulable, fungible and measurable. However, to be honest, it is not clear whether human capital fulfils them (Dasgupta, 2000).

To add a minimum of depth to the above criticisms, it is helpful to analyse how the conditions in the above definitions of social capital (socio-cooperative norms, social trust, and civic-mindedness) could be fulfilled.

a. *The existence of an investment process or "a "present sacrifice" for a future benefit"*. Based on the perception of the desirability of trust, civic-mindedness, and cohesion, it can be assumed that there is a personal investment that facilitates the internalisation of these, both because of the usefulness of acting according to ethics or moral commitments (Etzioni, 2007) and understanding the individual and collective benefit of their generalisation. All societies, through long processes of socialisation and education, try to spread these features. Moreover, it is a fragile investment by the very nature of social processes and not always a conscious one that could even be considered integrable in human capital.
b. *Depreciation.* Social capital does not experience depreciation like a physical asset, as it does not deteriorate over time in the same way as a machine or a building. However, it can experience declines over time due to various factors, such as changes in social relations, social participation, cultural norms and shared values, and institutions. In addition, social capital can be affected by external events that

affect its dimensions (disasters, political changes, or economic crises). Exploiting the analogy, social capital requires maintenance and renewal to keep its value and effectiveness precisely because it is subject to potential depreciation.

c. *Transferability or alienability*. Although social capital cannot be transacted, donated, or lent like other forms of capital, social norms, trustworthy attitudes, and civic-cooperative norms can be transmitted. This is the case of cultural inheritance that is transmitted through social structures (Bourdieu, 1986), of parents instilling civic values and a trustworthy attitude in their children (Uslaner, 2008), of religious organisations transmitting prosocial values, or of an association, following Putnam (1993), instilling civic habits for a good life in society. In this case, it could again be considered human capital.
d. *Productive*. Social capital is productive to the extent that it facilitates the achievement of various ends, although this productivity is less precise than the ratios customary in the study of physical capital (Coleman, 1988, p. 98; Hellerstein & Neumark, 2020). In any case, it cannot be denied that society's ends are welfare or aggregate economic efficiency, issues to which social capital contributes. It should also be noted that while micro-social capital can have negative returns at the aggregate level depending on the nature of the social network, macro-social capital relies on elements that are, in principle, positive. Consequently, we are faced with a severe definitional problem. Finally, social capital complements and sometimes substitutes for other types of capital (Eloire, 2017; Membiela-Pollán et al., 2019b).
e. *Durability*. This implies that the assets that constitute capital can maintain their value over time. In the case of macro-social capital, this can be durable. Trust and norms can persist over time and develop over generations. Even so, durability can be relative and undermined by cultural change, conflict, or unstable institutions. Indeed, one of the essential features of general social capital is its already noted asymmetric character. It suffers from long accumulation processes and potential losses in short periods.
f. *Accumulability*. This is a prominent feature in the case of physical capital. Notwithstanding, in general, or macro-social capital, it is more difficult to estimate, and its value is more complex to assess. Again, this condition is fulfilled to a greater extent in micro-social capital, with a subject able to accumulate and inherit social ties properly for different purposes (Pena-López & Sánchez-Santos, 2013, p. 36). In any case, the "stock" of macro-social capital, in the form of social trust and civic-cooperative norms, can be linked to cultural traits (Yamagishi & Yamagishi, 1994) enduring over time.
g. *Fungibility*. This term refers to the ability of a resource or asset to be substituted by another of identical nature, quality, and value without any loss of value. While in micro-social capital, this characteristic is relatively defensible, as the social network is the axis of exchange of tangible and intangible resources (Millán & Gordon, 2004), in macro-social capital, fungibility is ethereal because an individual or group cannot exchange aspects that are by nature intangible and consubstantial to the collectivity. However, when speaking of norms of generalised reciprocity (Putnam, 1993), this exchange of prosocial and cooperative behaviours induces their prolongation over time.

h. *Measurability.* The attributes identified as general social capital are measurable. Despite this, not all the indicators chosen are equally adequate and precise. This situation is linked to the degree of complexity compared to physical capital. Let us recall the widespread criticism of Putnam's (1993) approach when he takes social participation as a measuring instrument. Therefore, it can be said that the challenges of quantifying social capital are relatively high.

In sum, considering each of the definition's components, we think it is safe to say that the analogy with the concept of capital is forced.

4 Sources and effects of macro-social capital

Another of the building blocks referred to in Chapter II is that of its sources and effects. This is such a relevant issue that it is worth pausing and critically reflecting on the assertions made in this regard.

4.1 Sources of macro-social capital

Summarising existing work, the "sources" of social capital can be classified into two broad types: endogenous and exogenous (Membiela-Pollán, 2016).

Exogenous sources refer to any aspect external to social capital's cognitive and structural dimensions but can affect them. These include conditions such as religion, the political and legal system, the media, cultural identity, geographical context, lifestyles, economic conditions, or the intervention of authorities.

On the other hand, endogenous sources encompass aspects that are integral to social capital and exert an influence, often bidirectional, on each other. Cognitive and relational factors influence the structure and vice versa. For example, trust influences social structures, and their changes influence general trust (Durlauf, 1999).

Considering the problem of endogeneity in developing the sources of social capital, we will start from one of its dimensions, trust, to explain the possible causalities that have been proposed. In fact, practically all research has chosen this starting point.

4.1.1 The origins of social trust. Explanatory theories

The sources of trust can be multiple: membership in social networks and civic participation, personal well-being and satisfaction, perceptions of public and institutional security, cultural identity, personal success, favourable socioeconomic conditions, economic equality, and opportunity (Welch et al., 2005; Glanville & Paxton, 2007; Cais et al., 2021).

Systematising the various proposals as to what the ultimate determinants are, we can speak of four complementary explanations: (a) Theory of associationism or mainstream social capital, (b) Theory of institutional conditioning factors, (c) Theory of cultural conditioning factors, and (d) Theory of strong ties and the personal framework (Figure 4.3).

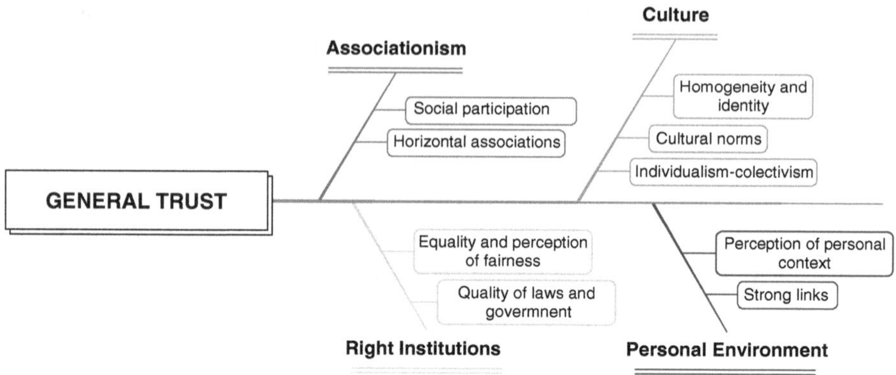

Figure 4.3 Sources of general trust.

Source: Own elaboration.

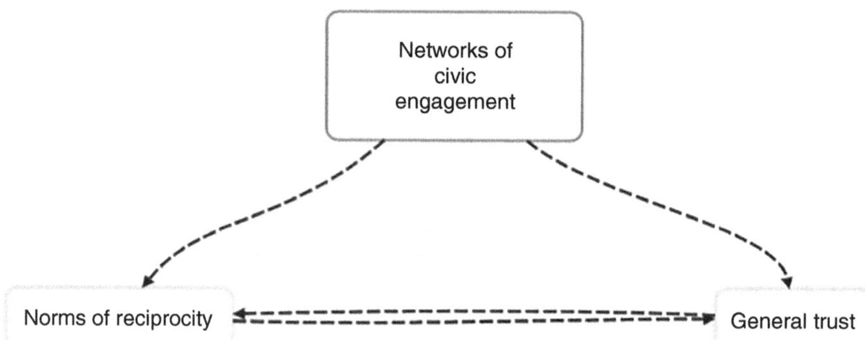

Figure 4.4 Causal relationships of Putnam's concept of social capital.

Source: Own elaboration based on Häuberer (2011).

4.1.1.1 ASSOCIATIONISM OR MAINSTREAM SOCIAL CAPITAL THEORY

This theory defends the existence of a link between social trust and civic participation in associations and voluntary organisations. Because of its diffusion, it can be identified as the "mainstream theory of social capital" (Stolle & Rochon, 1999; Pena-López & Sánchez-Santos, 2014), and its precedents can be found in Tocqueville's ideas taken up by Robert Putnam (1993). In its most straightforward formulation, membership in voluntary associations nurtures civic spirit and habits of cooperation, empathy, reciprocity, and trust, as well as understanding the common interest and good of the whole society (Putnam, 1993; Cook, 2003).

According to Putnam, trust is intimately connected with civic engagement networks and norms of reciprocity (see Figure 4.4). The frequent interaction characteristic of dense social networks involved in civic engagement, such as neighbourhood associations, purchasing groups, cooperatives, and sports clubs, facilitates establishing and spreading reciprocity norms, thus nurturing trust and cooperation (Putnam, 1993; Millán & Gordon, 2004). Then, this theory directs attention towards horizontal interaction where public interests prevail, thereby promoting generalised reciprocity and extending cooperative tendencies beyond specific groups. This horizontal associationism serves as a "didactic" force in shaping general cultural norms. It acts as a catalyst for social commitment, encouraging cooperation, solidarity, and civic-mindedness, ultimately leading to general trust.

The operation of institutions and the vitality of democracy hinge upon such civic engagement. In his seminal work from 1993, Putnam conducts a comparative analysis between Northern and Southern Italy. He discovers that regions in the North, characterised by greater civic participation and involvement of civil society and elevated levels of trust, exhibit superior governmental quality, enhanced institutional performance, and more favourable economic development outcomes.

Criticisms of these causal links are pretty evident. Some authors point out that it lacks empirical support, and the cited relationship is unclear (Herreros, 2004; Rothstein & Uslaner, 2005; Kleiner, 2021). Putnam does not take into account aspects such as the size of the network, the sociability within the network, the intensity of contact between its components or the values that inspire it (since there are violent, racist, criminal, secret, rent-seeking organisations, etc.) (Glaeser et al., 2002). Moreover, other authors argue that the informal social networks of family, friends, school, neighbourhood or workplace play a more critical role in the functions attributed to associationalism (Levi, 1996; Delhey & Newton, 2003).

In another sense, the role of associationism is unclear. Some researchers allude to the Olson-Putnam controversy to indicate that the influence of associations on subjects and trust varies depending on the nature of the associations (Paxton, 2007, p. 48). Interconnected associationism does promote general trust, as opposed to isolated and self-enclosed associationism, which can be detrimental to trust. The latter is because the norms and cooperative behaviours fostered in one association can be extended when linked to other organisations, thus fostering an overall network of associations or "community". This is to avoid the confrontational logic of "us" and "others" characteristic of isolated associations (Paxton, 2007, p. 51). Generally, individuals tend to perceive their group members positively, seeing them as more trustworthy than others.

In any case, it seems clear that the potential link – generalised trust-associationism – would be bidirectional, as not only does associative participation generate trust, but trust also favours participation in social networks, including voluntary organisations (Newton, 2001; Pena-López & Sánchez-Santos, 2014).

4.1.1.2 INSTITUTIONAL CONDITIONING THEORY

By institutional determinants, we refer to formal institutions (laws, regulations, rules) and the organisations monitoring them (government, administrations, public and private institutions) that affect social, political and economic functioning. This theory is rooted in neoinstitutionalism and highlights institutions' importance in reducing the risk and uncertainty associated with life in society by providing a stable or reliable environment (Cook, 2003; Ayala Espino, 2005).

Specifically, research establishes that a set of institutional variables favours social trust: the quality of laws and public institutions, citizens' perception of social and political order, a stable legal framework and the independence of courts, honesty of governments and the absence of corruption, strong democracy, economic development, equal opportunities, social peace, and public security. In the same vein, policies relating to economic equality and equal opportunities, universalistic social welfare programmes, and redistributive policies play the same role (Rothstein & Uslaner, 2005; Guiso et al., 2011; Frederiksen, 2019).

4.1.1.3 CULTURAL CONDITIONING THEORY

Trust can have a cultural component for three reasons.

- On the one hand, it is commonplace that cultural homogeneity, identity, shared interests, norms, and values are a source of trust. Whereas social and cultural diversity, heterogeneity and the absence of moral references in society favour social distrust (Bacharach & Gambetta, 2001; Welch et al., 2005). The reason is simple: behaviours that derive from a shared culture tend to be more predictable. Expectations are clarified, strengthening the normative structure (Zucker, 1986; Coleman, 1990; Goddard, 2003).
- On the other hand, it is influenced by the nature of the norms and values that shape the culture, that is, its degree of prosociality (e.g., honesty/opportunism and respect for moral commitments), which is the type of behaviour that favours the construction of social relations and leads to cooperation (Zamagni, 1995; Uslaner, 2008).
- Finally, the typology of one's culture (individualistic or collectivistic) affects social trust. Yamagishi and Yamagishi (1994) indicate that more individualistic cultures, such as North America, favour greater general trust since the subjects tend to establish relational bridges with other groups (bridging social capital). In contrast, in collectivist cultures such as the East, the subject is integrated into his or her rigid social network of strong ties – bonding social capital – which provides a higher level of commitment and security. Nevertheless, this investment tends to destroy social trust because it produces "encapsulated" relationships, with a high prominence of "intra-group" cooperation at the expense of undermining "inter-group" cooperation (Ermisch & Gambeta, 2010).

4.1.1.4 STRONG TIES AND PERSONAL FRAMEWORK THEORY

In this case, the roots of trust are sought in the focal subject's personal characteristics, including his or her psychological traits and network of strong ties (Glanville & Paxton, 2007; Membiela-Pollán, 2016).

Individuals to whom things "go well", the "social achievers", have more social trust (Newton, 2001). Trust positively and significantly correlates with income, status, life satisfaction, happiness, and overall positive experiences (Inglehart, 1990;

Feher & Tremblay, 2018). Optimistic people with self-esteem and self-control have also been identified as having higher social trust, linking trust to personality traits (Welch et al., 2005; Tulin, 2018). Finally, some studies find a significant link between trust and education (Delhey & Newton, 2003), while for other attributes (gender, age), the relationship seems less clear.

A theory that analyses the link between trust and the subject's framework cannot avoid the study of his or her network of strong ties (family, close friends), among other reasons, because the variables: satisfaction, happiness and the experiences associated with life have a lot to do with the relational environment in which the subject participates (Bubolz, 2001). The family and, in general, the network of strong ties (bonding social capital) provides the individual with security, a sense of control and certainty. It enables them to assume certain risks. In other words, it integrates the subject into society (Boulding, 1973; Nee & Sanders, 2003).

In the family, we have the first experience of trust, which is born with the satisfaction of specific basic needs associated with life, such as food, shelter, general support and affection (Freitag & Traunmüller, 2009; Membiela-Pollán, 2016). In the family and other strong ties, the result of interaction, cooperation, and reciprocity, which the subject will later extrapolate to society, is learned from childhood (Gui & Sudgen, 2005; Pena-López & Sánchez-Santos, 2014). These contexts go hand in hand with socialising norms and values in the family nucleus. In the latter sense, certain attitudes, such as social trust itself, can be transmitted in the family (Welch et al., 2005), as Uslaner (2008) explains, taking the case of subjects of Nordic origin who reside in the United States and who show the highest levels of trust in the ethnic analysis of this country.

Studies find that subjects who enjoy a stronger family, those who are married and have children, have higher social trust. It also indicates that people who had an unstructured childhood and childhood trauma, as well as divorced people, have lower general trust, which is due mainly to reduced expectations of the good behaviour of others (Rotter, 1980; Putnam, 1995; Paxton, 2007, p. 49).

Overall, we find that the origins of trust are not causally structured, so the proposals are surprisingly disjointed. As we proposed in Chapter III using the "Coleman boat", a general foundation of social capital that starts from the macro conditioning factors and builds an explanation through micro-mechanisms is critical.

4.2. *Effects of macro-social capital*

As in the case of sources, macro-social capital gives rise to several endogenous and exogenous effects. In general, we can distinguish three groups, sometimes interrelated: economic effects, institutional effects, and effects on well-being and quality of life.

4.2.1 *Economic effects*

In the first chapter, we already made a brief overview of the authors and schools that emphasise the weight of the social in the economic. We also pointed out that social capital seems to be an effective way to study embeddedness. The interest in this point in economics has always been based on the effects of both micro-social and macro-social capital (social trust, civic-mindedness, social cohesion, and civic participation) on sustainable growth and economic development. An overall effect is at least as strong as human capital (Whiteley, 2000; Sommer, 2019).

Using the terminology of neoinstitutionalists, the effects can be interpreted as a reduction of transaction costs, information costs, contract monitoring, conflict, etc. (Andriani & Christoforou, 2016) (see Box 4.1), leading to an increase in exchanges, investments, entrepreneurship, and innovation, as well as the diffusion of knowledge and information (Knack & Keefer, 1997, pp. 1252–1253; Thompson, 2018). This game positively affects the performance of other types of capital, such as physical, financial, and human capital (Membiela-Pollán et al., 2019a; Eloire, 2015).

The improved efficiency and market functioning are also reflected in a reduced need for regulation and oversight by the public sector, which would also reduce defensive public spending. This expenditure is aimed at maintaining welfare in the face of antisocial behaviour (from vandalism, violence, or attacks on property rights to fraud, corruption, tax evasion, or embezzlement) (Leipert, 1989; Moore & Recker, 2016; Membiela-Pollán et al., 2023).

4.2.2 *Effects on institutional functioning*

In Robert Putnam's study (1993), a comparison between Northern and Southern Italy revealed that increased civic engagement and trust within the northern regions were associated with improved institutional performance. Putnam even asserts that "good governance in Italy is a by-product of choral societies and football clubs" (1993).

Subsequently, numerous studies have used data at the national, regional, and even local levels, adopting social indicators (trust, associationism, social homogeneity, etc.) to support the existence of this empirical relationship.

The argument is self-evident: norms of reciprocity and solidarity, habits of cooperation, public spirit, and trust incline people to make society work (Coffé & Geys, 2005), reducing transaction costs, including enforcing laws and regulations. Within politics, greater cooperation between politicians, institutions, and organisations facilitates a higher quality of governance (Knack, 2002).

Simultaneously, greater associative and community participation tends to raise citizens' interest in public life and politics (Boix & Posner, 1998), so they become more active in demanding good governance and monitoring public management. Citizens' increased involvement in the political process (co-governance) and the production of public services (co-production) means that they come to perceive themselves as active subjects and not only as clients of the welfare state (Lawndes & Pratchett, 2008).

4.2.3 *Effects on well-being and quality of life*

Research on social capital frequently cites the effect of this variable on well-being, both subjective (more related to happiness) and objective (more related to quality of life) (Pena-López et al., 2017; Calcagnini & Perugini, 2019).

The causal relationship can come from different pathways.

Trust is a relevant element, as a feeling by which one appreciates the ability to trust others and as an instrumental variable that facilitates social interaction, cooperation, and reciprocity (Brehm & Rahn, 1997, p. 999; Glanville et al., 2016). General or social trust positively and significantly influences subjective well-being and quality of life (Dolan et al., 2007; Phillips, 2006). Similarly, perceptions of public safety and crime rates correlated with social trust and are strongly significant (Helliwell & Putnam, 2004).

Social cohesion, also identifiable with macro-social capital, is linked to a sense of belonging and trust and tends to affect well-being (Knack & Keefer, 1997). Associationism and civic engagement networks alone have an influence that, although generally positive, is more ambivalent and depends on the nature of the associations (expressive or instrumental) (Rodríguez-Pose & Von Berlepsch, 2012).

Indirectly, social capital's contribution to development and better institutional functioning influences people's well-being. Putnam (1993) noted that more civic-minded regions in Italy, where commitment was higher, were more responsive to issues such as creating clinics or promoting investment and development.

In short, general social capital's effect on well-being is intrinsic-expressive and extrinsic-instrumental. Human beings are social by nature, and sociability is a basic intrinsic need, as are security and a sense of belonging. It is, therefore, logical that trust, social interaction and participation, the presence of prosocial civic norms, cohesion, and even cultural identity impact well-being. This is because the individual's chances of living a whole life in society are enhanced. In addition, there is an extrinsic-instrumental benefit derived from macro-social capital since, as we have said, it facilitates cooperation, collective action, general economic activity, or institutional functioning.

5 Let us be critical: "what are we talking about?"

We have already outlined many criticisms of the concept of macro-social capital. Almost all of them are amply justified. However, as we indicated in the previous chapter when dealing with Coleman's boat, the problem is not the non-existence of macro-social capital but its articulation with micro-social capital, which we will deal with in the next chapter.

The first problem is the lack of a referent. Macro-social capital is an abstract and less delimited entity (Dasgupta & Serageldin, 2000). This situation justifies a first criticism that has to do with its categorisation as an "umbrella concept", for it stands for social trust and civic norms, associationism, or social cohesion. Despite the links that may exist between these aspects, the concept is less well defined than at the micro-level and, of course, less concrete than physical capital, natural capital, financial capital, or human capital. It is one of those notions where rhetoric often trumps logic, and the passionate use of descriptive statistics often replaces detailed analysis (Sobel, 2002).

Secondly, the circularity or tautology inherent in definitions of social capital invites criticism. At times, social capital appears to be both a cause and an effect in a way that makes it impossible to establish the direction of causality. From a logical standpoint, distinguishing between the *pars definie*ns and the *pars definiendum* proves elusive. For instance, the delineation between what social capital encompasses, its functions or outcomes, and its location remains blurred. Putnam (2000, p. 334) acknowledges the ambiguity surrounding the direction of causality, although most studies indicate that high levels of certain social activities indirectly contribute to favourable outcomes. A significant number of questions are open: Does social participation foster general trust, or does general trust facilitate social participation? Does social cohesion engender trust, or does trust subsequently foster cohesion? The concept of macro-social capital seeks to amalgamate all desirable societal attributes into a unified framework. In this sense, it is noteworthy that many studies concentrate on analysing successful cases under the presumption of possessing social capital. Yet, the group's success often indicates its social capital (Durlauf, 1999).

The third criticism arises from the two previous criticisms. The ambiguity and circularity derive a logical problem in measurement and testing. As a result, much of the evidence is questionable, and the possibility of advancing knowledge is diminished. To some extent, social capital is in danger, if it is not already there, of becoming a fashionable concept where there is no referent and whose success in political discourse destroys its analytical capacities. Research can make fundamental contributions in fields as diverse as organisational theory, education, health, economics, and sociology. Notwithstanding, the testing of the contributions needs to be articulated on a more solid basis than that proposed by the macro approach. The micro-level of the next chapter may be more interesting in this respect. The essence of the problem, its status as capital, is also in question (see Box 4.2). As far as the macro approach is concerned, this criticism is justified. As we have already seen, the analogy with capital presents serious problems. Social capital only relatively adheres to these assumptions, but objectively speaking, this is also true of human capital and does not generate as much criticism.

Similarly, the functionality of the concept comes under scrutiny. Social capital has a dark side, often called "bad social capital" (Warren, 2008). Its effects are not uniformly positive. While its constituent elements, such as social trust, civic-cooperative norms, social cohesion, and prosocial behaviour, are inherently positive, their particularistic manifestations can give rise to significant societal challenges. Moreover, this form of capital can create economic opportunities for members within networks while simultaneously excluding others. Networks can also act as barriers, restricting entry for those outside the network. Factors like race, ethnicity, religion, language, or shared economic interests frequently serve as bases for exclusion from both markets and society. Consequently, although social capital can serve as a catalyst for innovation and entrepreneurship, it can also foster individual complacency, impose rigid conformity, and exclude essential groups in society, generating poverty traps (Quibria, 2003).

Sociology and neo-Marxist economics criticise this approach as expressing economic imperialism (Fine, 2002). It is said to instrumentalise the social by coining it "capital" and simplifying and reducing it until it almost ceases to be "social"

(Claridge, 2018a, p. 3) (see Box 4.2). However, using "capital" and "neocapital" does not mean instrumentalising the social dimension but considering the social as a necessary asset.

Finally, the concept's treatment is open to criticism. Many studies show a disconnection between macro- and micro-social capital when the bidirectional, albeit complex, interplay between the two is evident (Pena-López & Sánchez-Santos, 2013; Membiela-Pollán, 2016). This is one of the big holes in social capital theory. Understanding the interplay between levels is vital to increasing this variable's explanatory capacity and credibility. This will be one of the critical points of the next chapter.

Box 4.2 Ben Fine and the perversions of the uses of social capital

Ben Fine stands out among the authors who are most critical of the uses of social capital. This researcher has developed an essential body of work analysing the surprising growth of publications on this concept, parallel to the lack of a common reference point and methodological rigour. His criticisms are fundamental and well-founded and deserve to be dealt with in a specific section.

Fine starts from an attitude of suspicion in the face of the concept's surprising success. Social capital is part of a confusion that is functionally useful in hindering the critical analysis of capitalist society. The concept's starting point is "laudable": to complement economic analysis with social analysis and show how the latter's success depends on the former, a kind of "precondition" of development (Fine, 2001a).

As we have seen in Chapter 2, the history of the concept can be revealing. Although in its micro version, it was introduced by Bourdieu in his analysis of the mechanisms of reproduction of power and social stratification, in the 1980s, it was reintroduced, stripped of its theoretical foundation, by Rational Choice. This shift involved rediscovering "socio-structural" resources that operate as capital. This macro reinterpretation equates to "internalised norms" that help individuals act according to collective interests (Fine, 2003). An atmosphere of mutual trust and reciprocal obligations makes it easier for individuals to make economic decisions that coincide with the collective interest. Putnam's (1993, p. 172) already studied definition is paradigmatic as it tries to give academic rigour to the social functionality of trust in economics.

This is a self-interested use of the concept of society, functionally helpful for neoclassical economics. This stock of "reciprocity" or trust derives in economic benefits: the reduction of opportunism, collective investments, and public welfare, etc. Social capital becomes something functionally useful from an economic point of view and even a way of relieving the state of its control over economic activity (Fine, 2010).

As we have seen in this chapter, the macro strands are often highly ambiguous about how they are created: they emerge from synergies between the economy, the state, and various organisations belonging to "civil society". For Fine, the concept's functionality lies in the fact that it expresses a way of understanding the economy, one of the key ideas of development economics as understood by the World Bank. In sum, this apparent success of the concept under its macro approach would have an obvious ideological undertone.

Looking more closely at specific aspects of the theory, Fine (2003, 2010) also highlights three significant flaws

i. Object delimitation is a problem; all kinds of institutions are mixed. Thus, the computation of formal and informal organisations in any society is very complex, from the family to political parties. Moreover, they are not static institutions. The supposed decline of one gives rise to others. If these are the potential sources to which Putnam alludes, it would be essential to delimit which ones and their causality.
ii. Social capital is anything else that contributes to individual or collective performance after other forms of capital have been considered: natural, physical, human, and financial. Surprisingly, all the authors start by acknowledging this chaos but then choose to use more generalised definitions or directly offer their own.
iii. Finally, as part of a ceremony of bewilderment, many papers recognise that the effects can be negative and positive. From the growth of regional economies to mafia problems, everything can be interpreted under social capital.

However, the problem for Fine lies in the very conception of capital in neoclassical economics. From this view, capital is an asset that enters the productive process and has to reproduce through this process, as with physical or even human capital. Applied to macro-social capital, this is understood as any social relations outside the economy that can be sustained and reproduced. Thus, a country's social capital exists in aspects as diverse as its sports, cultural, and neighbourhood associations, but also in community solidarity, etc. It is a bare-bones factor of production in society, which reduces transaction costs and contributes to product generation. For Fine, Social Capital is a "reification" of all social relations and the key to the closure of the arch of orthodox economics. For him, not all relationships can be included since not all involve economic contexts, such as trust, reliability, and familiarity. Accepting this reductionism would mean eliminating the specificity of the social.

Fine is not entirely misguided, the suspicion about the concept is that it tries to be a prism through which all social theory wants to be rewritten self-interestedly, losing all its critical capacity. Social reality loses its historical and conflict dimension, using the concepts of orthodox economics. Social capital is an ideological artefact that tries to integrate the social into neoclassical economics without altering its foundations. Throughout Chapter 5, in which we will delve into the micro-foundation of social capital, we will try to respond to the well-founded criticisms of Fine's work.

6 Recapping

Social capital has become a popular concept in academia and the public sphere. The macro approach, which focuses on general trust, civic-mindedness, or social cohesion, is perhaps the most prominent.

Talking about social trust is attractive and easy to approach for policymakers. The same is true in the field of research. However, this perspective brings drawbacks that the micro approach focusing on the social network does not have. Overall, social capital is less well defined, and its definitions suffer from a greater circularity, that is, there is a loss of clarity about what it is and does. As a result, measurement problems arise. It becomes more open to criticism when considered as a form of capital because it only relatively adheres to the assumptions that it should satisfy if physical capital is taken as a reference.

Even so, general or macro-social capital has significant consequences. We can understand that any society with a high degree of social trust and cohesion and in which norms of civic-cooperative behaviour are widespread will function better and be more productive than an unstructured or conflictual one. The effects of social capital can be grouped into economic, institutional, and well-being effects, which have been confirmed through multiple studies.

If anything, the macro approach lacks depth. As we have said, it is easy to praise the goodness of trust and civic behaviour and to communicate how desirable they are. However, there is no systematisation to approximate how such attributes are generated. In other words, what are the exact sources of this general social capital? The restriction affects even the detailed study of effects or returns; for example, it is seen in research that deals exclusively with the role of generalised trust.

Often, the macro is considered without considering its link to the micro; the same is true of the inverse relationship. Only with a holistic analysis of this interplay can social capital theory take a step forward and shed light on the mechanisms underlying this variable, thus gaining explanatory power and credibility.

5 Personal networks as capital

Individual social capital

> Social capital is the sum of the resources, actual or virtual, that accrue to an individual or a group by virtue of possessing a durable network of more or less institutionalised relationships of mutual acquaintance and recognition.
>
> (Bourdieu, 1986)

The criticisms highlighted in the previous chapter and the need for a general refocusing entail proposing some lines of restructuring the social capital theory on a more solid basis. As Portes (1998 p. 21) pointed out, the most significant theoretical promise of social capital is found at the individual level, rooted in the micro-mechanisms of social processes at the meso or macro level. Indeed, social capital has both a macro or collective and a micro or individual dimension. Then again, the nature of its investigation, following the explanatory logic of the social mechanisms we analysed in Chapter 3, requires studying individuals and their relationships within the constraints marked by the macro context.

In any example of a social relationship we want to propose, we always find the trilogy constitutive of social capital: a subject which interacts formally or informally with another or others, the particular characteristics of the relationship (in terms of norms and values) and a series of tangible (Hellerstein & Neumark, 2020) or intangible (Dodd, 2016; Mishra, 2020; Lee et al., 2018) resources, from financial support to psychological well-being. This trilogy opens up an "interpretation" of network and resource dynamics as a form of capital that we might call "individual social capital". The set of networks available to an individual is a form of investment, a productive resource, and a durable and culturally embedded form of capital. This analysis will be discussed in more detail in this chapter.

The foundation requires a micro approach, starting from the most elementary level: the individual and their relational fabric. In other words, the study of general social functioning and coordination implies the analysis of individual networks and their interactions.

By providing a starting point at the individual level, this conceptualisation of social capital allows us to study the mechanisms that can give rise to macro-social dynamics: stratification, institutional functioning, etc. Thus, the key to the definitions we will analyse is to treat social capital as a mechanism for establishing a connection

DOI: 10.4324/9781003375302-8

between individual interests and collective behaviours. The link lies in the fact that, at the same time, these networks are or can also be a form of local public good from the point of view of communities and society. This chapter is central and constructive. It aims to propose the micro approach as the starting point for Social Capital Theory. Then, we will try to answer the questions: Why are social networks a form of capital? How can we measure it? What is the capitalisation process of social networks?

1 A social "capital", relationships as assets

As discussed in the previous chapter, the concept of capital is highly problematic. Adopting that analogical perspective, which we have repeatedly alluded to, can be applied to areas beyond those for which it was initially formulated. Indeed, as Christoforou & Davis (2014b) suggests, capital can be understood as anything produced to enhance individual power. This analogy finds relatively smooth acceptance when applied to human and cultural capital. Nevertheless, regarding social capital, the matter becomes more contentious (Fine, 2001a, 2001b, 2010). Thus, it requires further clarification.

From a micro perspective, individual social capital pertains to an individual's capacity to access scarce resources by virtue of their membership in a particular social network (Lin, 1999a). This definition emphasises that social capital is a capability entrenched within social structures while simultaneously being influenced by personal objectives (Burt, 2001). In essence, social capital is inherently social yet individually managed. Like other forms of capital, it is owned by individuals who leverage resources from their networks, while also being a collective attribute of the group in which individuals are embedded, generating resources and externalities for both the group and society at large.

To extend the analogy further, social capital, as embodied in networks managed by individuals, is durable, cumulative, intra- and intergenerationally transferable (Waldstrøm & Svendsen, 2008), that is, it is alienable. If we study the configuration of personal social networks, they can be inherited by family or shared and managed as an exchangeable or alienable asset (Robison & Ritchie, 2010). To specify this last point, network resources are exchanged in labour markets and the family sphere; in fact, it is one of the determinants of individual payoffs (Erickson, 2021). It is the object of an inheritance the family receives, which the family strives to transfer. Similarly, it is a part of the assets that an individual shows when looking for a job or being hired (for example, companies are willing to pay for the network available to a worker).

Even more essential is that it generates a return, a flow of resources that can be material or non-material, expressive or instrumental (Lin, 2001). Social networks tend to be goal-oriented because they are generally created for specific purposes or returns: family, work, leisure, information or status (Verhaeghe et al., 2015; Pena-López & Sánchez-Santos, 2017).

At first glance, we are describing a more solid referent that fits the definition of capital, but taking up the criticisms we have referred to, some issues need to be addressed to focus on the approach. This will be our means of converging the various theoretical proposals from the rational choice underlying Coleman's approach to Bourdieu's post-structuralism.

1.1 Rational choice: the individual in Coleman's network

Coleman's (1988) functionalist approach defines social capital remarkably openly as qualities of the social structure that facilitate the activity of the people who constitute the structure itself. Social capital is a resource that resides in the social structure, a form of public good that generates returns and affects individual behaviours.

This position is intermediate between the "network" theory or sociology's paradigm and the adoption of explanations based on the maximising individual behaviour of neoclassical economics. Individuals have social relations at their disposal because of their insertion in the structure, while at the same time, they invest in them based on the expected returns in the form of resources. In other words, we are talking about an economic rationality conditioned by the social context in which decisions are made. The whole capitalisation process is based on this maximising behaviour on socially determined objectives (Coleman, 1988).

In this way, individuals arrange and create self-interested networks, and social capital resides in these relationships between people capable of providing resources. However, even starting from an individual network, Coleman sees social capital as a public good or at least a local public good, where individuals' self-interested and maximising actions benefit the whole. From this perspective, we cannot speak of a pure public good but rather a local and conditional one, to which individuals, depending on their position, have access to certain advantages provided by the relationships within this structure, but not all of them.

1.2 The Bourdieusian approach

Bourdieu's perspective can be understood as a confluence of neocapital and Marxist-rooted post-structuralism. For this author (Bourdieu, 1986), social capital is the sum of actual or potential resources linked to possessing a durable network of more or less institutionalised relationships (see Box 5.1). This network supports each social group member and simultaneously belongs to the individual and the group.

By adopting this definition, social capital is a stock of relationships oriented towards obtaining social resources. This makes it surprisingly close to rational choice, as it adopts a particular form of methodological individualism in which subjects are "optimisers". However, this option also considers the relational inequality and the weight of power relations that network analysis systematically neglects (Fine, 2001a, 2001b).

Despite this, acknowledging optimising behaviour does not inherently entail embracing rational choice theory. Contrary to this assumption, members of society are not perceived as constantly engaging in cost-benefit analyses, as individual actions may stem from non-maximising behaviours, such as ingrained social class habits. Agents shape their interests within a framework dictated by the dynamics of their social environment and personal dispositions, guided by what Bourdieu terms *the logic of field* and *habitus*. Nevertheless, in a capitalist society, this logic tends towards commodifying personal relationships.

Then, according to Bourdieu, social capital is a theoretical construct illuminating the mechanisms through which socioeconomic disparities between classes manifest (Fine, 2001a, 2001b; Adam & Roncevic, 2003). It represents one asset that contributes to establishing distinctions within the social structure. An individual's position within society is contingent upon their accumulation of economic, cultural, and social capital and the specific *milieu* in which their interactions occur, governed by what Bourdieu refers to as the "legitimate principles of the field" (Bourdieu, 1991).

In short, Bourdieu is considering a more holistic approach to the problem where agents construct their preferences. However, this perspective does not displace rational choice because, in developed capitalist societies, rational choice logic is considered the legitimate mode of action (Odabas & Adaman, 2014). We live in a capitalist society where relationships are progressively instrumentalised to maximise returns and, hence, individuals rationally accumulate them as a form of stock.

1.3 Nam Lin's neocapital approach

The neocapital approach we have already discussed allows for a kind of Hegelian synthesis of the two previous approaches. To a certain extent, it could be interpreted as a quantification of Bourdieu's approach, which was adapted to the neoclassical capital theory but incorporating social determinants. For Lin (2000, 2001, 2008), individual social capital is the set of networks that enable individuals to achieve market and non-market objectives by interacting with other individuals. Its value lies in the instrumental and expressive resources it can mobilise. That is, it is a stock with a return. As Christoforou (2014) points out, the individual social capital perspective shifts the "habit-field" framework to objective structures of social inequality.

Similarly, discussing investment strategies does not immediately imply directly adopting rational choice assumptions. Bourdieu's dispositions of origin and socialisation are conditioned by class, "habitus", and "field" and are reformulated by Lin in a practical way (Law & Mooney, 2006). Lin's approach to the problem is that relations are measurable capital facilitating social reproduction, where investment strategies constrained by social structure replace the abstract concepts of habitus and field.

The Marxist notion of conflict is replaced by strategies where inequality, social classes and their reproduction play a role in decision-making (Lin, 1999b). In other words, the maximising behaviours of agents in this investment in social relations are strongly conditioned by each subject's economic and social framework. This can be considered a rational choice perspective because it emphasises the individual and instrumental action, but, at the same time, it also introduces the social structure and considers the critical role of homophily, which we will discuss later in social reproduction.

Subjects' motivations are economic and maximising in the context of a particular field, which is a typical habitus in capitalist society. Economic motivations are not the only driver of investments in social capital (Robinson & Oliver, 2023). For example, Fine (2001a) questioned the nature of capital for certain relational expressions (trust, reliability, friendship, etc.). However, these expressive relationships (relational goods) can also have an instrumental character or be instrumentalised due to a generalised capitalist field extension. Finally, as Lin (2001) remarks, "without measurement, it will be impossible to verify propositions or accumulate knowledge". His proposal attempts to introduce an abstract concept into the realm of the testable.

From the three authors that we could identify as milestones in the study of individual social capital, we could propose a consensus definition of this micro-social capital or individual social capital that we will specify in the following critical review section: Social capital is the set of social networks that provide the resources, material or not, linked to the members of a social network that are accessible and mobilisable by an individual.

At this point, it is essential to reconsider whether we are talking about a form of capital and in what sense it is.

1.4 Is this a notion of capital? A critical review

As we saw in the first chapter, although crucial in economics, the notion of capital is far from univocal. Therefore, defining what we mean by capital when we talk about social capital is helpful.

Addressing the debate on what can be considered "forms of capital" from a neocapital perspective, we can draw a simple sketch: the result of an investment process subject to appropriation. Taking a micro perspective, the "analogy" we were referring to is obvious. Individuals of any class and social group invest in social relations, expecting a return. This factor of production also forms a stock, a productive capacity installed in the form of social networks, whose subjective value depends exclusively on the set of potential resources or expected returns. These returns range from the flow of information to exerting a form of influence or providing credentials and recognition. Thus, the returns can be either instrumental (material or status) or expressive (linked to personal identity).

The case of individual ownership or appropriation of investment in social networks as a feature of social capital is sustained by the implicit norms of any social relationship and implies coercion, like any form of capital. The trustworthiness of a subject depends on his or her respect for a set of norms specific to any society, ranging from the acceptance of a structure to the reciprocity of any bond. Thus, capital and its ownership are always measured by and depend on the rules of a given society (Piketty, 2014). In other words, recognising the ownership of relations lies in an external sanction derived from reciprocity rules. Repeated non-compliance is socially punished and constitutes a sufficient mechanism to delimit ownership.

1.4.1 Some remarks on what capital really is

The definitions of individual social capital that we have been collecting and analysing from an economic point of view present a series of inaccuracies that should be pointed out. The three versions analysed in the previous section indicate that individual social capital is the set of social networks and resources accessible to an individual. Strictly speaking, the productive factor that is the object of investment and intergenerational transfer is social networks and nothing more than networks.

Material or immaterial resources are the expected return on this investment. So, capital is only the object of an investment process; it constitutes a productive factor and a social valuation object as an asset due to the potentially mobilisable resources. We are, therefore, talking about a stock or endowment of social networks.

In the context of this review and combining sociological theory and economic theory, it is worth clarifying the elements that comprise it.

1.4.1.1 SPECIALISED SOCIAL TIES: STRONG AND WEAK TIES

Social capital is appropriately found in social relations that facilitate the mobilisation of resources. However, due to their functionality, relationships are not qualitatively equal: they depend on the objectives and are conditioned by the nature of the link and its structure.

Thus, for example, networks constituted by strong ties in which *alters* know and have strong bonds with each other tend to be more "closed" and preferentially associated with generating expressive resources of well-being and personal identity. These are the primary insurance in protecting the *ego* from mental and physical stressors. These accessible contacts have a high capacity for mobilisation and constitute strong relationships or close and long-lasting contacts (Hulbert et al., 2001). However, it is worth pointing out that the term relationship strength is remarkably ambiguous and depends on variables such as frequency of contact, duration, or relationship history. Nevertheless, all of them can be best summarised under perceived closeness (Wellman & Wortley, 1990). This is the case with relatives and friends with whom significant similarities are shared, so they tend to form denser and more homogeneous sets (Volker & Flap, 1997).

Weak ties are characteristic of more open networks that favour obtaining heterogeneous resources. These comprise less close and more diverse relationships that can provide resources that need to be bridged with other groups. Their functional specialisation is in instrumental objectives linked to prestige and status. Given their object, through the interplay of reciprocity, their effectiveness depends strongly on the prestige and status of the *ego* position (Lin, 2001).

Ultimately, and returning to Granovetter's (1973) traditional arguments, closed networks of strong ties can provide comfort and security more easily and are helpful when cooperation and agreement are needed. Open networks of weak ties can provide better opportunities and information, for example, when looking for a job (Burt, 2001; Lin, 2000).

Finally, and linked to this typification of relationships, there is a controversy over the attribute of closure in studies on social capital. By this, we mean a demarcation between those who are part of the group and those who are not. In Bourdieu, this is usually associated with the social stratum, which tends to be self-reproducing. In Coleman, from a more functional perspective, there is only a way of demarcating which set of relations can mobilise resources, that is, who is in the circle that mobilises and reciprocally mobilises them. The importance of closure is linked to the type of resources sought. Thus, objectives as varied as the maintenance of emotional ties imply closure in a family; the maintenance of class privileges implies group closure and delving into the negative expressions of social capital, and corruption networks imply closure vis-à-vis outsiders. Burt's classical work (1992) has strongly questioned the relevance of these closures because bridges are relevant to obtaining non-redundant resources.

1.4.1.2 INVESTMENT IN SOCIAL NETWORKS

Investment in networks has important social conditioning factors, the most obvious of which are ascribed ties such as family, which are interpreted as inheritance (Flap, 2004). In addition, it operates in a market with solid tendencies towards segmentation that could be encompassed under the term homophily. Based on gender, race, religion, and social class, individuals find it significantly easier to form networks with those with whom they have similarities (McPherson et al., 2001). Creating and maintaining this set of relationships entails actions that, in many cases, may not be deliberate but a by-product of social norms and directly linked to an expected future payoff (to attend a club, to keep a friendship, etc.). In other words, these actions entail the social structure and norms, costs, time, resources accessible and profitability.

1.4.1.3 RECIPROCITY AND EXPECTED RETURNS

Reciprocity is the system's foundation since it is built on the existence of generalised exchanges and transactions without immediate response based on trust. Consequently, any exchange takes place at the risk of opportunism. The history of exchanges can be transmitted among the network members and generate a reputation that favours future exchanges (Semmann et al., 2005). Like any other exchange form, it is conditioned by transaction costs (information, monitoring, etc.).

This approach to personal relationships may seem too "commodified" or, from a theoretical point of view, too biased towards the rational choice perspective. Thus, we would seemingly eliminate both altruism and personal relationships that arise for the sheer pleasure of sociality. In this line, Flap (1991, 2004) clarifies the nature of this micro-explanatory proposal: Individuals engage in social relations with a deliberate rationale. They actively pursue the enhancement of their quality of life and the advancement of their opportunities. Consequently, they allocate their personal resources strategically and cultivate relationships with others. The resources they allocate, that is, their investments in relationships, are contingent upon the anticipated returns and the perceived future benefits associated with each of these actions, some of them expressive or welfare-oriented. In sum, they optimise but under social constraints.

1.4.1.4 THE DISCOUNT RATE

From the point of view of economic theory, a stock's present value is derived from the discounted sum of all future expected returns, the net present value calculation:

$$NPV = \sum_{t=1}^{n} \frac{V_t}{(1+K)^t} - I_0$$

From the mathematical expression of Net Present Value, the existence of a discount rate is derived. This, by definition, incorporates the time adjustment of the expected returns in the future. The current investment must be contrasted with the expected resources and the time these could be perceived. Along with this time factor, perceived social risks should be incorporated since this expression refers to the probability of reciprocity, which is conditioned by time, but also by risk factors linked to trustworthiness, social and cultural norms, and social determinants such as inequality.

1.2 Is it really social?

Underlying the idea of ego networks and individual social capital is that an ego can access resources available to members of his or her network. This assertion assumes the existence of *quid pro quo* in the form of deferred exchange and, therefore, a particular form of social market.

Consequently, transactions with other actors under a shared interest occur. In this exchange, accepting its basic logic, it is verified that the present value of the resource to the recipient is usually more significant than the costs to the donor (Coleman, 1990). Simultaneously, the donor can expect something in return in the future to balance their efforts in providing the resource (Flap, 2004).

To achieve such transactions, there must be a socially grounded or non-formal conviction that there will be a *quid pro quo*. This basic understanding is at the heart of social capital transactions: the returns to social relations are enabled because of trust in one another.

Thus, we find the fundamental confluence between individual and social capital. This deferral rooted in trust in a particular bond is only viable in the broader group, community, or social context of trust. This, in turn, is only explicable within a common normative or value framework that depends on a cultural environment (Coleman, 1990).

Similarly, in the opposite sense, the returns derived from the exchange are not only individual but also group-based or social. The collective perceives a benefit that is not identical to the sum of the individual benefits. Here, we find the micro underpinning of the macro interpretation of social capital. This is the collective asset or resource that the macro perspective wants to capture. The mechanisms of this interaction are by no means precise. It could be said that the interrelation of individual networks and the generalisation of norms would favour reduced transaction costs. The expansion of networks facilitates social trust.

In other words, here, we enter the complex world of relational, cognitive, and structural dimensions that constitute the atmosphere in which these individual investments occur. Nevertheless, this macro asset is value-dependent. For example, strongly developed social networks could be associated with a greater capacity for improving a given group but not the social collective in general.

The great controversy we have already alluded to is the one between the macro and the micro that Portes (2000) spoke of. Practically, all the authors agree that social capital has both a micro and a macro level; the problem appears when social capital is approached as a collective, public good, establishing identities between them.

In short, there are relationships, but not identities, so it is essential to differentiate social capital as an individual asset from any expression of a supposed "collective asset" such as a common culture and trust.

The macro approach we studied in the previous chapter focuses exclusively on the "collective good" that ideally benefits the entire population in the form of general reciprocity (Putnam, 1993, 1995; Woolcock, 1998). As we have seen, adopting this one-size-fits-all approach presents serious problems, particularly as the effects can be positive or negative. Not all social networks pursue socially beneficial objectives (Durlauf, 2002) (see Box 7.1).

Box 5.1 Bourdieu, the forms of capital and socioeconomics

From our micro perspective, we feel indebted to neocapital theories but thoroughly in debt with Bourdieu's project.

At first reading, his work seems to reveal a certain economicism reflected in his sociological works' direct use of economic terms. Profit, capital, interest, and market are used outside the strict field of economics and are adapted to the sociological realm. Even so, his use is distanced from the neoclassical perspective. For example, the capital or the expectation of profit used in the financial sphere cannot be transferred to the cultural sphere. Nevertheless, there is an analogy between the two and even substitutability (Boyer, 2003; Christoforou & Lainé, 2014).

As we have seen in Chapter 1, neoclassical economics is under-socialised by reducing human actions to simple maximisation without social implications. The tradition initiated by Polanyi of the study of "embeddedness" has only highlighted this problem. For Bourdieu, *homo oeconomicus* is a sociological "aberration" designed to make the simplifications of economic theory practicable. Moreover, it shows a surprising lack of respect for empirical reality. On the other hand, he also highlighted the supersocialisation of culturalism or semiologism, which ignores "the general reducibility to economics" (Bourdieu, 1986, 1991).

Simplifying, Bourdieu seeks to detect the economic forces behind all human actions without necessarily deriving them from pure self-interest. A project that could be interpreted as an attempt to achieve "a more realistic definition of economic reasoning" (Bourdieu, 2003) that integrates the formal and informal economic and cultural spheres of human exchange into the analysis. The mode of integration will be through the notion of capital in its material and immaterial forms.

Bourdieu thus reformulates Marx's concept of capital with two original observations: (i) there are multiple forms of capital, from the material (physical and economic) to the immaterial (cultural, symbolic, and social) and (ii) it is possible to convert one form of capital into another.

In Bourdieu's (1986) terminology, economic, social, and cultural capital are different expressions of capital insofar as they are limited, valuable, and even quantitatively measurable and involve producing goods and services (Brewer, 1984). They all constitute dimensions of competition between individuals and groups, inherited through socialisation. As a result of this competition, individuals will make strategic investments that tend to reproduce inequalities.

Economic capital is relatively conventional within these forms, but others require a brief definition. Cultural capital is the individual's incorporation, institutionalised or not, of cultural products; symbolic capital is a more hidden form of capital reflecting "charisma" or recognised authority. The social capital we have been studying is a set of actual or potential resources accessible through a network of mutually recognised contacts. These three expressions can be converted into economic capital and derived from social strategies and calculation, although they cannot be reduced to this alone.

Actors have strong interests in these assets and consciously execute reasonable strategies (not rational) within the socially fixed logic of each historical moment. In other words, in the cultural or social sphere, individuals develop strategies and accumulate capital in all its forms following the legitimate (accepted) norms of each field that are historically conditioned.

These reasonable behaviours do not imply a determinism that structuralism might assume. Actors do not behave deterministically according to the dispositions of their social structure and field but adapt to a habitus. This disposition acts as a constraint on the decision-making process. It is a "natural" way of thinking that shortens the decision-making process towards those considered socially accepted.

Simultaneously, this does not rule out the existence of "maximising" behaviour. Paradoxical, though it may seem, Bourdieu is "utilitarian" in that he rejects idealised visions in which interests are denied. A norm, a habitus, a field… is inefficient if it does not incorporate the specific interests of individuals but does not fall into reductionism. As we have emphasised, he uses an economic analogy to understand the specifics of the cultural, relational world, etc. The interests within each area are specific, not economic in the strict sense, but socially established and subject to maximisation. This way, social evaluation is a more general phenomenon than economic evaluation but is also subject to interests, strategies, and forms of competition.

Accepting these assumptions, a general science of economics or a socio-economics capable of re-appropriating the totality of practices, economic or not, is possible. It must strive to understand capital and profit in all their forms and to establish the laws by which the different types of capital exchange with each other. In sum, Bourdieu's work can be interpreted as understanding social reality as forms of capital. Beyond the strictly economic, social realities help Bourdieu maintain a consistent point of view in his effort to generalise an "economic" discourse that will no longer be purely "economic" (Swedberg, 2011).

2 Measuring individual social capital

As we have already mentioned in the macro-social section, the problem of definition necessarily carries over to the problem of measurement. If we have problems specifying a definition, we will have considerable problems measuring and establishing acceptable contrasts of the proposals. In the micro approach, there is a measurable reference that allows us to find a way out of the problem of the profusion of *ad hoc* measurements that abound in the macro approach. As we have seen in the previous section, there is a kind of convergence in the definitions of what constitutes individual social capital, even among authors from opposing orientations, Marxist structuralism, and rational choice, allowing us to propose measurements all can accept.

Following the classic work of Flap (2002), an individual's social capital comprises the network at their disposal, the resources they can access through it, and the availability of those resources. In other words, it is the collection of resources owned by members of an individual's social network, which may be available to the individual due to the history of these relationships and social position (Lin, 2001).

This measurement entails a series of problems summarised in two questions: What social resources should we consider? And, should we consider access to or effective mobilisation of these resources?

Regarding the first question, it is necessary to bear in mind that a valuable social resource depends on the needs and objectives of the individuals. These needs are not homogeneous and may diverge by social group. This way, we can group them by areas or dimensions of life (domestic, work, etc.) that the general population may consider desirable or relevant, constitute and stock, and are not equivalent but oriented towards specific objectives.

This brings us to the problem of social network specificity or nonspecificity. In general, expressive resources are unspecific or can be provided by broad networks that are not directly linked to a concrete function but are generally more closely linked to strong ties. Whereas, instrumental resources are more specific and related to concrete contacts that provide access to a particular resource (Flap, 2002).

Regarding the second question, it is essential to clarify the distinction between accessibility and mobilisation. As we have defined, social capital is both potential access to social resources and the actual attainment or mobilisation of these resources. The links between both dimensions are apparent, but an essential set of micro and macro-social variables mediates between the two, which we will try to explain in the model we will develop in Section 4 of this chapter.

The two previous questions raised entail the use of two modes of measurement. On the one hand, accessibility to social positions that facilitate resources, and on the other hand, the effective mobilisation of these resources. This entails, firstly, selecting a set of resources linked to different dimensions of social life (e.g., work, daily family life, or leisure) and determining the social positions that could facilitate them. Secondly, consideration should be given to the practical possibility of mobilising resources (Snijders, 1999; Flap, 2002). We need to start by interpreting social networks (Marsden, 1990).

For instance, access to someone who works within the local administration may imply an advantage or privileged access to a series of resources (information, procedures, etc.). Nevertheless, whether you could get someone to facilitate the resolution of a specific procedure with the local administration is different. Still, it relates to the previous one and expresses mobilisation. This can be applied to multiple dimensions depending on the resources involved: obtaining funding, family support, etc. (Van der Gaag & Snijders, 2005).

In addition, it would be necessary to measure both the opportunity and the willingness of *alter* i to grant the focal individual access to resource j. The likelihood of granting access to the resource in question, and the willingness of alter i, will depend on various factors such as transaction costs to be surmounted, familial, affective, or physical proximity, frequency of interactions, the potential for effective reciprocity, and formal and informal norms, among others.

Gathering all the necessary data to measure social capital entails conducting an ego-centric network study encompassing extensive information about each *alter*. This includes metrics related to the characteristics of the *alter-ego* relationship, the *alter*'s inventory of resources, and the potential for exchanging each of these resources.

As the reader will think, the previous calculation presents more than notable biases; we are aggregating network members assuming that each one represents the same number of resources and the same probability of access to them. In part, this possibility of bias is limited by considering only the fact of accessing or not accessing an *alter*, that is, a subject associated with that resource.

Essentially, we would be doing no more than a weighted checklist of the social positions and resources available to a given individual. The major problem is considering the likelihood of effective access and mobilisation of the resource. The amount of information needed is not operationalisable in a simple answer.

These problems lead us to opt for three ways of implementing this methodological proposal for measurement. We will finally settle for a set of indicators that approximate the size of this network and the resources that can be mobilised using a checklist of social positions and resources.

2.1 Accessibility and mobilisation measures: names, positions, and resource generators

As we have already remarked, a distinction should be made between measuring access to positions and effective mobilisation. In the first case, measuring accessibility focuses on the possibility of access to a particular stock of individual relations that can constitute a good proxy for the social relations available to an individual. However, social capital is more than the networks of social relations available to a given individual since it implies mobilising the resources linked to these relations.

For this reason, it is necessary to quantify the accessibility of resources and, then, their capacity for mobilisation or effective access. Measuring accessibility provides us with the inventory of accessible subjects available to an *ego*. The measurement of mobilisation considers the effective obtaining of the resources considered. It should be noted here that the analysis of the determinants of resource mobilisation is more complex because it is causally linked to accessibility and individual decisions and their conditioning factors (needs, relational proximity, position in the social structure, etc.). Moreover, mobilisation requires social skills and the possibility of a deferred return or payment for the resource provided. Even generalised values and morals play a determining role in setting expectations for fulfilling commitments. Going more to the root of what we are measuring, accessibility is a stock, while mobilization is properly a return derived from accessibility management. It is therefore mediated by "efficiency" in its management.

Considering both measurement forms (accessibility to social positions and mobilisation of resources), we can propose three methods: the name generator, the position generator, and the resource generator. In the first two methods, the focal subject is asked about his or her contacts in various areas (Van der Gagg and Snijders, 2005, 2008), thus directly assessing accessibility. In the third method, we ask about effective mobilisation, which introduces a significant nuance we must analyse in more detail.

In the **name generator**, a list of contacts proposed by the focal subject is created for each resource considered by collecting their names. This method represents a social map of each interviewee by identifying a name for each dimension analysed. For example, for the question, "With whom would you solve a work problem?" The interviewee will propose a name if one exists. Leaving aside the complexity of the interview, the information suffers from two serious shortcomings: redundancies of persons and the over-weighting of strong ties. Additionally, the results are hardly comparable.

The **position generator** is a sample of socially useful positions for the focal subject's objectives (Table 5.1). More specifically, the individual (*ego*) is asked whether he or she has access to an alter occupying a specific social position in a sample of occupations based on social prestige in a hierarchical society. This sample of positions includes valuable resources, both instrumental and expressive. Additionally, by asking for access, we can assess the type of relationship the subject has with this *alter* (family, friend, and acquaintance) (Erickson, 1996; Lin et al., 2001a, 2001b, 2017).

In this way, the position generator would be computing the possibility of access to concrete structural positions ranging from a lawyer for advice on legal problems to help in a move. This method allows us to eliminate the redundancies of the previous method and the excessive weight of strong ties, limiting ourselves to direct computing access. At the same time, it would also allow us to measure not only the dimension of the network (the number of accessed positions) but also its rank in the structure. The set of positions can obey a structuring in social classes to distinguish a hierarchy of accesses.

Critically, we are obtaining direct information about access to a particular social resource not about the practical possibility of mobilising that resource (Van Der Gaag & Snijders, 2004). Therefore, position generator measures are specific for accessibility.

Table 5.1 Example of Position generator

		Family	*Friend*	*Acquaintance*	*None*
V1	That is a university professor	1	2	3	9
V2	Works in administration within the education system	1	2	3	9
V3	Works in the legal system	1	2	3	9
V4	Works in Finance	1	2	3	9
V5	(Non-political) works in local government	1	2	3	9
V6	Works in the banking system	1	2	3	9
V7	That is a doctor	1	2	3	9
V8	Works in the health system, but not as a doctor	1	2	3	9
V9	Is a policeman/woman	1	2	3	9
V10	Holds a political office	1	2	3	9
V11	Is a journalist or influences the media	1	2	3	9
V12	Has the opportunity to hire people	1	2	3	9
V13	Earns over 3,000 € per month	1	2	3	9
V14	Has more than 1 million in capital or you consider to be a wealthy person	1	2	3	9

Source: Pena-López and Sanchez-Santos (2017).

P1. Among your relatives are friends or acquaintances (acquaintance means someone whose name you know and who you could converse with on the street). Is there someone with the following characteristics? (IF HE/SHE HAS A FAMILY MEMBER THERE IS NO NEED TO CODE FRIENDS/ACQUAINTANCES, IF HE/SHE HAS A FRIEND THERE IS NO NEED TO CODE THE COLUMN OF ACQUAINTANCES).

In short, following this approach and for the sake of simplification, we resort to a simple aggregation of the contacts available to an individual, considering which resources would be accessible through them and the probability, given the level of existing relationship, that this position is accessible:

$$SC_{acc} = \sum_{i \in A} P_i \times p_i$$

Where i are the relations of the focal subject (network holder) with the agent i of the set of accessible positions P considered (chosen based on their links to a given resource), and p is the probability, interpretable as proximity or closeness, that the subject considered is accessible. For example, in the model we will develop later (Pena-López & Sánchez-Santos, 2017), we start from a limited set of 14 positions that allows an assessment of access to specific social positions (see table 5.1).

The third method, the **resource generator**, asks the focal subject about the possibility of effectively mobilising a set of socially valuable resources that cover the various dimensions of social life (Table 5.2). The range of resources that can be embedded in a network is extensive, ranging from those linked to the functioning of the family to those strictly linked to work and from the strictly material (the loan of money or a specific good) to the immaterial (information, influence,

Table 5.2 Example of Resource generator

		Family	*Friend*	*Acquaintance*	*Does not have*
V15	Find a job for a family member	1	2	3	9
V16	Advise on a labour dispute	1	2	3	9
V17	Help in moving	1	2	3	9
V18	Advise and/or help with educational issues	1	2	3	9
V19	Help you do the shopping when you are sick	1	2	3	9
V20	Provide medical advice when dissatisfied with a doctor	1	2	3	9
V21	Lend you a large sum of money (5,000 €)	1	2	3	9
V22	Offer a roof over your head while you cannot use your home	1	2	3	9
V23	Advise on tax issues	1	2	3	9
V24	Advise on financial issues	1	2	3	9
V25	Advise on legal matters	1	2	3	9
V26	Give good references when looking for work	1	2	3	9
V27	Care for children	1	2	3	9
V28	Care for elderly or other dependents	1	2	3	9

Source: Pena-López and Sanchez-Santos (2017).

Q2.Among your relatives, friends or acquaintances, is there anyone who you can ask for help to: (IF HE/SHE HAS A FAMILY MEMBER THERE IS NO NEED TO CODE FRIENDS/Acquaintance, IF HE/SHE HAS A FRIEND THERE IS NO NEED TO CODE THE COLUMN ACQUAINTANCE).

affection, etc.) (Van der Gaag & Snijders, 2005). Consequently, this measurement requires prior delimitation of the resources necessary for the focal subject and the probability of access to this resource or, in other words, the costs that the focal subject must overcome to acquire the resource mediated by the relationship. These are inversely proportional to the social proximity implied by the relationship (frequency of contacts, strong or weak ties, trust, etc.). Thus, in the same way as with the position generator, the subject will be questioned about the proximity of the "supplier" of this resource: relative, friend or acquaintance.

Ultimately, this resource checklist approach would aggregate the networks of relationships that an individual might need for his or her objectives (eliminating redundancies).

In this case, the mathematical expression would take the form:

$$SC_{mob} = \sum_{i \in A} R_i \times p_i$$

Where R refers to the resource that can be mobilised through a considered network and p_i is the probability, interpretable as proximity or closeness, that subject i gives access to this resource.

This is a more direct proxy measurement instrument since we are accounting for whether it is a resource that the person considers not only accessible but also among those effectively available to them. We are considering mobilisation, the expected return on available social capital. Whereas accessibility was the stock of a productive factor, this is a return of a social process. We will further develop this distinction and its determinants in the subsequent explanatory model.

Concerning the problems of comparability, like the position generator, it may have a specific cultural or social conditioning (social variability of needs and vital objectives). This leads us to the need to establish dimensions that group the resources and relationships that contribute to similar objectives (income, prestige, leisure, identity, etc.). Consequently, there is a specific or goal-oriented individual social capital. For example, there is a set of relationships linked more directly to family welfare (help in caring for children or the elderly, domestic arrangements, etc.), while others are linked exclusively to work achievements (help in dealing with the administration, specific knowledge, etc.) and therefore a different capacity for mobilisation in each area. This could be solved by proposing a priori the various objectives that can be achieved through social relations or, through internal correlations, using a principal components technique, that is, observing how the answers to the questions on access and mobilisation of social resources are grouped (Van der Gaag & Snijders, 2004).

After examining various measurement methods, we have to highlight an aspect that could impact subsequent modelling. The position generator serves as a valuable tool for representing accessibility, while the resource generator, though similar in some respects, offers more nuanced information for measuring mobilisation. In essence, the position generator indicates the potential access to specific social positions, whereas the resource generator focuses solely on the ability to mobilise particular resources. Thus, an individual might be acquainted with someone occupying a certain social position, but it does not guarantee automatic access to the associated resources.

Furthermore, it is also essential to acknowledge the presence of measurement biases in these instruments. Firstly, there is the possibility that ego-reported relationships with *alters* may not be reciprocated or experienced in the same manner by the listed alters, either due to asymmetrical relationships or the tendency to over-report interactions. Additionally, there exists a cognitive bias and the presence of hidden social capital, where relationships may offer resources that the individuals themselves may not recognise or consider having the potential for mobilisation.

2.2 The value of social capital

The concept of the value of networks beyond their concrete instrumentality, specifically, the economic value of the resources that can be mobilised through them, depends on their effect on welfare. One way of interpreting this is to adopt Becker's concept of the household production function. For Becker, the welfare maximisation objective that we can generalise to all individuals is also part of the production function in which the individual himself participates. In this way, the individual is simultaneously producer-consumer, producing the welfare he consumes (Becker, 1976, 1996; Stigler & Becker, 1977; Lindenberg, 1996).

This approach is based on three fundamental contributions

a. from psychology takes the idea that there is a link between goal achievement and well-being.
b. from Becker's household economics, studies of the domestic production function linked to the proposal of universal and instrumental or intermediate objectives.
c. from micro price theory, substitution between intermediate objectives according to cost-benefit considerations.

Briefly summarising this model, individuals define their well-being based on achieving a series of intermediate individual and social objectives that are supposed to contribute to a universal objective. These instrumental objectives are hierarchically ordered based on culturally defined needs. Individuals seek to maximise their well-being based on these intermediate objectives regarding constraints, particularly the endowment of means of production.

For example, we can assume that welfare is subdivided into two broad sub-goals: physical welfare and social approval. The explanatory variables related to these two broad goals may be multiple, have limited substitutability and are subject to diminishing marginal returns. Thus, a pleasurable stimulus such as comfort positively relates to physical well-being but with diminishing marginal productivity. Logically, the more physical well-being a person has, the less valuable an additional unit of stimulation or comfort is. Social welfare, in turn, is directly related to the social nature of man. To quote A. Smith again, "Nature, when she formed man for society, endowed him with an original desire to please and an aversion to offend his brethren. She taught him to feel pleasure in his favourable regard and pain in his unfavourable regard" (Smith, 1997 [1759], III-2). Such social well-being is achieved through intermediate goals such as status, behavioural confirmation, and affection (Figure 5.1).

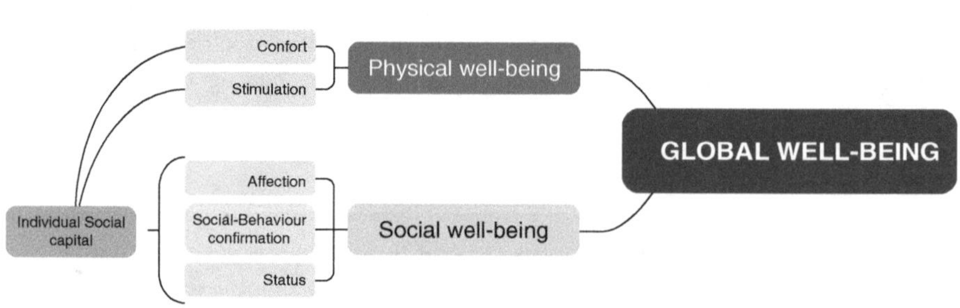

Figure 5.1 Social production function theory explaining the hierarchy of well-being.

Source: Own elaboration based on Lindenberg (1996).

Status pertains to an individual's position relative to others, primarily determined by their control over scarce resources. Behavioural confirmation involves the sensation of having acted according to societal expectations, even without direct reinforcement. Affection encompasses emotions like love, friendship, and emotional support, typically exchanged within caring relationships, including intimate, familial, and friendly connections. By logic, akin to physical well-being, all three instrumental goals exhibit positive and monotonic associations with social well-being, with diminishing marginal returns as their production increases.

The achievement of intermediate goals entails instrumental actions for their production in which the various types of resources available to an individual are applied. The relative importance of these factors in the production function is variable. It depends on micro and macro conditioning factors that would be very lengthy to analyse, for example, why, for some subjects, social achievements may be more critical than individual physical well-being or, more specifically, why status may be more important than comfort. Social values, norms and preferences play an important role in this.

Regarding the characteristics of the function, production factors undoubtedly impact more than one objective, there is limited substitutability between objectives, and there may be new "fits" of the function in the face of vital changes (Ormel et al., 1999).

As we have pointed out, the concept of the production function entails the study of the particularities of the factors integrated into it and their relationships. It is necessary to recognise the existence of a productive technology, the limited possibility of substitution between factors, and diminishing returns. Considering the theoretical background of this welfare production function, social capital is a factor with its logic (Flap, 1999, 2004; Lin, 1999a, 2001). Thus, for example, it is evident that managing a network of relationships entails a specific human capital, like the knowledge of how personal networks are created, maintained, and managed. This management entails knowledge of social and cultural norms and social skills that will affect both the generation of well-being and the investment process, as well as physical and time resources.

The functionality of social capital in generating returns lies in resource facilitation and assurance (Lin, 1999) insofar as it provides access to a broader pool of resources than the individual's own, channels information about opportunities and provides a reputational framework (Figure 5.1). Moreover, the pool of accessible persons constitutes a form of social certification of the ego, even apart from its actual mobilisation. For example, from a symbolic point of view regarding ego-assurance, social relations reinforce identity, recognition, and affective relations (Lin, 2001).

Starting from this production function of subjective well-being, it would follow that the product is only measurable in subjective terms. This will be one of the essential points of analysis when we come to the study of relational goods, social capital and revealed subjective well-being (happiness). Thinking about the subjective component and the social character of the construction of value, attempts to make a monetary translation of the value of social capital, even if econometrically feasible, are a purely theoretical exercise. Against this, as we shall see in chapter eight, the study of its influence on a subjective welfare function is more relevant.

3 Capitalisation. An extended model

Once the "analogue" nature of social capital has been defined, the next step is to explain the logic of the capitalisation process to clarify the micro part of the mechanisms considered by the "Coleman boat". This underlying logic of the capitalisation process is simple. This is derived from the welfare function in the previous section. Individuals invest in social relations by actively and intentionally trying to produce a good life and improve their opportunities. To do so, they use their resources or invest in relationships, which facilitates their access to those of others. Consequently, their investments in relationships depend on their expectations about returns (perceived future value) and the resources they have at their disposal (Flap, 1999, 2004).

Following what we proposed in the third chapter, this general approach to neo-capital necessarily entails that the dimensions cannot be considered in isolation, and neither micro nor macro analysis alone is sufficient. It is a form of individual and collective investment, where the individual is not necessarily reflected in the collective, nor vice versa, but there is a two-way linkage.

The micro must be considered within its macro context, a social investment framework. For instance, social norms and generalised trust strongly influence the nature of micro-level social relations. Similarly, social stratification systematically affects individuals and the nature of their micro-level relationships. Conversely, the macro level is not a mere aggregate of the micro. The extent of networks is critical, particularly in weak links, but cognitive factors like cultural values and institutional context play an important role.

At the macro level, individuals exert less direct control over relevant factors, as they are just one among many social actors, each wielding varying degrees of influence and power, while beliefs and values become more standardised and institutionalised. Consequently, micro-level dynamics are more fluid and subject to change as ongoing actions and interactions continually shape and reshape factors. Conversely, at the macro level, inertia is more pronounced, with social capital typically rooted in historical, cultural, and institutional frameworks that evolve slower, barring significant social upheavals.

3.1 A review of the general capitalisation model of N. Lin

The interpretative schemes of capitalisation processes that can be considered as a reference are those of Flap (2002, 2004) and Lin (1999a, 2001). Both approaches opt for a three-block model that distinguishes access to networks from the actual mobilisation of resources and, in turn, from the returns to the social capital mobilised (Flap, 1999; Lin, 2001).

Focusing on Lin's proposals (1999a, 1999b, 2008), these three blocks encompass precursors, capitalisation, and individual and social effects (Figure 5.2).

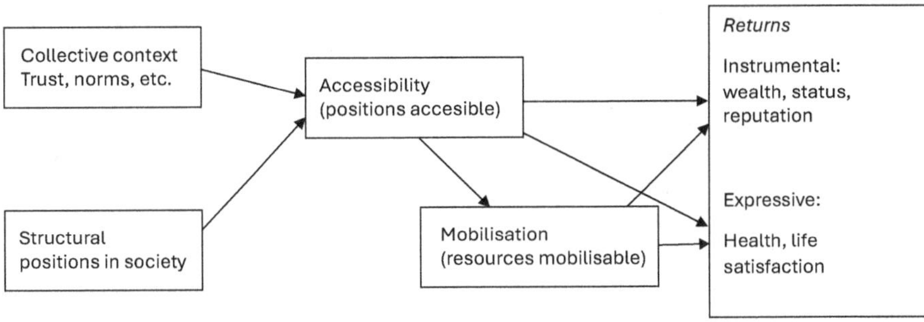

Figure 5.2 Lin's model on individual social capital.

Source: Own elaboration based on Lin (1999a, 1999b).

Firstly, precursor conditions of social capital consist of factors within the social structure and context that either facilitate or constrain its capitalisation, from general traits like social trust to specific ones, like position in the class system. The second block involves the generation of this capital, distinguishing between accessibility and mobilisation. The causal relationship between the first and second blocks elucidates the inequality in individual social capital endowment.

The opportunity for a greater or lesser endowment of individual social capital is tied to positions within the social structure and social determinants such as trust and the strength of familial institutions. Thus, understanding this inequality requires contrasting multiple factors.

Finally, the third block includes effects derived from the disposition of relational networks, encompassing returns on individual investment in instrumental terms (e.g., income and social status) and expressive terms (e.g., personal fulfilment, life satisfaction, and identity).

As we have pointed out, the distinction in the second block between accessibility and mobilisation is critical. An individual may occupy a particular position in the social structure and have accessibility to a series of resources embedded in the network to which he or she belongs but may not be able to mobilise these resources for specific finalist actions. In this block is the distinction between accessible networks and their effective use or mobilisation, which we will study in more detail. Our interest will now focus on the first two blocks, that is, the determinants of capitalisation and capitalisation itself.

The first block, or precursors, includes the macro conditions in which an individual develops. These conditions directly influence the development of personal social networks, such as cultural factors, social stability, and value consensuses. They also directly impact generic variables of a cognitive nature; such as trust itself.

In addition, the structural conditions of the individual are decisive in terms of their investment capacity. These are socio-cultural and institutional contextual factors that Lin (1999a, 1999b) considers decisive in explaining initial individual endowments and subsequent investment and, consequently, the key to explaining inequality in the endowment of this form of capital. Think, for example, of a caste system. It determines both the possibility of investing in relationships and the expected outcome of that investment.

The initial social evidence is that our relational environment is strongly influenced by a conglomerate of social institutions, personal, cultural, and historical factors together with social stratification itself. A more developed general social capital (trust, generalisation of values or social norms, an associative framework) favours the investment process and the capitalisation of social relations.

In the revision we seek to make of this model, the central point is to be found in the capitalisation block. As noted above, social accessibility and mobilisation are related but not an identity. An individual occupies a particular position in the social structure and has access to a series of social positions embedded in his or her network membership. This access can come from an intergenerational transfer (inheritance) from the group of belonging or a socially mediated investment process (Glaeser et al., 2002).

Notwithstanding, this disposition does not imply that the focal subject can mobilise them effectively. Mobilisation focuses on actions and achievements, and its determinants are more complex because they are associated with individual decisions and social context (needs, relational proximity, own resources, etc.). Moreover, it requires specific social skills and the possibility of a deferred return or payment for the resource provided. In this sense, even values and morals play a decisive role in establishing commitment expectations.

It is evident that the management of social capital is based on an expectation of reciprocity and creates obligations for repayment in the future (Van der Gaag & Snijders, 2005). Implicitly, behind mobilisation lies access and the ability to mobilise and bear the costs of future reciprocity or the repayment and cancellation of previous debt. Furthermore, there is also an ethical component to this decision-making process, as it may involve subverting procedures that are considered "normal". By way of example, a child who receives a broad set of social networks from an upper-class parent requires management of this network to obtain resources, be they expressive or instrumental. Along with access, he or she needs the social skills to manage these networks, the possibility of a deferred return or payment for the resource provided, and a reputation for meeting commitments. In this sense, even values and morals play a decisive role in setting expectations. Ultimately, the effective use of these networks depends on variables that reinforce accessibility.

The latter brings us back to the macro institutional framework by considering the possibilities of conflict between individual networks and institutional channels. This conflict can be expressed in different ways. For example, the trade-off between expressive social resources and the expansion of the welfare state. The extent to which institutional response substitutes for the relevance of expressive individual networks and vice versa. On the negative side, as we will see in chapter 7, how closed networks can be a mechanism for establishing forms of social corruption. In societies with few opportunities for institutional goal achievement, high levels of individual trust combined with low levels of general trust and a conducive cultural climate, one can expect much greater use of "individual" social capital.

Concretising the variables influencing mobilisation capacity given a level of accessibility, these are social determinants of the extraction of resources from the network (see Figure 5.3) or, in economic terminology, determinants of the efficiency of using the social capital factor in the productive process. As Lin proposes, precursors influence accessibility, that is, the extent of the available network. Individual network mobilisation is directly related to accessibility. Nevertheless, the effective use of these networks depends on variables that reinforce accessibility and the type of resources involved because networks are goal-specific (Flap & Volker, 2001; Verhaeghe et al., 2015). Two orientations can be delineated within the functional specialisation of networks towards resources: expressive and instrumental. These orientations differ in network typology, explanatory variables, and the nature of mobilised resources.

This way, instrumental mobilisation is more susceptible to status and contextual environmental variables and is directly associated with achieving economic, employment, and social stratification objectives. In this scenario, the capacity to mobilise resources hinges on human capital and the availability of extensive interaction possibilities (urban context), influencing the reciprocity and profitability of relationships. Exchange relies on the potential return of comparably valued resources, hence the significance of the member's status (human capital and class) within the network. Moreover, the multitude of interactions in urban settings facilitates such exchanges.

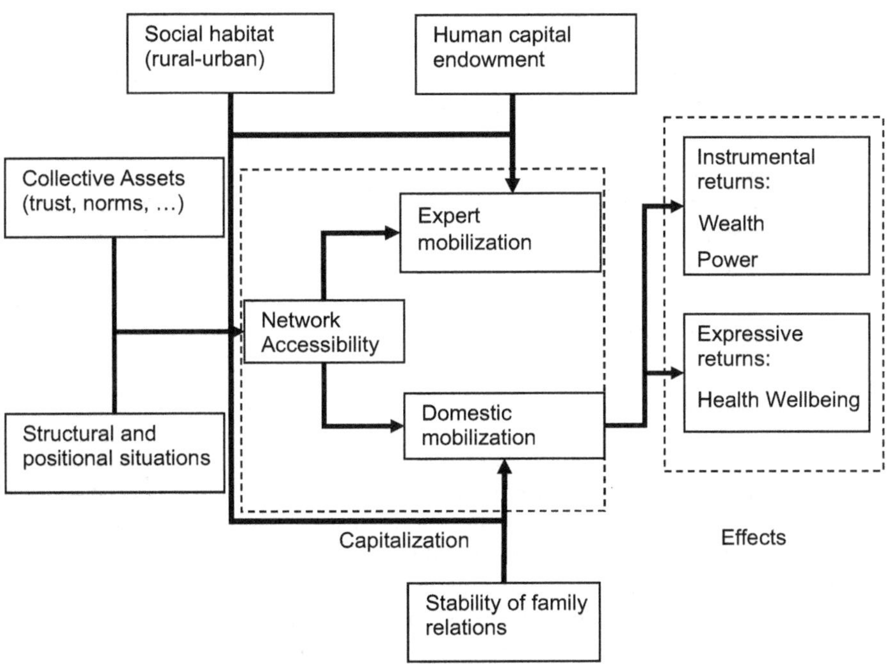

Figure 5.3 Adaptation of Lin's model.

Source: Own elaboration based on Lin (1999a).

Conversely, expressive mobilisation is more intertwined with strong ties, family size, marital status, and their impact on subjective well-being and health. Here, the backdrop of familial institutions and close social circles plays a pivotal role.

In this sense, to some extent, this expanded explanatory model is directly linked to Granovetter's classic proposition (1973) that weak ties are crucial, providing access to non-redundant resources (mobilisation of "expert" resources from positions with high human capital). Weak ties effectively broaden an individual's resource pool beyond what is already possessed by their group with strong ties. Strong ties, on the other hand, are more associated with expressive resources, health, and personal well-being.

Finally, the third block gathers the effects or returns from providing relational networks in instrumental and expressive terms. Networks aligned with instrumental goals yield three fundamental effects: economic (e.g., income), social (e.g., status), and political (e.g., reputation) (Lin, 2001). Networks linked to expressive goals aim to maintain personal identity, self-realisation, and family life, where redundant, dense, and cohesive (strong) relationships hold significance (Lin et al., 1981a, 1981b, 1982, 1990). This applies to communities, families, etc., influencing physical and mental health and life satisfaction (Kobayashi et al., 2013). A mutual interaction exists between expressive and instrumental dimensions, although both evolve within distinct "markets".

At this point, we are again dealing with generating macro-social capital. The proposed model interrelating micro and macro approaches is close to the one proposed by Lin (1999a, 1999b) and contributes to understanding the interrelations between individual and general social capital. Between the two, there is a clear link: general social capital is a contextual factor in the generation of individual social capital, as well as a conditioning factor of the investment process, and finally, general social capital is also the result of an extension of individual social capital that influences both the cognitive, the perception of generalised trust and the structural, the extension of social and organisational networks.

Overall, it is important to emphasise two aspects of this extended model. This investment follows a logic of "optimisation" and individuals make investment decisions with socially determined objectives that may be instrumental (status, income, etc.) or expressive (well-being, health, etc.).

3.2 A proposal of an empirical model for Spanish society (2017)

A review of the application of our extended model to Spanish society may be illustrative.[1] Following the indications pointed out in measurement and the theoretical approach of the model, and based on the survey results, our empirical strategy was developed mainly in three stages. Firstly, through a survey, we analysed the accessibility and mobilisation of a significant sample of the Spanish population, using the measurement methodologies indicated (position and resource generator) as presented in the previous section on measurement. Secondly, we study the underlying dimensions of the accessibility and mobilisation variables using a factor analysis, which allows us to define the structures of the networks and their function, in order to map individual social capital. Finally, we use a system of structural equations to test our extended model.

As we have already insisted, the study of a network's accessibility and mobilisation requires the adoption of a specific measurement methodology, different from the methods generalised in the study of general social capital. These variables cannot be a simple aggregation of the responses; we seek the construction of dimensions for which it is more appropriate to consider the Principal Component Analysis (PCA) scores of the underlying dimensions of these responses.

In this approach, we streamline the various forms of accessibility and mobilisation into a concise set of variables that reflect the development of different dimensions within personal networks (Pena-López et al., 2017). This methodological approach offers two advantages over previous studies (Flap & Volker, 2001): firstly, it avoids aggregating relationships into predefined or *a priori* categories, and secondly, the PCA scores of each individual represent their specific endowment of individual social capital.

The results enable us to establish network structures oriented towards both positions and resources, revealing two particularities: while the position generator, serving as an indicator of accessibility, constitutes a single dimension or latent variable, the resource generator, more focused on mobilisation, yields two differentiated factors that can be classified as expressive and instrumental mobilisation, consistent with our previous model, that is, the personal endowment of social networks is goal-oriented.

Examining the loadings of variables on each factor, the mobilisation of expressive resources pertains to collaborative efforts in familial and personal care contexts, where individuals receive personal support. In this context, these resources could also be termed domestic, as they involve obtaining assistance through a network associated with the household's welfare production function (such as childcare, eldercare, and relocation assistance). On the other hand, instrumental resources encompass goods and services that require significant human capital and mastery of intricate procedures (e.g., fiscal and financial support), logically resulting in instrumental outcomes like income and status.

Networks within each dimension exhibit distinct objectives: expressive mobilisation is aligned with identity and domestic production functions, whereas instrumental mobilisation aims to leverage valuable resources to enhance status. These findings suggest the presence of two manifestations of individual social capital that correspond to the strong-weak ties dichotomy. Both manifestations are characterised by the distinct nature of deployed resources and their objectives (e.g., income, prestige, leisure, and identity).

In summary, while accessibility uniformly expands, mobilisation displays differences between expressive and instrumental networks. Furthermore, at the empirical level, it is crucial to consider the existence of a trade-off relationship between them, as indicated by the negative correlation between the two.

Evidence derived from constructing the empirical model suggests that the behaviour of the accessibility variable conforms to the logic of investment processes. Moreover, each form of mobilisation has its determinants (Glaeser et al., 2002).

Constructing our models for each indicator demonstrates that both forms of goal-oriented mobilisation dimensions (expressive and instrumental) correlate positively with accessibility. This serves as a precondition for mobilising resources embedded in a network. However, as mobilisation is socially conditioned and depends on variables beyond accessibility, assessing the extent to which the latter variable mediates the relationship between other variables and mobilisation is pertinent. To this end, we conducted two structural equation models in our empirical analysis to test a model that includes a mediating variable.

In the first structural model (Figure 5.4[2]), instrumental mobilisation is the dependent variable. The results show that it depends on accessibility, but educational attainment and municipality size have a strong explanatory power. As noted above, instrumental mobilisation is associated with human capital and the urban context; that is, instrumental mobilisation can be seen as an extension of human capital (Bowles & Gintis, 2002), taking place in urban networks and with effects on income and social position. In this sense, it is an expression of what Bourdieu (2001) called a system of social class reproduction.

The nature of the influence of these determinants opens up an exciting line of research. Far from a compensatory effect, we find a Matthew effect or cumulative advantage, that is, inequality is reinforced by the direct relationship of the variables at the level of studies (which is also related to income). This will be the subject of our study in Chapter 6.[3]

The second structural analysis (Figure 5.5) focuses on expressive mobilisation or those resources more linked to the sphere of strong ties. These types of mobilisation networks are linked to the stability of the network of strong ties, which reflects marital status, and the frequency and closeness of interactions, which reflects the size of the municipality. Note that, in contrast to the case of instrumental mobilisation, the sign of the influence of municipality size on expressive mobilisation is negative. The development of these networks depends on the household production function (in a Beckerian sense of the term). Given the greater proximity and the predominance of strong relationships, they are favoured in a rural or semi-rural context.[4]

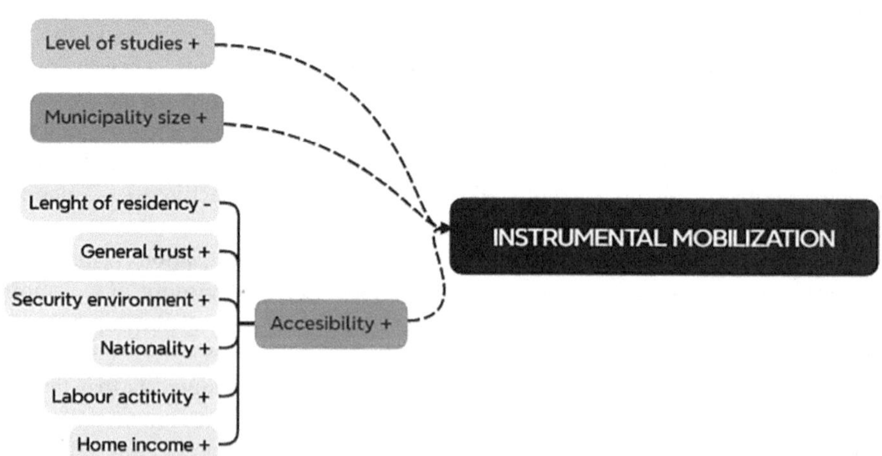

Figure 5.4 Structural model of instrumental mobilisation.

Source: Own elaboration. Survey on the use of social networks in Spain (2011).

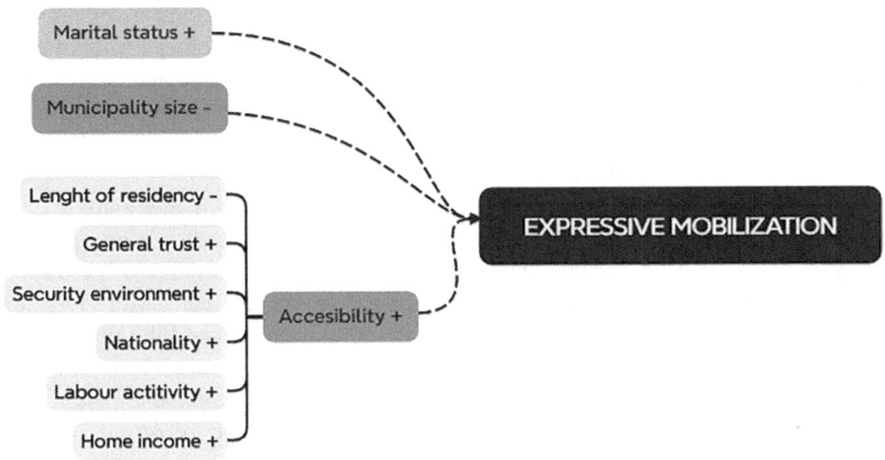

Figure 5.5 Structural model of expressive mobilisation.

Source: Own elaboration. Survey on the use of social networks in Spain (2011).

In short, accessibility (the set of networks that an individual accumulates) responds to the logical conditioners of social investment, the precursors to which we alluded in the general model proposed: from social stratification to the context of social trust. Mobilisation shows additional determinants that depend on goals. In this sense, it is necessary to distinguish between instrumental and expressive mobilisation. This leads us to propose an extension of the model by Lin (Figures 5.2 and 5.3) that reinforces the "analogy" with the notion of capital. Firstly, in the precursors of individual social capital, we find factors derived from individual conditions and social structure (income, age, nationality, etc.) that influence network investment, together with the proxy contextual variables of general social capital, trust, security, etc. In parallel, mobilisation incorporates another set of variables linked to the possibility of returns and the capacity to manage social networks, which we could interpret as conditioning factors of efficiency in managing relationships.

Overall, following the analogical interpretation of the notion of capital, the individual endowment of social networks fits a socially conditioned rational investment model (Glaeser et al., 2002). Individuals invest in social networks from an inherited stock based on both instrumental and expressive expected returns.

4 Recapping

In this chapter, we have focused on developing the micro approach to individual social capital. This is the set of social networks accessible to an individual that facilitate the achievement of market and non-market objectives through interaction with other individuals. Thus, the ultimate referent of the notion of capital is the social network, as it results from a process of inheritance and investment, is involved in productive processes and is interchangeable with other forms of capital. As an asset, its value lies in both instrumental resources (income, status, etc.) and expressive resources (recognition, mutual aid, well-being, etc.) that an individual draws from his or her network consciously or unconsciously (Pena-López & Sánchez-Santos, 2013; Membiela-Pollán, 2016).

As argued in the third chapter, adopting a micro approach is methodologically essential to grounding a social capital theory. On the one hand, it is an approach adapted to a notion of capital. Thus, it allows us to take advantage of neocapital derivations in this field (investment, capitalisation, inequality, etc.). Moreover, this approach integrates both the perspectives of rational choice and the critiques of structuralism.

In this way of analysis, the referent is clearly defined as personal social networks. This "objectivity" is also reflected in the way they are measured. The distinction between accessibility and mobilisation leads us to opt for a position and resource generator to determine personal networks' size and resource extraction capacity.

Studying these indicators makes it possible to define and map two expressions of individual social capital: accessibility (the extent of the network) and mobilisation (the ability to draw resources from these networks). Mobilisation is explained as resource-oriented. Regarding the issue raised at the end of Chapter 3, in this chapter, we have proposed an explanatory model that, extending Lin's initial model, tries to approximate the mechanisms underlying investment in this form of capital at the micro-level, linking it to the macro levels.

Overall, it provides a reference point for the study of macro dynamics in the following chapters.

Notes

1 The data used for the empirical study come from a survey on social capital and inequality conducted between November and December 2011 on a universe of residents aged 18 and over in Spain. The sample size was 3,400 face-to-face interviews. The survey was conducted using a computer-assisted telephone interview (CATI system). Households were randomly selected from telephone lists with a selection of respondents from random tables among the members of each household. Stratified sampling with mixed allocation was chosen: 1,700 interviews by simple allocation to ensure a minimum of 100 interviews per region and 1,700 interviews by allocation proportional to the size of each region. In each Community, there was a proportional distribution of interviews according to the size of the municipality. The questionnaires were also weighted according to sex, age, and region size. The sampling error is ±1.7% for the overall data, for a confidence level of 95.5% ($z = 2$) and assuming $P = Q = 0.5$. The questionnaire is available on the OSIM Group website: http://osimudc.es/

2 The full estimate is in the reference article for this chapter (Pena López & Sanchez-Santos, 2017).

3 Model fit (RMSEA = 0.07; CFI = 0.968; IFI = 0.968; NFI = 0.967). This result is optimal, considering the sample size (n = 3,400).

4 Model fit (RMSEA = 0.08; CFI = 0.924; IFI = 0.925; NFI = 0.922). This result is optimal, considering the sample size (n = 3,400).

Part III

Constructing from individual social capital

6 Inequality, homophily, and individual social capital

> The social world is accumulated history, and if it is not to be reduced to a discontinuous series of instantaneous mechanical equilibria between agents who are treated as interchangeable particles, one must reintroduce into it the notion of capital and, with it, accumulation and all its effects.
>
> (Bourdieu, 1986)

The so-called "Great Gatsby Curve"[1] (Corak, 2016) is purely an observational correlation highlighting the complexity of the mechanisms that generate and perpetuate inequality. The persistence of inequalities leads us to a complex social reality. Using the terminology of previous chapters, it involves a diverse set of stocks transmitted intergenerationally from cultural to social capital and their interactions.

Specifically, Figure 6.1 represents an empirical relationship between the concentration of wealth in one generation and the ability of the next generation to move up the economic ladder compared to their parents.

If we think about the cases shown in this figure, we can extract a "surprising" regularity that may contradict our initial expectations. Countries with higher levels of inequality or higher concentration of wealth have lower social mobility. Consequently, we find a correlation between current inequality and that of the following generations. In other words, inequality and social mobility are intimately linked, so we can affirm that self-reproduction exists.

There is an essential set of criticisms of what this curve expresses. So, for example, it is sensitive to the unit we consider. We are measuring inequality within nations, and Denmark is not a directly comparable country to the whole United States, and so on. Nevertheless, these first thoughts aside, the question that naturally arises is the logic behind this correlation: cultural attitudes, unequal investment in education, social influence, social stratification, etc.

The simplest way to explain the set of intergenerational linkage mechanisms of inequalities is in terms of opportunities. Existing inequality helps to define the opportunity framework of the new generation and affects the social environment into which this generation is born. In this explanation, micro-inherited social capital and investment in social networks are decisive factors in its capacity to accumulate information and opportunities (Andersson, 2021).

DOI: 10.4324/9781003375302-10

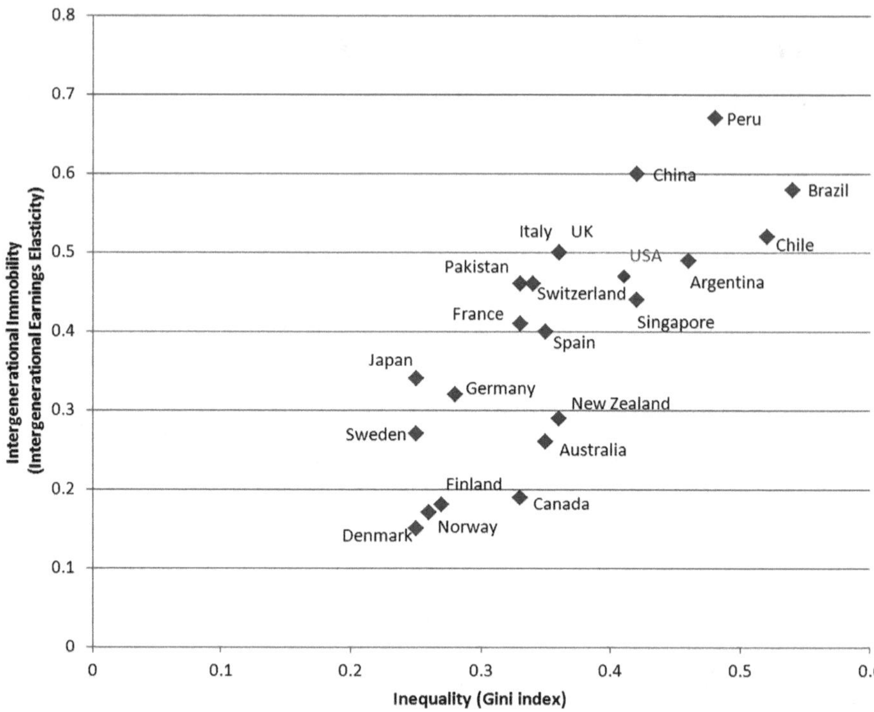

Figure 6.1 Great Gatsby Curve.

Source: Based on Corak (2016).

From the neocapital approach we have adopted, access to the most valuable resources is contingent upon one's position in the social structure. As delineated by Bourdieu, social, economic, and cultural capital form enduring differentiation because social classes are not solely economic constructs but are intricately intertwined with social reproduction (Doob, 2013). Indeed, understanding the formation of social classes necessitates an examination of how the possession of these types of capital interacts to perpetuate a cycle of reproduction (Savage et al., 2013). This chapter aims to explore how the stock of social relationships available to individuals serves as a mechanism for self-replicating the social inequalities that persistently manifest in our societies. We start applying our perspective to particular social problems, and the questions we will answer are: What is the relationship between social capital and persistent inequality? How are the forms of capital interrelated? How can social networks favour a Mathew effect?

1 The social determinants of persistent inequality

From a macro perspective, our economies depend on an increasingly intricate functional specialisation. These dependencies link the evolution of economies to the evolution of societies. At the micro level, the mobility and fate of individuals depend on their initial position in the structure and the position and fate of their friends, family, and acquaintances. We rest on our networks of relationships for resources, information, and opportunities. These networks also play a decisive role in acquiring norms of behaviour or even the formation of expectations. Simultaneously, these networks may constitute a mechanism for reproducing inequality.

Despite political activism, economic inequality endures because of its multidimensionality and entrenchment in the social environment and in this process, social capital plays a decisive role (Atkinson & Morelli, 2014). We refer to socially embedded inequality when disparities among social groups stem from wealth or factors such as language, ethnicity, social background, and access to social networks, which shape opportunities.

If a person is socially segregated for whatever reason (cultural, social structure, racial, etc.), this will lead to lower performance in any form of capital and create substantial obstacles to social mobility (Fang & Loury, 2005; Oxoby, 2004). This is obvious and can be identified as a form of discrimination. Even so, as Loury (2002) points out, these mechanisms are notably subtler since they operate as a simple optimisation logic. Inheritance and differential investments between social groups due to markedly divergent expected returns reproduce social inequalities.

Focusing on our perspective on social relations, two immediate causal links arise: Inequality can be related to the social configuration of networks and the resources that can be mobilised through them. Simultaneously, inequality in social networks can be related to other forms of capital and facilitate circular accumulation processes.

The macro approach we have critiqued in chapter four is unsuitable for this analysis because it consistently underestimates or overlooks society's conflictual nature (Fine, 2010). Society is organised into groups, and intragroup social capital is not necessarily correlated with intergroup ties. To rephrase it, prosocial behaviour is segmented, and networks can function as a mechanism of social closure restricting access to perceived out-groups. Race, ethnicity, religion, language, friendship, or shared economic interests often serve as the basis for these exclusions in market and non-market contexts (Quibria, 2003; Fehr et al., 2020).

The outcomes generated by these social networks depend on power relations (Martin, 2009). Ignoring these considerations leads to an overly simplistic treatment of inequality and poverty. This is the case of the contributions of the World Bank (Dasgupta & Serageldin, 2000) or the canonical works by Putnam (1993, 2000). For example, the answer to the World Values Survey question often used as an indicator of social capital ("In general terms, would you say that most people can be trusted or can be trusted by most people?") is related to status and quality of life. When controlling for these variables, the link between this indicator and associationism loses all significance (Herreros & Criado, 2008). Another example, if we focus on associationism, Hall (1999) shows how participation is strongly linked to social class to the extent that the upper class in British society is between two and three times more likely to belong to an association than other classes.

Evidence contradicting this integrative or equitative view of social capital is already prevalent. An increasing body of literature utilises the neo-Weberian class model to examine the relationship between social capital, cultural capital, and class

(Pichler & Wallace, 2009; Bennett et al., 2008; Savage et al., 2013). These studies demonstrate that social trust and civic participation are also socially stratified. Nevertheless, this phenomenon is not the root cause of the influence of social capital on inequality but rather its outcome.

As we have already remarked, the mainstream macro approach overlooks the quality of capital and its social structure. What we have called the "meso" approach allows for some nuances to be introduced, such as the recognition of group social capital. Das (2006) proposes the notion of class social capital, which acknowledges the presence of trust, reciprocity, networks, and organisations within each social class, yielding specific effects. For the working class, systems of mutual aid, neighbourhood relations, and proximity networks form a type of capital similar to expressions of social capital, such as bridging or bonding (Migheli, 2017). Nonetheless, these working-class groupings suffer from a lack of heterogeneity, which is pivotal in accessing instrumental social resources, particularly those linked to valuable ones and class mobility (Burt, 2001).

Studying these inequalities brings us back to a micro approach since, although they are reflected in class constraints, they are ultimately related to the personal constraint to social mobility. This is crucial because the concept of individual or micro-social capital can elucidate the exercise of economic power within the class framework, particularly in the self-reproduction of the class system.

2 Social networks, inequality, and social capital

Opportunities and information and access to them are not distributed homogeneously in the social fabric (Van Tubergen & Volker, 2015). Extensive literature on network analysis has recently expanded around authors such as Chetty et al. (2022a, 2022b), who have made relevant contributions in this regard.

To summarise, These authors highlight two mechanisms – direct and statistical discrimination – that could facilitate the persistence of inequalities through social networks.

The first is a *direct expression of discrimination*, in which a social group is excluded from a particular type of opportunity. People segregated based on gender, race, culture, ideology, etc., will have lower returns on their human capital and even on their economic capital. Therefore, a social background can hinder social mobility (Fang & Loury, 2005).[2] Slavery, racism, segregation, and even sexism (see Box 6.1) would fall under this heading. In all these cases, one social group has privileged access to resources and explicitly prevents access to non-members. In this case, the effects of persistent inequalities are evident (Bertrand & Duflo, 2017; Hangartner et al., 2021; Huber et al., 2021).

Still, the same effects can occur without direct and intentional discriminatory action. In the case of *statistical discrimination*, a privileged group has negative expectations of another group, for example, in terms of its human capital, productivity, etc. The pigeonholing into these expectations diminishes the adequate access opportunities of this non-privileged group and, thus, the probability of its access to the labour market. These expectations reduce the adequate access opportunities of this non-privileged group and, consequently, the likelihood of returns on investment in any form of capital. The effect is a reduction in investment and a confirmation of the initial expectation, effectively discriminating (a self-fulfilling prophecy).

In short, the dynamics of social networks can exert a powerful influence in cases where discrimination is not manifest in the first place. Nevertheless, as Chetty et al. (2022a, 2022b) note, this second case, which is much more evident in developed societies, can be interpreted as homophily and social network segmentation.

2.1 Homophilia

As a subtle form of statistical discrimination, inequality in the networks of relationships, combined with the segmentation of these networks derived from homophily, leads to information and opportunities remaining concentrated within one part of society (Jackson, 2021).

By homophily, we mean the natural tendency to associate with those with whom there is some link of social resemblance. As such, a social selection mechanism operates outside any discriminatory process. Nevertheless, as Chetty et al. (2022a) note, up to two-thirds of differences could be explained by pure status homophily.

It should be stressed that the term homophily refers to something socially evident that reflects a tendency in any form of society to generate groups based on affinities of various kinds (from having the same school to practising the same sport or following the same club), and that may not even be intentional. They even may not expressly desire to exclude those who are not similar for reasons beyond the bond that makes up the group (McPherson et al., 2001).

As we remarked, Individuals in society tend to get closer to and maintain ties with those with some similarities. These can range from language, ethnic or cultural origin, education, gender, or more apparently specific aspects such as hobbies. For example, an old study by Verbrugge (1977) found substantial homophily in all the characteristics he analysed, including age, years of schooling, profession, religion, marital status, and employment status. In particular, he examined 240 categories (obviously, many dimensions correlate). What is genuinely relevant about this truism is that affinity groups can be relatively isolated from each other socially.

Being more penetrating in the analysis, we realise that at least two types of homophily must be distinguished: exposure or, contact and choice.

The first is nothing more than natural proximity to those who are physically or virtually close, such as schoolmates or members of the same religious community. This is homophily, which arises from physical and virtual proximity spaces due to characteristics or interests that can generate homopsychology or cultural and educational homogeneity.

Conversely, choice is a decision to gravitate towards individuals with a community of interests, norms, or preferences (Lobel & Sadler, 2016; Aybas & Jackson, 2021). The outcomes of the two are not necessarily the same since, in the latter case, it may be a sought-after or imposed homogeneity. An individual, out of self-interest, may ascribe to a group that he or she considers advantageous, so there may be an intentional strategy of ascription to a particular group.

The most studied effects of homophily are in the labour market since using networks to obtain a job is crucial (Rubineau & Fernandez, 2013; Zeltzer, 2020). In the context of uncertainty that characterises this market, where information costs are very high, the instruments available to link offers and demands can be precarious. Thus, given that any selection for recruitment is subject to the risks arising from information asymmetry, the employer tends to look for someone with homophily links through recourse to a social network. This option allows them to reduce risk and obtain credentials and assurance of the process. Moreover, in societies where signalling systems are not abundant, or information is more limited, employers tend to give free rein to homophily. The result is a trade-off between diversification and insurance, and the logical consequence is the dominance of a particular group in each work environment, along with its perpetuation in a particular place on the social ladder.

If we analyse the problem from the point of view of labour supply, this effect can also be reinforced through expectations. The greater or lesser likelihood of being hired in a particular stratum provides incentives or disincentives for investment in human capital and influences job search processes. Thus, for example, homophily in low-strata groups reinforces learning and habits that can impair their mobility and vice versa (Lobel & Sadler, 2016; Aybas & Jackson, 2021).

Undoubtedly, the starting macro context will affect the outcomes of these mechanisms. An integrated and "homogeneous" community with strong cross-cutting relationships can facilitate the flow of information and opportunities between groups and thus facilitate social mobility. In contrast, a heterogeneous, unequal community lacking cross-cutting relationships will progressively exacerbate the differences between the various strata and inequality (Chetty et al., 2022a, 2022b; Dederichs, 2024). We leave this discussion for when we address the problem of universalistic moral capital in the next chapter.

In short, homophily will generate an accumulation of opportunities linked to information and certifications in those groups that occupy privileged positions, which will have derivations in the investment in other forms of capital: human, cultural, symbolic, etc. (Bowles et al., 2009; Bolte et al., 2020). These findings do not imply the existence of a perceived form of discrimination, nor do they imply an absolute dominance of a particular stratum. Notwithstanding, As Arrow and Borzekowski (2004) argue, minor relative differences of homophilic groups in each stratum may give rise to a clear trend towards dominance over a longer or shorter period.

Then, the structure of social networks plays a crucial role in the persistence of inequality and social mobility. This influence is exerted by itself and by its relationship with economic and human capital and limits the capacity of any equalising policy. As we have been anticipating, we must consider the interaction between the various forms of capital to study the persistent inequality problem. That is, how inequalities in economic, human, and social capital interact and reinforce each other in the form of a "Matthew effect" and how the problem of inequality becomes socially embedded.

Box 6.1 Homophily, gender, and other non-spoken forms of discrimination

One of the pieces of evidence we want to highlight in this chapter is that a higher endowment of individual social capital improves life chances and favours the provision of instrumental and expressive resources such as income, power, social status, and well-being (Lin, 2001, 2008). It will be especially significant in improving labour market opportunities. At the same time, however, the social constraints that facilitate or hinder the development of networks may give rise to a source of inequality. To the extent that our inheritance or investment in networks may be unspokenly biased by race, gender, age, etc., it can be a source of inequality and facilitate subtle forms of discrimination.

The homophilia of which we have spoken can take many forms that go beyond the social class to which they belong and can be linked in many ways to traits (tastes, hobbies, origin, education, etc.) that, without constituting an express form of discrimination, end up being so.

The literature on social capital has limited itself to emphasising diverse patterns of associationism between men and women or between racial or age groups (Addis & Joxhe, 2017). Suppose we adopt the perspective of neocapital theory. In that case, the mechanics of capitalisation processes discussed in the previous chapter can account for much of the observed inequalities in the case of gender, the denominated "glass ceiling".

Men and women, for example, have different socialisations, live in different situational contexts, and have different associative lives. Men's and women's social networks differ in nature, size, depth, and functionality (Gidengil & O'Neill, 2006). Suppose we add to this evidence the tendency of classes to self-reproduce. In that case, accumulating more extensive stocks of individual social capital by one social group, gender, or race constrains social mobility.

The "non-privileged" groups would find themselves in relative isolation, which implies a starting inequality and limits the incentives and capacity to invest in generating networks. In this context, gender or race gaps will always be more significant in the higher strata of society, where stocks are more relevant and have more differentiating potential.

Going deeper into the argument, networks can constitute a form of segmentation of society. Mechanisms of social closure manifest themselves in preferences over gender, race, ethnicity, religion, language, etc. These homophily trends converge with economic interests and limit access to non-similars while facilitating the hoarding of opportunities by insiders (Chetty et al., 2022a, 2022b; Christoforou & Davis, 2014).

Focusing on gender as a particular expression of homophily, previous empirical work has shown that women have smaller, more homogeneous networks centred on a more immediate and even domestic environment and with a more significant presence of family members (Lowndes, 2004, 2006; Addis & Joxhe, 2017). Men's networks, on the other hand, are more instrumental and more effective in providing information about potential jobs, business and career opportunities due to the predominance of weak links and more diverse social positions (Granovetter, 1973).

These observed differences can negatively affect career development and be oppressive because they are predominantly linked to obtaining resources for traditionally gendered roles (Bezanson, 2006). In short, groups are "trapped" in gender-segregated networks that isolate them from circulating information, influence, and status (McDonald et al., 2009).

Figure 6.2 illustrates the strong differentiation in instrumental social network endowments by gender, considering social class, in Spanish society. The differential in resources accessible through networks is more significant as social class rises. Men have more extensive networks and greater mobilisation capacity.

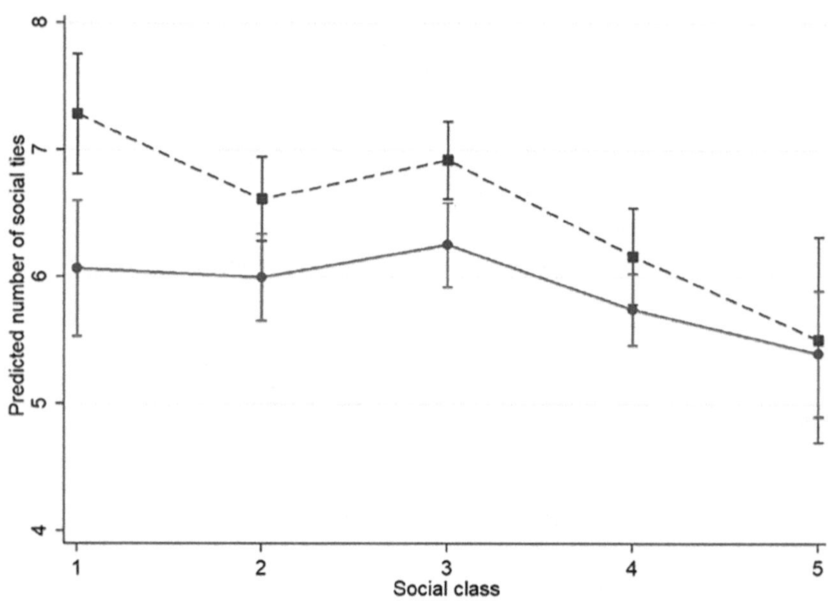

Figure 6.2 Number of social ties by gender and social class.

Source: Own elaboration.

Females: solid lines; males: dashed lines (social classes: 1, higher salariat; 2, lower salariat; 3, intermediate class; 4, working class; 5, never worked and long-term unemployed).

Suppose we return to our extended investment model. In that case, social networks respond to a conventional maximisation and capitalisation logic

(Glaeser et al., 2002) in which differences in gender composition do not "only" fall in the field of preferences (Leeves & Herbert, 2014). In this capitalisation process, women are disadvantaged by homophilic and cohesive gender networks ("old boys' networks") where men are dominant. Logically, as we have seen in the previous chapter, investment in networks is conditioned by expected returns, is sensitive to contextual variables, particularly social stratification, and is closely linked to human capital endowments (Martin, 2009).

As we have seen, inequality in network accessibility arises from two mechanisms: inheritance and investment. Both processes are socially conditioned. If we incorporate both male dominance, especially in the higher strata, together with homophily, the low expected returns to investment in social networks will result in a broad gender disadvantage. Women start from a smaller inherited network of relationships (dominated by women and close relations) and anticipate lower returns so that they allocate fewer resources (in terms of, for example, personal effort and time) to expand their network. Explained with everyday reality, by homophily, organisations and institutions where valuable information and influence are shared (from social and sports clubs to professional associations) are dominated by men. Therefore, social networks at the top are "old boys" networks. In this regard, let me tell an explanatory anecdote. A female executive who was asked directly about the lower agenda that women tended to have answered bluntly: "We do not play golf".

3 Persistence of inequality and the forms of capital

When economics analyses the sources of inequality, it immediately thinks of the unequal returns to the factors of production. Thus, Piketty's (2014) central point is the finding that the return on capital is greater than the growth of the whole economy "r>g", so the group of capital holders accumulates wealth in a self-sustaining process. More straightforwardly, having access to a scarce factor guarantees a privileged position.

This process of accumulation cannot be observed only in economic capital. For Piketty, a higher level of education and, therefore, a higher accumulation of human capital also explain an essential part of the accumulated inequality. Human capital integrates an aggregate of education, experience, knowledge, skills, etc., and is the product of an extensive accumulation process starting at an early age, a process mediated by a comprehensive set of social variables where the family's social status is decisive.

Consequently, low mobility could be explained by the lack of access of the new generations of low-income groups, who no longer participated in accumulating financial capital, to better (more expensive) education. Other determinants of the investment process may be decisive, such as the parents' availability of human capital, the characteristics of the education systems, and credit constraints. If we add to this health, which could participate in the analogy we have been using with the concept of capital, differences in health care can limit education and employment. Poorer health reduces both productivity and the scope for investment in human capital (Brighouse & Swift, 2014; Lazenby, 2016).

Considering other variables, such as space and the lack of mobility of resources, we could discuss problems of poverty traps (Carter & Barrett, 2006). Space is a key variable in growth, and geographical immobility can lead to social immobility. In sum, opportunities are not homogeneously distributed across space, so productivity, health, and human capital can be trapped in a poverty trap in a given geographical environment.

Previous explanations neglect the social environment in which these processes occur. Leaving aside strictly economic variables, social variables can also play a decisive role by channelling information and opportunities that Piketty does not consider. What is the role of social capital?

3.1 *The forms of capital: a bourdieusian way of understanding society*

We begin by explaining what we mean by the other forms of capital, adopting a bourdieusian perspective and recapitulating what they are and their most elementary features to understand their interactions.

Leaving aside the concept of economic capital, which is not under discussion, our starting point is social capital, already analysed and interpretable as "the value of social networks as an asset" for the functioning of the economy and society. The ultimate referent of this notion of capital is consequently the social network insofar as it results from an investment process, is involved in productive processes and is interchangeable with other forms of capital: human (cultural) and symbolic.

3.1.1 *Human capital and cultural capital*

The concept of human capital is no stranger to controversy and presents the same problems as social capital. In seeking a consensus definition, we adopt Cameron and Neal's (2005) proposal of integrating the competencies, skills, and knowledge of the labour force accumulated through schooling, lifelong learning, and experience.

Again, we can confront both a micro and a macro dimension, an instrumental, and an expressive aspect. These knowledge, skills, and competencies are embodied in individuals and groups and are oriented towards producing goods, services, and ideas under market conditions (OECD, 2007) as well as personal fulfilment and well-being. This last characteristic is relevant because, like social capital, human capital can have an expressive aspect. However, due to the biases inherent in economics, the emphasis tends to fall more on the instrumental or productive aspect.

Although we can find precedents as far back as A. Smith, the introduction of the study of "human capital" dates to Schultz. His seminal 1961 paper notes that investment in this factor answers questions about economic growth, wage structure and personal income distribution (Savvides & Stengos, 2009). When considering the factors that influence the increase in human capabilities, Schultz (1982) highlights five determinants: investment in health services and their influence on life expectancy, formal education at all levels, on-the-job training, including extension programmes, and migratory movements that allow for the adjustment of work capabilities.

The macro approach to human capital is generalised and focuses on proving its determinant character in growth. It shows how the countries that have reached the highest levels of education in the 20th century also have had the highest economic development, even in circumstances of low natural resource endowment in proportion to their territory and population (Barro, 1997, 2001). For these, the privileged proxy or the best indicator is the level of education attained in formal terms.

If we opt for a micro approach, the referents that can be integrated under this definition extend beyond the mere accumulation or stock of formal knowledge. At this point, it is worth reflecting on some parallels in sociology, where analogical interpretation possibilities open up again. Pierre Bourdieu coined and popularised the sociological concept of cultural capital and first used it in his book *Reproduction* (1970). When he refers to the various forms of capital (1986), he defines it from a micro perspective, essentially linked to social stratification. The forms of knowledge, education, skills, and social signals reflect a higher status within society. This stock is partly the result of inheritance from the family environment and partly from investment in the educational system. Concretely, this stock is not limited to functional knowledge but encompasses attitudinal and objectified aspects, like knowledge, habits, and attitudes. At the same time, objects such as titles or cultural symbols can be possessed by individuals and recognised by cultural and educational institutions.

The "moulding" to the characterisation as a form of capital parallels social capital. It is a transferable and exchangeable stock resulting from inheritance and investment. This form is achieved through investing time and resources in cognitive and educational processes. It has effects on the labour market and is easily transferable to economic value.

Finally, aware of the problems involved in delimiting the set of factors that influence the perception of inequality, Bourdieu includes a more diffuse concept that denominates symbolic capital. This could be interpreted as a social conjunction of previous forms of capital or a form of "social alchemy" that translates or legitimises the other forms. In other words, this form expresses how the holders of the other forms of capital exercise social domination. Thus, for example, cultural capital refers to using culture to create social inequality. In contrast, symbolic capital can be cultural capital and any other type of capital if it is perceived as legitimate or "socially considered".

Having reviewed both concepts, it is evident that the Bourdieusian concept of cultural capital is notably more interesting when it comes to understanding social reality than the concept of human capital, but it is also difficult to operationalise (Sullivan, 2002).

Opting for its institutionalised part, assimilated to the most common ways of approaching human capital, may constitute a good proxy for appropriate cultural capital and its role in social inequality. Bourdieu himself rebelled against this interpretation because he rejected the model of social representation that Rational Choice sociology had adopted. Nevertheless, to facilitate both the use of the concepts and an empirical approach, we will henceforth use the concept of human capital as an acceptable proxy for cultural capital. Similarly, for the sake of empirical simplification, we will choose not to address symbolic capital directly. In conclusion, we will reflect directly on the social, human, and economic trilogy.

3.2 Are these forms interrelated? The complexities of inequality

As we saw in the previous chapter, from the micro approach, individual social capital is embodied in personal agendas. It is assimilated into networks of relationships that facilitate access to social resources and, therefore, generate returns. In this sense, individuals are social entrepreneurs who consciously invest in relationships because of expectations of instrumental or expressive future returns (Ostrom & Ahn, 2003). These returns are conditioned by their social environments by inheritance and by the contacts accessible to them through the environment in which they operate. As the reader will already be considering, this endowment is not homogeneously distributed. Consequently, it can be an enabler or an alleviator of social inequality.

If we now focus on the particularities of their distribution. According to the model we have studied in the previous chapter, the endowment of instrumental relations depends on inherited status and personal investment, and both factors are not independent. The inherited endowment influences the expected returns to this investment in networks. Let us simultaneously consider that there is class homophily and a stratification-based starting inequality. It follows immediately that the expected returns to investing in networks will be unequal and, therefore, the inequalities in that personal stock of networks are inherited, self-replicating, and self-reinforcing.

We had already arrived at the assertion that social groups differ in their access to social resources because social interactions occur preferentially within these groups. Previous studies have demonstrated high levels of homophily in social interactions, which have decisive effects on economic inequalities. Notwithstanding, as we pointed out above, the effects of this fact are more evident if we consider them within the dynamics of the various forms of capital.

Starting from the bare assertion that society is characterised by a pyramid structure, where the most valuable resources are located in the upper strata (Figure 6.3). In this general context, high-income groups participate more in social networks and have higher social trust because of the expected returns to these networks. In contrast, the lower strata of society have less extensive, less adaptive, and more informal networks (Van Oorschot & Arts, 2005; Lin, 1999b, 2000).

The initial logical consequence is that information and the ability to influence others are not evenly distributed. Homophily by social strata implies that interactions are more frequent among individuals of the same hierarchical level, facilitating the bidirectional circulation of expressive and instrumental resources.

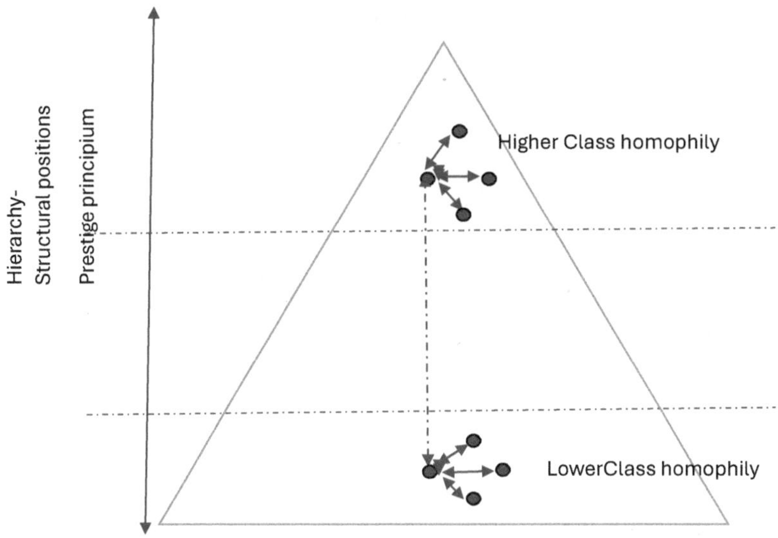

Figure 6.3 Social stratification pyramid and homophily.

Source: Own elaboration, based on Lin (1999)

Under inheritance, individuals inherit two social characteristics, notably a level of wealth that tends to categorise them into a social class and a set of relationships tied to a specific social status and identity and vice versa for lower strata. Then, high-income groups hold a distinct advantage, particularly concerning instrumental relationships. Recognition of the potential of accessible resources and socio-economic proximity (homophily) facilitate interactions. Thus, higher anticipated returns encourage the formation of weak ties and non-redundant relationships, enabling access to valuable resources (Laumann, 1966; Granovetter, 1973, 1983).

Conversely, disadvantaged groups have minimal ties with more privileged groups and little expectation of establishing them through homophily. This results in low anticipated returns and diminishing investment in instrumental social capital (Loury, 2002) and a specialization in expressive relations. However, the differentiation potential extends beyond social capital.

This stark inequality, which we will empirically analyse below, can impact other forms of inequality in three ways. Firstly, it shapes preferences, aspirations, and goals regarding employment and income (Rungo et al., 2024). Secondly, it facilitates privileged information channels or social certification. Lastly, networks imply the capacity to influence the decision-making of others due to the "sympathy" or interdependence of utility functions.

3.2.1 Inequality in social capital and human capital

When analysing the factors that influence educational outcomes, the immediate social environment is a determining factor, particularly the social support networks

(Hanushek, 1972; Glasman & Biniaminov, 1981). Coleman (1988), in one of the foundational works on social capital studies, points out that the time and effort devoted by parents to their children, the structure of the household (the bonding network), its composition, and its residential stability affect the academic results of the youngest students.

Similarly, the "educational investment" made in the household depends directly on the stock of social networks. In the family, altruistic relationships and unconditional reciprocity prevail, so parents seek to maximise their children's utility and well-being, and that of the whole family unit, by investing in their human capital (Becker, 1987). Beyond the family social network, closer community ties (bridging ties) also impact education. Links between parents of pupils lead to "closure" and mutual monitoring (Coleman, 1988, p. 113). The peer group thus plays a significant role that is hardly separable from the family and the community and influences the student through expectations, motivations, values, and habits (Manski, 2000, p. 23).

This relationship also operates on the expected return on investment in human capital. The individual's insertion into social circles of high income and social influence is decisive for the expected "reproduction" of status. To be specific, the expected return on human capital investment (Bourdieu, 1986; Flap & Boxman, 2001). Members with higher status by their social contacts have more opportunities to attain higher positions in the labour market. Hence, the returns to investments in schooling and networks are higher regarding future (expected) income. Simply put, a well-connected family will transfer connections to the next generation; these social contacts will allow them to extract the maximum return on their investment in human capital.

In sum, individual social capital, both strong and weak ties (bonding and bridging social capital), affects individuals' investment in education and, thus, the configuration and performance of their human capital.

On the latter, despite being a repeated finding, the lack of general studies analysing the social segmentation of the labour market and how social capital conditions the productivity of human capital is somewhat striking (Flap & Volker, 2001; Verhaeghe, 2015). But, more strikingly, the inverse relationship, how human capital affects social capital, is less analysed.

In the model in the previous chapter, we saw how human capital, like all status-related variables, is a precursor of the stock of relationships available to an individual. Education is a precursor of social capital that affects "accessibility". In this sense, through the educational process, the social network is strengthened, increasing the endowment of social capital based on weak ties. These offer resources that the individual does not find in his or her network of strong ties (family and closest social circle) (Szreter, 2002). Despite the lack of studies in this sense, Glaeser's classic work (2001) concluded that there is no better predictor of individual social capital than human capital and proposes considering that much of the theory on human capital applies to social capital. Specifically, the most robust correlation of this variable is with years of schooling (Glaeser et al., 2002).

There are three possible explanations for this evidence.

First, a higher level of education may reflect a higher future orientation translated into the discount rate. This means, the higher expected return on education is also a higher expected return on social relations.

Secondly, just as education gives individuals access to the higher strata of the population, social relations also facilitate upward mobility.

Finally, social relations are also part of the educational agenda, so those with greater investment processes in human capital have more personal capacity to develop these networks (Martin, 2009, 2012).

Although this issue is less studied, following Bourdieu's approach, both forms of capital participate in social distinction and are inseparable. Investment in education and, particularly, the selection of the educational environment, in other words, the network of relationships formed in an educational system, is part of the transmission of inheritance and investment in networks to the next generation. Going further, both the encouragement to advance in the education system and the selection of a particular school is a way of selecting both the size and the structure of the network of relationships available to sons and daughters. To take the most obvious example, the choice of school can be determined by knowledge but much more by the social selection of the educational centre (Figure 6.4).

In essence, the combined dynamics of human and social capital and their interdependencies can play a crucial role in the emergence of a Matthew effect, which elucidates social and economic inequalities.

Examining these dynamics enables us to delve into the mechanisms by which inequalities, once established, perpetuate themselves and widen social and economic

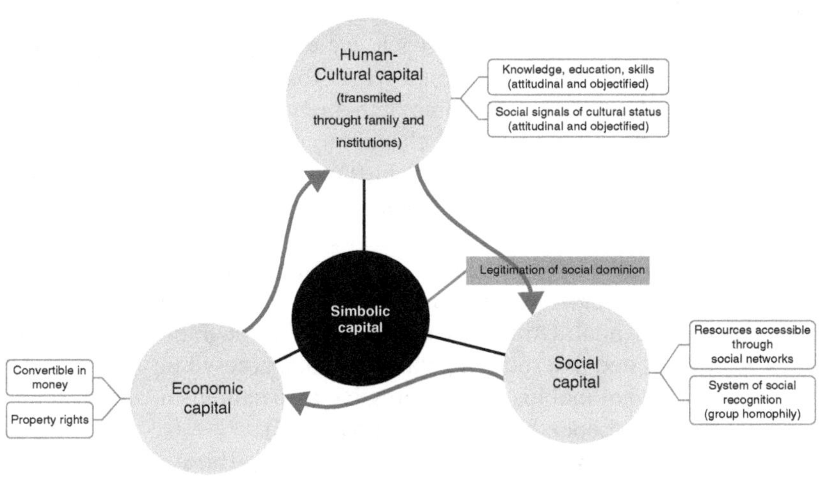

Figure 6.4 The interactions of the forms of capital as Mathew effect.

Source: Own elaboration.

disparities (Rigney, 2010). As Myrdal boldly asserted, "Circular causality is valid in the entire realm of social relations. It should be the primary hypothesis when examining economic underdevelopment and development" (Myrdal, 1957, p. 23). In our context, the Matthew effect is a self-reinforcing mechanism favouring the upper echelons while disadvantaging those excluded from instrumental social networks. Through continual investments in social networks and education, the affluent and well-connected may maintain higher relative incomes and social status, and, vice versa, for the lower strata. In other words, the level of social capital can serve as the ultimate determinant of persistent inequality, even as educational levels converge (Rungo & Pena-López, 2019).

4 Individual social capital and inequality in Spanish society[3]

Intending to ground what we have been pointing out in the chapter, we will develop analysis, as simple as possible, of the survey data we have already proposed as an example in the previous chapter. This is an analysis of the case of Spanish society; however, there is no reason to suppose that it cannot be at least partially transferable to any other developed society.

The reasons for choosing this case for our empirical work are that, in addition to being our country, it has been presenting a persistent growing economic inequality together with an erratic evolution of the conventional figures of macro social capital. According to the AROPE indicator (Llano Ortiz, 2015), during the 2008–2014 crisis, 29.2% of people in Spain were at risk of poverty or social exclusion. On the other hand, this situation showed the central role of social ties for the personal and economic (Jaraiz & Vidal, 2014). Indeed, the economic crisis in Spain led to a paradoxical increase in trust in other people (Bolancé et al., 2018). The survey was developed to extract as much information as possible on the various capital indicators at the micro level to analyse their interrelationships.[4]

Regarding our methodological approach, we employed a two-step analysis to create a series of individual social capital scores for each respondent. Initially, we utilised a battery of questions, including both a position generator and a resource generator, as detailed in the preceding chapter, to gather data on accessibility and mobilisation. Concurrently, the survey yielded information on macro-level indicators of social capital, from trust to associationism (such as trade unions, sports clubs, and NGOs).

Following the methodology already explained in the previous chapter, we derived individual indicators of social capital from this combined dataset of individual and general social capital. Utilising scores obtained through principal component analysis, we formulated five social capital indicators: accessibility, expressive mobilisation, instrumental mobilisation, expressive associationism, and instrumental associationism (Pena-López & Sánchez-Santos, 2017).

The variable "accessibility" measures access to a broad array of social positions. The findings from the factor analysis reveal the presence of a singular dimension. In simpler terms, all variables within the position generator load onto the same factor, indicating the absence of trade-offs in accessing various social positions.

Consequently, accessibility tends to grow simultaneously in every kind of social position without trade-offs.

The variables associated with "mobilisation" assess the effective utilisation of network resources, in other words, the practical possibility of getting them. Through factor analysis applied to the resource generator, two dimensions emerge, consistent with Lin's model, along with a trade-off between them. One group of variables, closely tied to expressive resources (such as assistance with childcare, eldercare, or household tasks), loads onto the first dimension that we will call expressive. On the other hand, variables reflecting instrumental resources (such as aid with public administration or assistance in tax procedures) load onto the second dimension. As per Lin's framework, expressive mobilisation is more closely linked to strong ties and activities within the domestic realm. In contrast, the instrumental dimension, negatively correlated with the first, is more closely associated with economic attainment and social status (Pena-López & Sánchez-Santos, 2017).

The negative correlation between expressive and instrumental mobilisation is unsurprising when considering the opportunity cost of individual investments in social networks (Table 6.1). Investing in cultivating one type of network (such as instrumental) entails costs in developing alternative networks (such as expressive), leading to a trade-off. Moreover, due to resource constraints, investing in weak social ties incurs costs in maintaining strong family relationships.

Similarly, we identified factors reflecting individuals' varying degrees of integration into associative networks (see Table 6.1). In this analysis, two dimensions emerged. Firstly, there is an instrumental dimension, wherein high scores are associated with membership in trade unions, political parties, or general associations focused on advocating for specific or group interests. Conversely, membership in expressive associations, which encompass more traditional forms of associationism in Spain, such as religious, sporting, cultural, and NGO associations, align the same axis. These represent more expressive forms of associationism, with instrumental functions taking a secondary role (Pena-López & Sánchez-Santos, 2017).

We also include general trust in our analysis, which, as previously discussed, is widely recognised as a fundamental aspect of social capital. General trust is represented as a dichotomous variable, taking a value of 1 when respondents affirm that "it is possible to trust most people".

Table 6.1 Pearson correlations of individual social capital stocks and associationism

	Accessibility	*Expressive mobilisation*	*Instrumental mobilisation*	*Instrumental associationism*	*Expressive associationism*
Accessibility	1	.164**	.482**	.283**	.158**
Expressive mob	.164**	1	−.279**	.071**	.004
Instrumental mob	.482**	−.279**	1	.188**	.104**
Instrumental assoc	.283**	.071**	.188**	1	−.192**
Expressive assoc	.158**	.004	.104**	−.192**	1

**Correlation is significant at the 0.01 level (two-tailed).

Source: Own elaboration.

In addition, we consider income and social class indicators of economic conditions. Five income groups with different net monthly income ranges are considered. Our models utilise this variable as a proxy for economic capital.

4.1 The relationship between the various forms of capital

A simple analysis of the correlations between the variable "education" – a proxy for human capital – and different indicators of individual social capital (Table 6.2) shows the intertwining between human capital and any dimensions of individual social capital. In this sense, we would like to stress that although social structure can influence the distribution of social capital, it is also possible that social capital can affect economic and human capital. For this reason, we have focused on the associative nature of the relationship and have not attempted to draw any causal conclusions.

The level of studies is linked with access to specific social positions, but mainly with those of an instrumental nature that make social mobility or status possible (Figure 6.5). Similarly, the link between educational level and instrumental associationism is significant. The bidirectional link is evident, and the causality referred to above is multiple.

The higher the level of education, the greater the access to a set of social nodes with the potential to provide a return in the form of multiple resources. This evidence fits in with Lin's (1999a, 1999b) theoretical approach, which places socio-economic status as a precursor of accessibility. However, it is also worth noting the inverse relationship: greater access to the network favours the agent's education

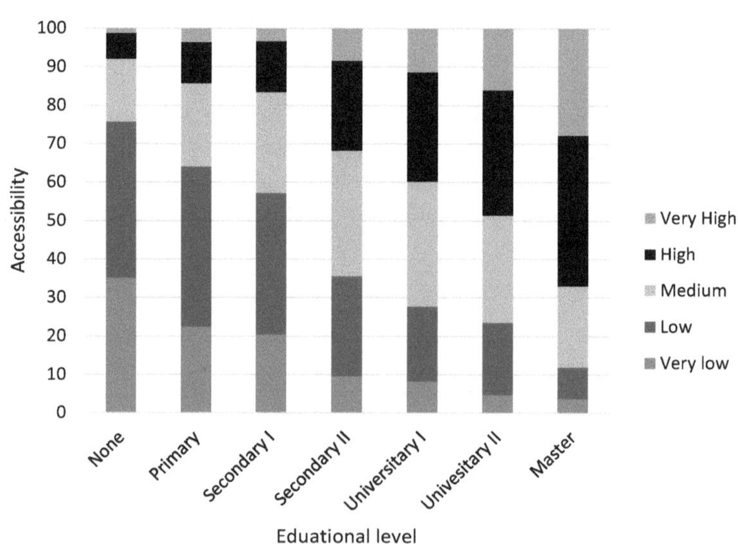

Figure 6.5 Educational level versus accessibility.

Source: OSIM. Survey on the use of social networks in Spain, 2011. Own elaboration.

Table 6.2 Spearman correlations of the social capital variables

	Accessibility	*Mobilisation*		*Associationism*	
		Instrumental	*Expressive*	*Instrumental assoc.*	*Expressive assoc.*
Level of education	.381***	.294***	.153***	.279***	.030*
Income level	.263**	.175**	.200**	.250**	.050*

Source: OSIM. Survey on the use of social networks in Spain, 2011. Own elaboration.

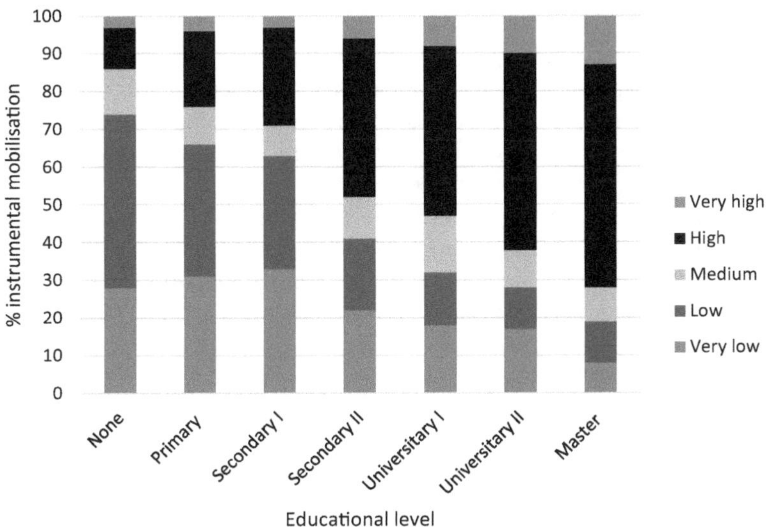

Figure 6.6 Educational level versus instrumental mobilisation.

Source: OSIM. Survey on the use of social networks in Spain, 2011. Own elaboration.

level. As we have explained, social capital impacts education because social networks play an important role in educational investment, generating expectations, monitoring and helping the focal subject (Hanushek, 1972; Bourdieu, 1986; Coleman, 1988; Buchmann & Dalton, 2002).

For its part, the effective mobilisation of instrumental resources (Figure 6.6) depends again on the position within the network or the relational proximity of the subject to the other nodes and, thus, on the possibility of exchanging resources. The individual's education conditions these elements. Someone with a higher education will, ceteris paribus, be more likely to have people to advise them on medical, financial, fiscal, or employment issues.

In short, we can affirm that a higher level of education (a proxy for human and cultural capital) has a clear, direct relationship with social capital in any form. In other words, having a higher level of education provides greater accessibility and capacity to mobilise social resources, primarily instrumental and expressive ones.[5]

Similarly, a higher level of education is linked with greater associative participation and social trust.

The tie between the level of education and macro expressions of social capital, such as associationism, is very significant in the case of instrumental associationism (Table 6.2) and weaker in the case of expressive associationism, which is more cross-cutting. Both educational level and income positively influence the decision to invest in formal and informal social relations. If we carry out the same analysis for income level, the results show an almost identical trend.

Continuing with this simple empirical exercise, we can directly study social stratification without theoretical preconceptions by analysing the combination of capitals in the Spanish population using a clustering technique (Table 6.3). This will provide us with a grouping of the sample according to their proximity based on the endowment of the various forms of capital (Pena-López et al., 2021).

As shown in Table 6.3, all dimensions of social capital seem relevant to the composition of the groups. However, accessibility and instrumental mobilisation explain most of the differences between groups.

The cluster analysis results reveal the presence of two equally sized social groups, each characterised by distinct levels of individual social capital (Figure 6.7). Cluster 1 exhibits high levels of accessibility and mobilisation, albeit with a stronger emphasis on instrumental relations. On the other hand, Cluster 2 demonstrates a relatively higher emphasis on mobilising expressive resources alongside lower levels of accessibility and instrumental mobilisation.

Specifically, the group emphasising instrumental mobilisation boasts more than double the accessibility of the second group. Moreover, the level of instrumental resources is over three times higher than that of the second group. Regarding expressive resources, no significant differences were observed between the groups.

Furthermore, there are minor disparities between the two groups regarding association membership, with Group 1 displaying a higher degree of association. This limited ability to distinguish between the groups raises doubts about the efficacy of formal expressions of associational participation as substitutes for individual social capital endowments.

To elucidate the connections between social capital and other forms of capital, particularly the capacity to convert one form into another, we investigate the factors influencing the probability of belonging to the high accessibility group.

Table 6.3 Post hoc ANOVA on the cluster classification

	Cluster mean square	*Error mean square*	*F*	*Sig*
Accessibility	87.616	0.046	1,894.594	0.000
Expressive mobilisation	1.188	0.040	29.620	0.000
Instrumental mobilisation	196.050	0.018	10,801.357	0.000
Instrumental associationism	1.996	0.011	175.196	0.000
Expressive associationism	0.727	0.016	46.676	0.000

Source: Own elaboration from the survey.

Figure 6.7 offers an initial descriptive insight into this issue without accounting for personal attributes that could also influence individual social capital endowments. Individuals in Group 1 (characterised by high accessibility and a strong emphasis on instrumental relationships) exhibit higher income and education levels. They are more inclined to belong to the upper classes. This finding indicates that social networks are intricately intertwined with the broader social structure.

We have developed a series of regression models to explore the observed relationships in greater depth, controlling for the remaining potential explanatory variables. Specifically, we seek to analyse which variables explain membership in this group of greater accessibility, with a clear predominance of instrumental relationships (see Table 6.4).

As observed in the first two models, higher education and income levels increase the probability of belonging to the high accessibility group. Expressed in terms of social class, following Goldthorpe's functional classification, the middle or intermediate class, and especially the upper or service class, show a high probability of belonging to that group. These results are highly robust concerning education (see Model II) when we remove the income variable from the explanatory variables.

The classical macro social capital variables' results are redundant. Thus, generalised trust positively correlates with membership in a highly accessible and instrumental resource-intensive group (Pichler & Wallace, 2009). On the other hand, the effect of control variables is interesting. For example, as neocapital theory would

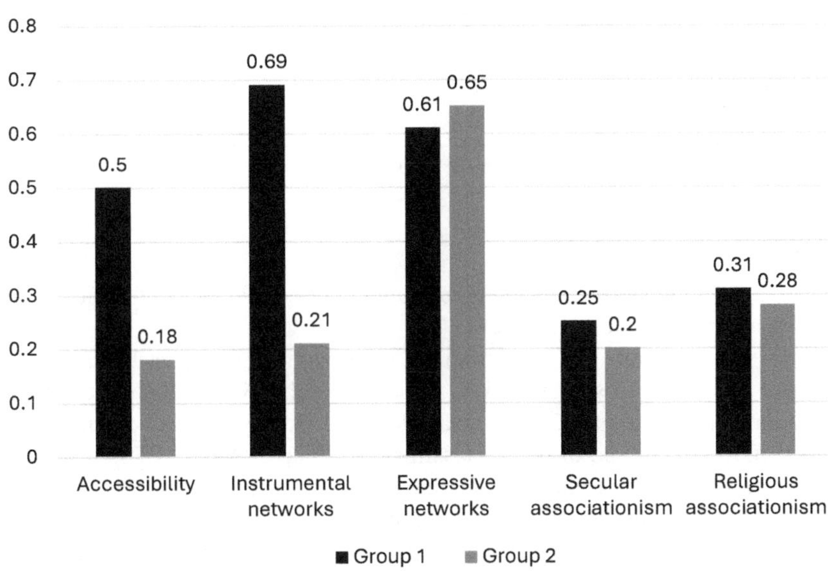

Figure 6.7 Group 1 (instrumental resource-oriented group) versus Group 2 (expressive resource-oriented group); means by group.

Source: own elaboration from the survey.

Table 6.4 Determinants of the probability of belonging to Group 1. Binary logistic models (average marginal effects).

	Model I	*Model II*	*Model III*	*Model IV*	*Model V*
Education					
Secondary	0,070**	0,104***		0,062**	0,092***
University	0,174***	0,229***		0,151***	0,200***
Income group					
2	0,031			0,039	
3	0,132***			0,134***	
4	0,154***			0,148***	
5	0,208***			0,202***	
Social class					
Intermediate	0,107***	0,118***		0,099***	0,112***
Salariat	0,155***	0,206***		0,15***	0,195***
Social class-parent					
Intermediate			0,061***	0,034	0,018
Salariat			0,229***	0,092***	0,090***
Trust	0,042**	0,069***		0,043**	0,069***
Urban context	0,024	0,032	0,056***	0,021	0,031
Female	−0,002	−0,018	−0,042**	−0,005	−0,021
Age group					
2	−0,097	−0,063	−0,007	−0,095	−0,058
3	−0,064	−0,048	−0,022	−0,055	−0,048
4	−0,075	−0,056	−0,031	−0,062	−0,050
5	−0,088	−0,099**	−0,132***	−0,080	−0,096**
6	−0,161***	−0,176***	−0,246***	−0,153***	−0,173***
N	2,025	3,079	3,165	1,954	2,952
	272	359	205	266	346
Wald Chi² (p-value)	(0.000)	(0.000)	(0.000)	(0.000)	(0.000)
Pseudo R^2	0,113	0,100	0,053	0,114	0,101

**Significant at the 0.05 level; ***significant at the 0.01 level.

Source: Own elaboration from the survey.

anticipate, the only significant age is retirement due to the decapitalisation process after abandoning the labour market.

When focusing our analysis on social stratification, particularly on variables related to belonging to specific social classes, we observe a clear pattern of self-replication. Individuals from upper-class families exhibit a 22.9 percentage point increase in the likelihood of being classified as Group 1 (Model III). Furthermore, even when considering education, income, social class, and the social class of origin simultaneously, as demonstrated in Model IV, we continue to observe an effect of the reference parent's class, indicating the persistence of structural factors across generations. Finally, in Model V, despite excluding the income variable, the associations between various forms of capital remain significant.

In summary, the group characterised by greater accessibility and a higher prevalence of instrumental social networks, alongside higher levels of trust in their environment and greater participation in associative activities, also possesses a more substantial endowment of economic and human capital. This group occupies a privileged position in the social structure and originates from similar backgrounds. Thus, the social structure is intricately intertwined with social networks, where individuals with higher education, income levels, and superior social positions are more likely to have better access to social networks, especially those rich in instrumental resources.

In Spanish society, and likely applicable to other societies, an individual's position within the class structure significantly correlates with the formation of individual social capital, representing the personal accumulation of social networks. Moreover, the distribution of social capital exposes substantial inequality closely intertwined with economic and human capital endowments. Individuals occupying higher strata in society, possessing elevated levels of economic and human capital, experience greater accessibility, with their social networks characterised by a prevalence of resources associated with instrumental relationships. Education, income, and social background crucially influence both accessibility and the capacity to mobilise instrumental resources within social networks. These findings support the notion that individual social capital inequality exacerbates economic inequality and potentially contributes to its perpetuation over time. Social capital replicates and reproduces existing inequalities, akin to the Matthew effect, rather than mitigating them, thus challenging Putnam's notion of macro-level social capital as a levelling force.

This evidence raises doubts about the supposed equalising effect of macro-level social capital advocated by Putnam. Instead, it suggests that macro-level social capital may reinforce or perpetuate inequalities, resembling also the Matthew effect. This perspective aligns with Bourdieu's concept of class reproduction and the evidence presented by Chetty regarding the relationship between social capital and social mobility. These assertions question traditional redistributive policies for their limited efficacy in addressing deeply entrenched social inequality. A critical question arises concerning the impact of education policies on cultivating human and individual social capital.

Box 6.2 Class, relationships, and opportunities: revisiting Wright

Studying social classes from a neocapital approach implies considering social strategies in managing individual endowments of any form of capital. As we have seen, giving primacy to a micro-level analysis implies studying social strategies. At this level, individuals follow an "optimising" logic on the various forms of capital given social constraints.

Purely economic approaches are insufficient to analyse the problem of inequality and its persistence. For example, however sophisticated, an analysis such as the one proposed by Piketty (2014) lacks a relational approach (Wright, 2015) where individuals invest in social networks. This leads to paradoxes such as an executive and a worker only differing in possession of income or even economic capital when the social reality is considerably more complex.

Few issues are more contentious than the notion of social class. We can generally find three broad theoretical perspectives (Wright, 2015). Class is either a derivation of individual living conditions, a consequence of the ability to appropriate opportunities, or a form of domination. For the first, or individualist, the critical point is how individuals acquire the educational, economic, and social resources that give them a position of privilege. For the second, the focus is on how some social groups present a position of privilege that allows them to take advantage of social opportunities. Finally, for the more normative, one group exercises control over the situation of another.

Following Wright's three proposals, the second, the Weberian approach to opportunity hoarding, seems to be the response that presents a "pragmatic realism" that reconciles the causal mechanisms of the other theoretical traditions. Persistent inequality aligns with this as it remarks an organisational perspective on inequality, emphasising that the advantages of certain groups are constructed through relationships (Tilly, 1999).

Permanent inequality is due to individual processes of accumulation of social opportunities of various kinds that facilitate both reproduction and exclusion. This way, social classes are analytical constructs, but they are based on social foundations. A multidimensional social space exists with various differentiating factors, social powers, or forms of capital: economic, cultural, and social. They cannot be defined exclusively by the connection between individual attributes and material living conditions, which follows the stratification approach (education, cultural resources, and social connections, among others). They are defined by mechanisms of accumulation of opportunities, which, while benefiting some, exclude others (social closure mechanism) and, in a non-exhaustive way, define relations of domination.

Thus, social capital is crucial in stratification processes because its impact is not only a product of accumulation but is reflected in interactions. The value of social networks derives from mobilisable resources, but their capacity to perpetuate inequalities also lies in their impact on other forms of capital. Social relations operate as intermediaries, constructing horizons of expectations and beliefs and providing information on contacts, resources and services that allow opportunities and determine stability in a position of privilege.

At the same time, the selective and homophilic nature of networks is a determining factor in establishing mechanisms of social exclusion that reproduce positions of privilege by keeping opportunities and resources out of the reach of the lower strata and limiting social mobility. Upward social mobility, in turn, entails investment in building networks within these groups and circumventing closure mechanisms.

Having analysed the interaction of social capital with the other forms, it remains to consider the relationship with what Bourdieu (1986) calls symbolic capital. This is the form that different types of capital take once they are perceived and recognised as legitimate. Since social capital, governed by mutual knowledge and recognition, is the natural channel for expanding symbolic capital, institutionalised recognition in exchange relations implies the recognition of homogeneity or belonging to a particular group.

Finally, a further reflection on this interrelationship is needed. Social capital is not reducible to the other types of capital, but neither can it exist independently. Similarly, social capital exerts a multiplier effect on symbolic, economic, and cultural capital, which refers us to the existence of a Matthew effect (Merton, 1988; Rungo & Pena-López, 2019) in which the processes of self-sustaining accumulation of material and immaterial forms of capital result in an increasingly polarised society.

Overall, social capital has a structuring character in an integrative class definition. It determines the capacity to take advantage of opportunities for the remaining forms of capital and establishes the mechanisms of class replication and exclusion.

5 Recapping

In this chapter, we have tried to show how social capital from a micro approach questions the supposedly egalitarian character of the macro approach. In contrast to the latter, access to and extraction of resources from social networks through mobilisation depends primarily on the position in the social structure. Moreover, individual social capital is a determinant of the persistence of inequality.

Our approach builds on neocapital theories to consider the inequality in social networks and then the interrelationships between the various forms of capital and their inequalities.

Firstly, there is inequality in the arrangement of networks, both in size and composition, which is not necessarily the result of intentional discrimination. The dynamics of investment in social networks linked to expected profitability combined with homophily favours a segmentation of sociability.

This inequality interacts with the other forms of capital as it facilitates the accumulation of opportunities, which has a multiplier effect on them. Social capital is related to economic stratification and has a bidirectional relationship with human capital.

In sum, a notable inequality exists in the distribution of network accessibility and mobilisation, mainly instrumental mobilisation. This distribution correlates with other forms of capital and the social structure.

To encapsulate the findings of our research on Spanish society and offer an empirical contribution to this debate, we observe a clear and direct relationship between social capital and other forms of capital, as well as social positioning within the class structure. Individuals in the upper echelons of society, possessing higher economic and human capital levels, tend to enjoy greater accessibility to social networks. These networks exhibit a prevalence of resources associated with instrumental relationships. Education, income, and social background play significant roles in shaping accessibility and the capacity to mobilise instrumental resources.

Social capital perpetuates, reproduces, and aggravates existing inequalities when embedded in society. This evidence contradicts Putnam's notion of social capital as a levelling force at the macro level. Thus, it is possible to affirm the existence of a Mathew effect.

Finally, the approach of the interrelation of the various forms of capital as a determinant of the persistence of inequality could facilitate a pragmatic way of integrating class studies by reconciling the study of individual endowments with a relational perspective.

Notes

1 The name of the curve refers to the novel *The Great Gatsby* (1925) by Scott Fitzgerald. As many will recall, this novel highlights the social gap between inherited wealth and the nouveau riche during economic growth (the Roaring Twenties).

2 However, as Loury (2002) points out, this is a much more complex social phenomenon than simple segregation. Inheritance and differential investments between social groups due to divergent expected returns may play a role in the persistence of inequality, especially in more homogeneous societies.

3 This empirical example is based on the research already explained in Pena López et al. (2021).

4 The social capital survey was conducted in November 2011 among individuals aged 18 and older residing in Spain, with a sample size of 3,400 face-to-face interviews. The sampling error was approximately ±1.7%, with a confidence level of 95.5% ($z = 2$). The survey was administered using computer-assisted telephone interviewing (CATI). Within each geographical area (Spanish Autonomous Community), interviews were proportionally distributed based on the size of the municipality. Additionally, the sample was weighted by sex and age.

5 The graphs have been compiled based on five social capital variables as plotted.

7 Is there a negative social capital? Social capital and corruption

> Blood is given for friends; blood is taken away from enemies. All others are subject to administrative law.
>
> (Spanish saying)

Corruption is a persistent and complex socioeconomic phenomenon. Its complexity is rooted in the fact that it is submerged or semi-hidden but also in the fact that it is a socially embedded problem. Consequently, as far as economics is concerned, corruption did not enter the research agenda until the last quarter of the 20th century, as international data on the problem emerged. In this sense, the seminal works of Rose-Ackerman (1975, 1978) are an essential reference, marking the starting point for a purely economic approach to the problem.

In this line of work, the question most addressed and with the most significant convergence of results is the effects of corruption. Practically all studies coincide in establishing an inverse relationship between corruption and economic growth, to the extent that the former seems to constitute one of the main obstacles to growth (Mauro, 1995; Lambsdorff, 2002; Hall, 1999; Jain, 2001) and human development (Akçay, 2006).[1] Nevertheless, there is no definitive consensus in the field of causality. The socioeconomic complexity mentioned above calls for an approach to social, cultural, and institutional variables. A broad set of factors that reflect a particular prior configuration of society and are difficult to alter through policy actions explain why a given society is more prone to "informal solutions" in the economic sphere (Treisman, 2000; Paldam, 2002). This approach seems to lead us to some form of neoinstitutionalism and to concentrate our attention on studying the interaction between individuals and the formal and informal rules that govern life in society. Agents will succumb to corrupt practices if they have discretion, weak accountability, and a substantial monopoly of power. There is simply a rule they can break; they do not have to account for it, and they perceive a particular benefit in return. This approach shows that reformers could reduce corruption by restricting this discretion, increasing control over officials, and reducing the state's power. In other words, by reducing benefits and increasing costs. What is peculiar is that despite the clarity of this typically economistic approach, the measures have proved to be largely ineffective. There is also a problem of persistence despite

DOI: 10.4324/9781003375302-11

political activism. Once again, the social rootedness of the problem, which we alluded to in the previous chapter, may play a key role. In this sense, introducing the concept of social capital can enlighten and open up some interesting questions about its interpretation.

This chapter will study the interrelationship between social capital and corruption, mainly how social networks constitute the substratum on which these problems are rooted (Baycan & Öner, 2023). This review will also introduce a broader problem, the Olson-Putnam controversy. Thus, this chapter forays into the dark side of social capital, and we will try to answer the following questions: What are the causes of corruption? What kind of social capital is linked with corruption? Is there negative social capital?

1 Corruption: definition and some clarification to the mayhem of causality

Corruption is a global phenomenon that, to varying degrees, is present in any form of society or organisation and is closely linked to its institutional conditions. In the simplest explanation, when any legally constituted authority sets a rule, circumventing it with the connivance of some instance of that authority can be profitable.

In the search for definitions, there is no convergence on what we mean by corruption. We will follow an orderly sequence to arrive at a consensus proposal that allows us to delve into the complexity of the phenomenon we are studying. As starting point, it is expected to use the definition proposed by Goode (1984) based on the Penal Code. For this author, an individual commits corruption when

> being or expecting to be a public official, he accepts or obtains from someone, for himself or another person, remuneration other than that legally established as a motive or reward for some official act derived from the exercise of his functions, in which any individual or group of individuals is favoured or disfavoured.

From a legal point of view, this is a complete or closed definition. However, a wide range of more diffuse situations, whether they are corruption, must be clarified. Philp (2006), from a sociological perspective, proposes a broader definition, not limited to legal demarcations, as an action deviating from general normative expectations oriented by the pursuit of personal or narrow group benefit, mainly through the misappropriation of a public resource. It is a transgression of a normative expectation in pursuing a benefit that need not be individually derived from handling a public resource.

This link to "normative expectations" is closely related to the characteristics of a particular society. A simple comparison of two extreme models of society is illustrative. For this purpose and following the classic terminology of Tönnies (1947 [1887]), a cold society and a warm society can be contrasted. In the first type of society, there are practically no relationships between individuals and consequently, interpersonal knowledge is minimal, even within families. In contrast, a warm society assumes the existence of a vast network of personal relationships as well as mutual knowledge. In these societies, family contacts are widespread, and the family constitutes a strong mutual support network.

Both societies have clear implications for the functioning of government. Purely economic relationships that maintain social distances are more likely in a cold society. In this case, respect for the norm is more likely without considering the link to the individual. On the contrary, in a warm society, the strict application of the norm to any circumstance encounters difficulties. Social distance could even be seen as contrary to normative expectations and even "immoral". In other words, it is a double system of expectations linked to social proximity. Moreover, these "proximity arrangements" are hardly observable at the social level. In general, it is difficult to distinguish an act that can be labelled as corrupt and its consideration from any other social behaviour since there may not be a direct payment but a long-term circulation system of favours.

In these societies with strong ties in close groups, the bonding social capital, the expectation that the official will be impartial in applying the rule is non-existent, making the Weberian claim of achieving a technical bureaucracy unfeasible (Weber, 1964 [1922]). In this case, the rules of respect in small circles will be safer forms of behaviour than those based on universal and impersonal principles. In extreme cases, we might even see social acceptance leading to the entrenchment of such behaviour; society prefers the other "norm". These relationships between officials and individuals may become socially accepted so that any corrective attempts by the government are ineffective. In such cases, we may face a clear obstacle to the economy's growth by not being able to guarantee the impartiality of the administration and the enforcement of contracts (Tanzi, 1994).

Another aspect or variable to be taken into account is that corruption is linked to a decision taken by the public administration. Then, it is also related to some characteristics of the state, its size, and the regulatory framework itself. The size of the public sphere and the characteristics of its exercise are decisive insofar as a more interventionist state is more likely to transgress.

At the same time, there is the problem of administrative system development or interpretative discretion. Corruption involves breaking a rule, which requires a precise definition of the rules so that public officials have no room for discretion. Leaving these decisions in the hands of the agents means placing them in a monopoly regime with the capacity to appropriate the consumer surplus. It is clear then that the greater the power of discretion, the greater the likelihood that it will be used for individual benefit or the benefit of close associates and "customers".

This duality leads us to a particular trade-off. On the one hand, there is a need to establish rigid rules to avoid discretionary decisions. However, the extension of these rules may be an attempt by public officials to take advantage of this discretionary power and increase the possibilities of transgression. Often, the very excess of rules creates fertile ground for corruption. To a certain extent and by analogy, corruption can be interpreted as privatising the state without giving the role back to the market but rather to the bureaucracy (Tanzi, 1998).

If we consider both aspects, the problem of the social impartiality of the rule's application and the need to "increase" the rules to control irregularity, we find a surprising paradox that could be behind a social entrenchment of the problem.

After this demarcation of the territory, we will revise the diverse causal approaches to corruption, later incorporating the social capital analysis of the problem.

1.1 The causality of corruption

It is very ambitious to propose a causal model of the determinants of corruption. If we had proven causality, it would be "relatively simple" to tackle the problem, and the results show that it is not. A quick look at the main theories on corruption leads us to conclude that some of them converge because they include contextual factors that favour the appearance and spread of this type of problem. In simplified terms, we can speak of four explanatory proposals that we could simplify into three: one closer to economics, a second closer to organisation theory and, finally, a third more sociological.

Institutional economics, specifically Public Choice (Rose-Ackerman, 1999), proposes an explanation centred on individual rational calculation of highly predictable outcomes. Public agents are corrupt because the benefits outweigh the expected costs, considering the probability of being caught. Derived proposals will logically focus on reducing the benefits and increasing the costs of such behaviour (Schinkel, 2004).

Traditional analyses of the economics of crime (Becker, 1968) stress the need to reduce the probability and incentives derived from crime. Thus, the reduction of discretion by public officials and the decentralisation of authority has significantly reduced corruption. More open economies that are less public and penetrated by market relations are less prone to corruption (Treisman, 2000; Kranton, 1996). Similarly, increased penalties, transparency regulations, and competition in the press and politics effectively reduce incentives. Despite the advantages of this approach, the object of criticism is apparent: Why is there a prevalence and persistence of corruption in organisations and society in general?

Organisational studies respond by analysing the culture and structure of the organisations under which corruption is most likely to occur. For them, corruption is about behaviours that, for various reasons, may be accepted at some organisational level.

It is then necessary to understand how the organisation functions and how perhaps a corrupt organisational culture has been generated from a sour apple (Punch, 2000). In this case, it is a group culture that can be traced and intervened. In its elementary expression, corruption is translatable into an agency problem that can be expressed through a three-actor model, a principal-agent relationship and a third actor that we will call the "client". The principal (authority, businessman, state, etc.) delegates decision-making power and resources to the agent, and the agent breaks the rules that the principal has established to give the client a benefit. Corruption, therefore, involves the breakdown of a principal-agent relationship, both formal and informal, in which the agent receives some form of deferred payment from the client for the abuse of his decision-making power. Obviously, under this analysis, corruption is not necessarily limited to public administration but can occur in any area where there is a contract and a normative expectation, including private business.

Looking deeper into this principal-agent relationship, it is evident that corruption entails an asymmetric risk. As a behaviour against the regulatory framework, the agent is in a peculiar "contractual" context. The agreement between client and agent is not enforceable in case of breach by the former. This support is informal, so its assurance requires informal institutions, particularly when the agent has a clear risk of being penalised if he is discovered. In this way, we can speak of a tacit contract between the two, whereby it is more "profitable" for the agent to bypass the link with his principal. Therefore, it is necessary to redefine this organisational framework, eliminating discretionarity, aligning interests, etc.

However, the study of this relationship does not penetrate the social or normative conditioning factors that underlie these behaviours and make them persistent, even in the face of these organisational changes, nor into the true nature of the underlying contract. By way of example, a police officer may avoid giving fines to friends and acquaintances, receive a few gifts for doing so, and not consider this to be in any way "corrupt" or outside the norm. In other words, it is necessary to investigate what lies behind these stable behaviour structures.

A third group of studies from **Socioeconomics** emphasises the social and normative constraints surrounding this problem, specifically the particular-universal normative conflict (Uslaner, 2005; Svendsen, 2003; Graeff & Svendsen, 2013). This conflict is generated when private values and close networks collide with those attributed at the public level and considering society in general to a given agent. As in the case proposed in the previous example, the clash of particular morality or the norms we apply to those who are close to us, family and friends, and social morality, the behaviour expected at the global level. This conflict consequently arises in the clash of expected social roles. This problem is typical of economies in transition that come from patrimonialist, traditional or "warm" societies where strong ties can be particularly significant.

Previous solutions are of little relevance in these cases. Becker's proposal to prosecute crime as a means of control in the first way of analysis would only be effective in the case of a modern state in the Weberian sense.

A synthesis of the various theories would be attractive. They are not mutually exclusive but have a complementary component that we will contrast in the empirical section. Huberts (1998) has already proposed a triple-level analysis. At the micro level, they deal with individuals and their work. At the meso level are the characteristics of the organisation, which are distributed among leadership, organisational structure, personal politics and organisational culture. Thirdly, there is a range of macro-level factors, including changes in criminality, norms, and laws.

The study of Macrosocial capital and, surprisingly, its inconsistencies may constitute an explanatory path. This facilitates the analysis of the socio-cultural conditioning factors we have proposed in the third approach and the explanation of the entrenchment of the corruption problem.

2 Social capital as a determinant of corruption

The description we have developed on corruption refers to situational aspects related to the dimensions included in the definition of macro and micro social capital: norms, networks of relationships and forms of trust. Precisely, the functioning of any corruption network presupposes the existence of shared norms and closed networks of mutual trust between clients and agents. In a way, we are dealing with unique forms of social capital that could be described as particularistic linked to micro and meso expressions. This can have extreme expressions, such as the case of kleptocracies, to wit, the existence of a "culture" of corruption based on norms and trust rooted in closed groups.

In these networks formed through an "informal contract" to the defining features of any relationship, such as reciprocity or interdependence of the utilities of both actors, closure and concealment are added. The reason is straightforward: either has something to lose in the case of non-compliance and must conceal that link since it goes against the general rule and causes negative external effects for non-participants.

Under these circumstances, norms and trust in restricted groups are the social institutions that can support the spread of corruption. Then, the homophily discussed in the previous chapter, or simply the expectation of repeated interactions derived from a network of relationships, can generate the opportunity to reinforce the contract (Husted, 1999).

In essence, the extent of corruption within a society is closely linked to specific types of trust and norms ingrained within social networks. The enduring nature of this issue over time appears to stem from socio-cultural factors. Societal attributes, the presence of particularistic or closed networks, hinder the impartiality of public endeavours and the ability to penalise such behaviour. For instance, a society with a strong family culture can derive from corruption networks.

To grasp the motivations behind corrupt practices, it is imperative to deconstruct the underlying social framework and examine the influence of norms, trust, and, consequently, social capital on a micro and macro scale (Lambsdorff et al., 2005).

2.1 Trust and corruption

From the social capital perspective, we are analysing a confrontation between micro and meso social capital and macro social capital, reflected in networks, values and trust. Corruption is based on a predominance of particularist trust or trust in the narrowest circles and, in parallel, an absence of generalist trust (Rose-Ackerman, 2001). At this point, it is worth specifying what particularistic trust means within the various trust forms: unilateral, reciprocal and organisational.

Unilateral trust means that one person trusts another person or institution based on information about the latter's incentives, motives, and competence.

Reciprocal trust or trust in micro and meso networks, implies that agents need to trust each other that the other party will perform the intended or expected action.

This implies a lattice of components in the relationship in which there is a mutual calculus of interests, personal affections, responsibility, and mutual values (Hardin, 1999). This type of trust can be ambivalent. On the one hand, it overcomes cooperation problems generated by situations analogous to the Prisoner's Dilemma, that is, it facilitates a system of social pre-coordination (Warren, 1999). On the other hand, it creates networks based on stable relationships of sympathy and shared goals that facilitate breaking laws.

Finally, trust in an *organisation*'s rules is based on the assumption that the rules will be followed predictably and neutrally, regardless of who occupies positions in an institution and in the spirit in which they were formulated.

This simple classification isolates the trade-offs and complementarities between the various trust forms. The most apparent tension arises between reciprocal trust and generalised trust and can have wide-ranging effects on the functioning of public institutions and markets.

Interpersonal or reciprocal trust based on sympathy, a sense of duty to family and friends, is very different from the general trust that, for example, someone may have in the neutrality of governments. In a world where reciprocal trust based on personal ties predominates, there is little chance for general trust to expand or vice versa. In a world without generalised trust, in societies that are defective in functioning, particularistic trust in closed networks is the great escape route to a "controllable" environment. Similarly, as Luhmann (1988) highlights, social evolution towards complex societies increases the benefits of general trust but undermines the roots of trust in family and friends.

As a result of this trade-off, some forms of particularistic reciprocal trust create links between actors that are favourable to their rent-seeking but have serious negative externalities at the societal level. This conflict can become so embedded in society in what the Italians call the culture of "Raccomandazione" that it can materialise in forms of corruption that are stable and immune to any change in the political system, where particular agreements take precedence over social ones (Uslaner, 2005; Lambsdorff, 2002).

2.2 *Norms and corruption*

What we mean by a norm is somewhat less clear than it might first appear. A norm about a particular action exists when there is a socially defined right to control that action, not by the actor but by others (Coleman, 1988). Consequently, as something "socially defined", we may encounter contradictory norms, such as written and socially accepted norms.

This ambivalence means that in the case of corruption, one socially accepted norm may increase the probability of corrupt behaviour. For instance, the written norm may favour meritocratic personnel selections. However, a non-formalised but powerfully influential social norm accepts and positively weighs up respect for family ties to the point of reproving anyone who refuses to hire a relative.

To clarify the relationship between norms and corruption, we must establish distinctions within these coexisting normative systems following the same criteria we adopted when analysing trust.

Firstly, and closely linked to the concept of informality, there are *particularistic* norms established in membership or primary groups in the traditional terminology of Cooley (1909), that is, those small groups defined by the existence of association and cooperation characterised by their proximity and permanence (family, clan, etc.). These groups have an enormous capacity for influence and are neither status nor person-neutral. The particularistic norms of these systems are not usually codified, as they regulate habitual interactions in which "wrong" behaviour is immediately responded to (Schweitzer, 2005).

By contrast, *universalist or generalist* norms refer to secondary groups, such as those established on a contractual basis, which are codified and should be status- and individual-neutral. In addition, their level of knowledge, although it should be generalised, requires a coercive system and a considerable number of resources for its defence, given that detecting irregularities is more complex (Granovetter, 2005).

Particularistic norms have a clear functionality that gives them priority over universalistic norms. The satisfaction of fundamental needs, including affective and recognition, occurs within primary groups and groups of belonging. Consequently, the protection generated by particularist norms is so relevant that it can only be prevented by imposing severe sanctions and generating a new symbolic system, sometimes through religion, which re-evaluates the costs of breaking the universalist norm.

This last trait means that when a society finds itself with a diffuse hierarchy of values, both particularist and universalist systems can come into conflict, and the particularist one can become the priority. For example, this problem is evident in the transition from patrimonialist societies to modern states. For Weber (1964 [1922]), in the former, there is no clear separation between property, public and private. Thus, in a particular agent, the defence of the family or friends can come into contradiction and take precedence over the execution of a social norm. In this sense, societies that have undergone a rapid growth process tend to present higher levels of corruption by facilitating the confrontation of traditional and progressive value systems (Olson, 1965; Hirschman, 1985).

Based on this normative conflict, we can find two levels of corruption in terms of normative penetration. Firstly, particularist corruption derives from the primacy of particularist norms over universalist norms, as in the case of an agent who does not fine a member of his immediate circle, family, and friends.

Notwithstanding, corruption could even arise at a higher level in the conflict between universalist norms. In extreme cases, particularist norms have been constituted as social norms that conflict with the written norm. Continuing the example, the norm that family and friends should not be fined is socially accepted. The latter case leads in its extreme expression to forms of systemic corruption resulting from prolonged situations of generalised corruption that eventually generate conformity with the social system to the point of constituting the actual system of social organisation. For example, in some countries, it is considered obvious that promotion to public office is associated with the whole family being incorporated into the public sector regardless of meritocratic consideration.

2.3 Synthesising: corruption and social capital

As can be seen from the previous analysis, the ambivalence of norms and trust facilitates the emergence of corrupt relationships. This same ambivalence is transferred to the notion of social capital, leading us to consider the relationship between corruption and social capital and the ambivalence of the concept of social capital itself.

As we have already discussed at length in the previous chapters, several definitions of social capital attempt to explain the concept. Among those framed within the macro perspective, Putnam's (1993) stands out for its generalised adoption. From this perspective, social capital can comprise social networks and social norms. The former refers to the social networks where individuals are inserted, which can be communication networks and social and economic support. For their part, social norms refer to social rules of reciprocity or mutual expectations of cooperation or trust.

As discussed in the fourth chapter, this characterisation encompasses at least three forms of social capital under the same concept. On the one hand, there is a relational capital of family or peer ties (bonding), members of the same family or set of strong ties. There is also bridging capital or relations with members of other groups, both in ethnic and socioeconomic matters. Both levels would fall under the micro and meso approaches. Finally, there is an essential institutional linking capital, or the relationship between individuals and groups of individuals with any form of general community of belonging, then, a macro approach (Woolcock, 2001).

Even so, taking up the findings of the previous sections, these three expressions can generate contradictory results. As we have seen, the causality of general trust is far from evident. It should be noted that general trust would constitute positive social capital. In contrast, the particularistic expressions of social capital (usually placed between bonding and bridging capital) may constitute negative social capital when they facilitate establishing reciprocal trust relationships outside society and the market (Villalonga & Kawachi, 2017).

Consequently, we may find a trade-off between trust in family and friends and general trust, which could reflect a tendency to subvert general norms and favour, for example, shadow economy solutions. Some forms of micro and meso networks may facilitate an illegal or corrupt exchange. However, it is essential to note that this distinction between positive and negative is made solely by the values and norms governing these particular networks and their social effects (Graeff, 2005; Graeff & Svendsen, 2013).

This point will illustrate the problem we have already pointed out when dealing with "Coleman's boat" that we studied in chapter three. The problem of the leap from personal networks to social functioning entails dealing with values, trust, and network configuration aspects. What we have called general linking capital involves extending social networks and universalistic norms and should be associated with increasing generalised trust. In some cases, this may be related to forms of trust but ultimately depends on the type of norms and values reflected in these networks. The latter leads us to consider revising the term general social capital (Box 7.1).

This **negative social capital** is deeply linked to proximity relations and is more dependent on relationships than on informal systems of norms. Thus, it could be argued that trust over norms is prioritised. Norms are an unstable expression of this form of capital, as they are unspecific in providing information about actions. Trust, on the other hand, generates specific information about the intervening subjects. Then, developing corruption-friendly norms will depend on the closeness and trust between groups that allow reasonable behaviour expectations to be established.

The closed character of which we have already spoken gives these particular networks a stability that positive social capital lacks. The very nature of the group's activity and purpose implies its closure insofar as everyone has something to lose. Simultaneously, growth in the group size would imply the need to increase the possibilities of coercion, as the defection of one member poses a risk to the others (Moore & Recker, 2016).

Ultimately, social capital positively influences social functioning if linked to ethical attitudes. These attitudes and rules oblige subjects to evaluate their behaviour, taking into account the gains and losses perceived by non-participants. These are, therefore, universalistic expressions of trust. In contrast, particular trust does not necessarily imply positive social and economic outcomes.

3 Are there good and bad forms of associationism? The Olson-Putnam-Paxton controversy

The argument we have developed above refers to a more general problem: the formation of social capital from individual social capital. This is a remarkably complex issue, but we believe it is worth making some initial reflections that will allow us to put this last link of the "Coleman's boat" into context.

As observed, the mainstream perspective shares a significant consensus: the acknowledgement of trust and cooperative or pro-social behaviours as fundamental pillars of both the economy and society. There is no dispute over trust's crucial role in economic development (Zak & Knack, 2001). It is evident that transaction costs (such as information costs, contract monitoring, and conflicts) are markedly diminished within an interconnected community due to the expansion of trust networks.

However, the role of social networks is as ambiguous as the definition of social capital. For example, we find two seemingly contradictory propositions in an elementary literature review. Putnam (1993) attributes the greater success of regions and countries in terms of economic growth to a robust associative framework. These networks develop habits of cooperation, solidarity, and interest in res-publica, which are fundamental to resolving collective problems and agency. Consequently, for him, there is an identity between networks and general trust (Putnam, 2001) without testing the internal causality of these links (Bjørnskov, 2006). Applied to the Italian case, his classic work argues that the significant growth differential between southern and northern Italy stemmed from the different tendencies to generate horizontal associations with derivations in trust and citizen cooperation. As we have already remarked, for Putnam (1993), good governance is a by-product of civic associationism. Notwithstanding, as we have seen, how social networks affect economic activity is neither self-evident nor always positive.

In contrast, Olson (1965, 1982) offers a seemingly opposite interpretation. Social organisations, acting as specialised interest groups (lobbies), can limit the possibilities for growth. If the interests of some of these organised groups conflict with those of society at large, the effect on trust and, thus, on economic activity would be negative. Due to the logic of collective action, minority groups with specific interests are more successful than generalists. The success of these minority "rent-seeking" coalitions will result in regulations affecting the allocation of resources (investment, labour, etc.) and limiting growth (Knack & Keefer, 1997; Knack, 2003).

A first reading of both seems to lead to an *aporia*. However, both perspectives can be compatible if we distinguish social groups based on their goals, using the considerations of the previous sections. Olson is talking about closed (with a particularistic interest) networks, whereas Putnam is considering cross-cutting (universalistic) networks. Therefore, only a particular type of closed and vertical group acts as rent-seekers.

These specifications allow integration of both hypotheses (Sánchez-Santos & Pena-López, 2005; Pena-López & Sánchez-Santos, 2007, 2014). From what has been studied in the chapter, it is possible to speak of a particularistic social capital, a particularistic configuration of micro and meso, that may have negative effects, as opposed to a generalistic one with very different macro effects, particularly on levels of trust.

Nevertheless, an underlying problem must be clarified: What is the relationship between associationism and generalised trust? Theoretically, it is possible to argue that trust generates a greater propensity for associationism and that associationism favours generalised trust and endogeneity. We find evidence in both directions: those who affirm the existence of a direct relationship (Claibourn & Martin, 2000) and those who question it (Sønderskov, 2011; Van Ingen & Bekkers, 2015). Based on the latter, we could argue that there is no conclusive evidence that causality runs from associationism to trust. However, it is true that associationism brings together those individuals with higher levels of trust and constitutes a "pool of democracy".

3.1 What kind of associations create social capital?

Let us try to answer the question posed in the previous section. Trust arises from a bond between individuals based on an inferred knowledge of the norms we expect others to comply with. Thus, social homogeneity in norms, values, interests, and identities favours trust, and diversity harms it (Hardin, 2001, 2002). Logically, the frequency of interactions increases overall trust because of better inferred knowledge (Bacharach & Gambetta, 2001; Stolle, 2001).

As we saw in chapter four, explanations on trust can be divided into two groups. Some theories emphasise the existence of a psychological predisposition that can be altered by everyday experiences (Uslaner, 2002, 2008), while others emphasise social learning (Paxton, 2007).

For the *psychological predisposition*, trust is based on previous learning and is related to the sense of control over one's own life. In this case, current experiences would be less relevant (Uslaner, 1999, 2002, 2008). Determinants are the weight that structural variables can have on the levels of generalised trust, such as ethnic and cultural heterogeneity, perceived security, income, and life expectancy (Delhey & Newton, 2005; Delhey et al., 2011). In short, trust is a product of socialisation in which individuals must have support that guarantees subjective well-being and control over their environment. This first proposal does not contradict the second.

The *social learning* approach suggests that individuals continuously extrapolate their repeated personal experiences into their general estimates (Yosano & Hayashi, 2005). Generalised trust is a sum of individual experiences across life domains (Glanville & Paxton, 2007). Thus, association membership would enhance generalised trust by multiplying the possibilities for interaction and the practice of trust. Norms spread through groups influencing attitudes and behaviours, and associative interaction facilitates diffusion and generalisation (Morales & Mota, 2006).

However, at this point, it is essential to correct the simplicity of Putnam's proposal. It is not possible to assimilate all forms of associationism and all forms of trust with general trust. As Paxton (2007) points out, the extension of trust derives from the interconnections between the associations themselves. It is the vertebration of associationism, multiple memberships, and their open character what is decisive.

A chain of closed associations facilitates a minimal number of interconnections between individuals. In contrast, the interrelationship between associations multiplies them, facilitating the generalisation of values and norms and general trust.

Simply put, individuals categorise others into two groups: us and them. Those who are integrated into the "us" are perceived in terms of trust. An individual who is integrated into various groups tends to generalise the conception of the "we" and consequently increase his or her perception of trust (Herreros, 2004) (see Figure 7.1).

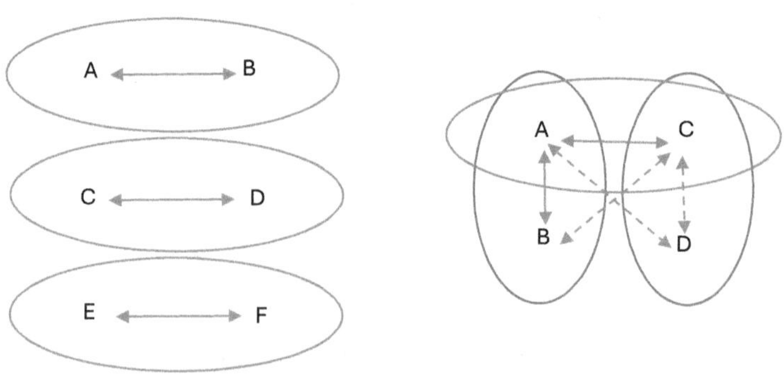

Figure 7.1 Closed versus open partnerships.

Source: Own elaboration based on Paxton (2007).

This argument leads to the distinction between open and closed groupings or associations. The former facilitates integration into a broad associative network of diverse natures and is beneficial for general trust. The latter, by contrast, is exclusivist or limiting and does not affect generalised trust. In other words, generalised trust cannot be linked exclusively to membership in any association but only to those considered more open. The closed ones, based on particularist trust forms, have no derivations in general trust.

Consequently, generalised trust is not based solely on the multiplicity of associations and their diversity, as would follow from Putnam's (2000) or Granovetter's (1973) proposals. In reality, such trust appears to be more linked to the diversity of groups, the diversity within groups, and the interconnections within this diversity of groups.

At this point, Paxton's (2002, 2007) hypothesis can be summarised as follows: Greater incorporation of individuals into interconnected or open associations will positively affect generalised trust and, thus, the generation of social capital. In contrast, membership in closed associations does not affect generalised trust.

This hypothesis, which explains a specific conditioning factor in the capitalisation process of general social capital, places us on a different level from the mere development and expansion of social networks. It is not an aggregate of networks of relationships or forms of individual associationism but the particularist or universalist-generalist content of these networks of relationships. Even as a mere exercise in reflection, we believe it is worth thinking about the cognitive and relational dimensions of general social capital and the ethical basis of human behaviour in society (Box. 7.1).

Box 7.1 Social capital or moral capital? An alternative concept

As discussed in the third chapter, one of the first impressions after analysing the various concepts of social capital is perplexity. There is an apparent lack of integration of the three major dimensions and a total split between the micro and the macro, the particular and the general. This is evident when we address the issue of trust.

As a reaction, it could be asked whether there is a potential redefinition of the concept to overcome the inconsistencies we have mentioned. Guiso et al.'s (2011) notion of moral capital, or even civic capital, could, to some extent, overcome the problems outlined above.

As we have seen throughout the chapter, although the relationship between trust and social capital is evident, the relationship between associationism and social trust is not (Sánchez-Santos & Pena-López, 2005, pp. 148–149). By qualifying the concept of social capital, we could propose a definition of what "moral capital" or civic capital might be. This focuses on the behaviours that underlie the formal and informal relationships established within civil society and the ethical attitudes predisposing to general reciprocity and cooperation. Then, the central matter is on the values and beliefs that internalise the common good, encouraging cooperative behaviour.

Overall, through this shift, we would be giving more prominence to the normative component that we previously placed in the cognitive and relational sphere, which was reduced to the trust variable. In fact, we are restricting the relationships that constitute general social capital to only a special kind.

Moral capital may reduce ambiguities

Moral capital is translatable as generating a consensus on social values and extending and deepening networks of personal ties (sympathy) between individuals. It implies the exclusion of forms of particularistic closure. This does constitute a prior coordination system that reduces transaction costs (Koslowski, 1991, 1999).

This concept has some advantages for several reasons:

It is not indifferent to individual networks' characteristics, content, and behaviour. In this case, there is no proper notion of negative social capital. Simply, particularistic networks are not capital in a general sense. As Olson argued, closed networks conflict with society to the extent that they are an obstacle.

Moral capital embodies a readiness to engage in social cooperation and direct interactions towards collaborative solutions, including participation in associations. This concept aligns with the notion of civil society, which represents the foundational structure of society distinct from the coercive authority imposed by the state. While networks may serve as platforms for exchange and oversight, they do not inherently ensure that individual behaviours are universally beneficial (Ratnapala, 2003).

Moreover, moral capital can be viewed through an economic lens. While all forms of capital involve resources owned by individuals, firms, or groups utilised in producing goods and services, moral capital encompasses conditions that facilitate production, such as coordination among parties involved in transactions. In this context, the accumulation of moral capital arises from individual investments, which could be a kind of reputational capital, and group investments aimed at reducing transaction costs. Investment in human capital and developing an appropriate institutional framework are part of this process.

This refinement of the concept of social capital enables the synthesis of micro and macro perspectives. Moral capital pertains to an individual actor's investment decisions and is intertwined with social norms, conventions, associations, preferences, etc. In both scenarios, an economic approach rooted in optimisation principles can be applied analogically (Glaeser et al., 2002).

Therefore, this "new" concept has a reference, namely the framework of personal relationships, which consists of social ties and can separate what it is (a normative consensus-based universality) from what it does or facilitates (trust, cooperation, agreements, etc.). Moreover, sympathy is the elementary unit in the constitution of formal and informal social networks and differs from them (Robison et al., 2002).

This recourse to morality removes the ambiguities in the definition of social capital, especially for its link to economic development that we saw in the Olson-Putnam controversy, questioning particularistic groups and amoral familism.

4 A brief exercise on the relationship between social capital and corruption[2]

To verify what we have been pointing out, we will propose a simple empirical model that analyses the relationships between socio-cultural factors and perceived corruption rates at the national level.

In the preceding sections, we anticipate an inverse correlation between corruption and general trust and a positive correlation with particularistic manifestations. Moreover, drawing from Olson's (1965) classical argument concerning the adverse effects of interest groups, we would predict a direct link between indicators of interest group strength and the prevalence of corruption.

Furthermore, our model will include control variables that have demonstrated explanatory power across different research approaches. These include cultural dimensions and indicators such as openness, property rights, economic freedoms, and human development, all previously identified as influential factors in the literature.

The data used in our applied econometric model for this analysis come from various sources. Firstly, the Transparency International (2022) Corruption Perceptions Index (CPI) serves as a proxy for the level of corruption. This index aggregates survey and institutional data from multiple countries and rates perceived corruption on a scale of 0–10, with higher scores indicating lower levels of corruption, that is, transparency. The Human Development Index (HDI), calculated using data from the World Development Indicators (WDI), provides insight into the development levels of the countries under study. Additionally, statistical information on economic and social factors was obtained from the 2022 World Values Survey. This survey yields general and specific trust indicators, which can be interpreted as proxies for the bonding and bridging aspects of social capital. Institutional characteristics such as regulatory approaches and interventionism versus free-market principles (including property protection and capital mobility) are captured by civil liberties indices from Freedom House International (2018).

Table 7.1 Corruption versus institutional variables and proxy variables for social capital

Correlations				*Relational dimensions (bonding, bridging)*					*Institutional Trust*	
	General Trust	*Corruption (Transparency)*	*Global freedom*	*Importance friendship*	*Importance religion*	*Cultural associationism*	*Trade union associationism*	*Political associationism*	*Trust in political system*	*Trust in economy*
Corruption (transparency)	0.6151**									
Ind. freedoms global	0.3615**	0.7732**								
Importance friendship	0.2673*	0.4440**	0.3736**							
Importance religion	−0.5914**	−0.3734**	−0.1816	0.0434						
Partnership cultural	0.2836*	0.4425**	0.4722**	0.2548*	0.2836*					
Partnership trade union	0.3874**	0.3220*	0.1393	0.1804	0.0039	0.5189**				
Political associationism	−0.0921	−0.0524	0.0784	0.0241	0.4751**	0.4688**	0.2815*			
Confidence in politics	0.5020**	0.6738**	0.4941**	0.4900**	−0.2140	0.1718	0.2565*	0.1451		
Trust in economics	−0.0256	0.0685	−0.0441	0.1335	0.4901**	0.2956*	0.2314	0.2815*	0.1943	
IDH	0.3985**	0.7116**	0.6287**	0.3370**	−0.6145**	0.0885	0.1209	−0.0974	0.5307	−0.2763*

*Significant at 0.05; **significant at 0.01.
Source: Own elaboration.

Examining correlations among the critical variables analysed in the econometric study highlights the significance of the interaction between institutional factors and general trust and corruption. However, an intriguing observation arises when considering particularistic trust, as shown in Table 7.1.

As expected, the trustworthiness of the legal system and indicators of freedom are directly related to general trust and the absence of corruption. The correlations between general trust and the absence of corruption also suggest a link between both variables, so high levels of corruption (low levels of transparency) are associated with low levels of generalised trust. Nevertheless, at this point, we must introduce a *caveat* that seems to agree with Olson. The extension of horizontal associationism, as in the case of cultural, leisure and even NGOs, seems to enhance trust and transparency, but not vertical expressions, as in the case of political and trade union associations. The latter could be identified with Olsonian interest groups and often negatively affect general trust and transparency (Pena-López & Sánchez-Santos, 2007; Paxton, 2007).

Regression analysis will allow us to determine the explanatory power of institutional, cultural, and social variables on observed levels of corruption controlled for the remaining influential factors (Table 7.2).

Model I (Table 7.2, Figure 7.2) reveals a notable association between general social capital, as indicated by the variable "generalised trust", and transparency or the absence of corruption. However, examining this relationship in light of the previous discussions, the macro, meso, and micro-level expressions of trust are crucial. Initially, general trust correlates with trust in the political system and the lack of corruption (transparency). Conversely, the significance of strong family bonds operates in the opposite direction (see Model II in Table 7.2). Therefore, in a more comprehensive model considering various forms of trust, trust expressions

Table 7.2 Corruption versus cultural and institutional variables

Dependent variable: corruption (Transparency)
Sample size: 60

	Mod I	*Mod II*	*Mod III*	*Mod IV*
General trust	0.1049**		0.0595**	0.0516**
Political trust		0.0864**	0.0728**	0.0493**
Importance of the family		−0.0913**	−0.0661**	−0.0465**
Trust in Trade Unions			−0.0302*	−0.0168*
Trust in political parties			−0.0361**	−0.0146**
Trust in market			0.0332*	0.0271*
Global Freedom Index				0.6455**
C	1.711817	8.196602	6.142601	0.615729
R^2	0.378304	0.526499	0.701019	0.848384
R-Adjusted^2	0.367585	0.509588	0.665844	0.824264
Prob (F)	0.000000	0.000000	0.000000	0.000000

*Significant at 0.05; **significant at 0.01.
Source: Own elaboration.

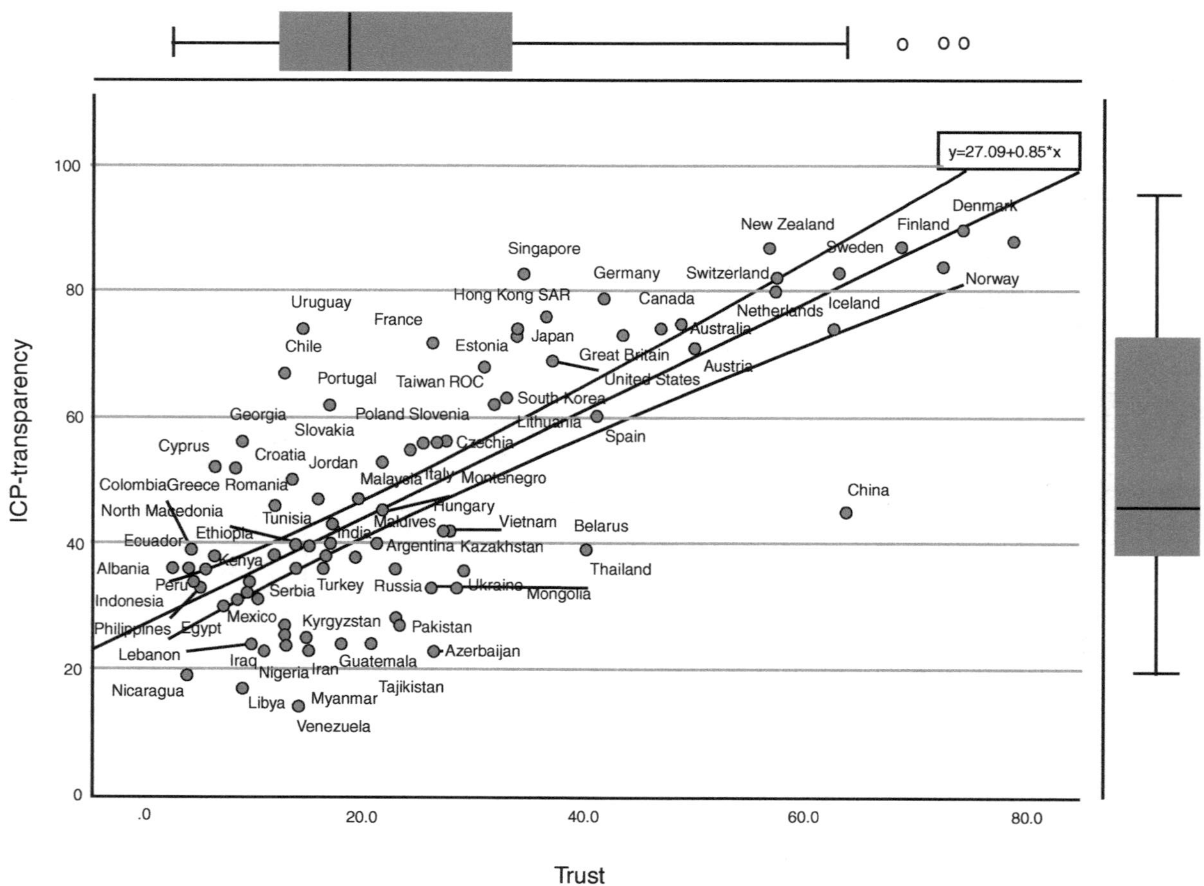

Figure 7.2 General trust versus corruption (transparency).

Source: Own elaboration.

within small (particularistic) groups are linked to issues of corruption (see Model III in Table 7.2) (Uslaner, 2002).

This can be interpreted as evidence of the importance of family ties or strong links in interest groups (political parties, trade unions, etc.) that favour corruption. The weight of amoral familism or the absence of a generalised universalistic morality determines the lack of transparency or corruption. In societies without generalised trust with institutional problems, group or family reciprocity relations offer a second-best alternative solution. This aspect also has an interpretation in terms of the dimensions of culture.

Following this perspective, broadening market mechanisms could likewise mitigate corruption. Notably, the significance of the "trust in business" variable merits attention. Trust in the market and its operations appears to correlate with general trust rather than its particularistic manifestations. This observation would support Kranton's (1996) notion of system confrontation (Griesshaber & Geys, 2011).

Finally, Model IV (see Table 16) integrates institutional and socio-cultural dimensions, demonstrating high explanatory power and supporting the ambivalence of social capital and the influence of institutional variables. First, it confirms the correlation between different forms of trust (particularistic and general) and levels of corruption. It underscores the relationship between corruption and interventionism. Within this relationship, a significant link emerges between the absence of corruption and the Global Index of Economic Freedom, particularly concerning property rights. However, the magnitude of public expenditure (public expenditure/GDP) proves insignificant. This suggests that the determining factor is not the size of the state but rather its regulatory activism. Politically, this result indicates that the lack of clarity regarding property rights is pivotal in explaining high levels of corruption. Furthermore, this aligns with Kranton's (1996) and Tanzi's (1998) assertions regarding the conflict between market and patrimonialist systems in exercising public authority.

In sum, the distribution of countries in the sample highlights the influence of socio-cultural, historical, and institutional factors as determinants of corruption. Nevertheless, it shows the different influences of the levels of social capital and the confrontation between particularistic and general or universalistic values.

5 Recapping

This chapter examines the determinants of corruption to highlight how the persistence of this problem is directly related to the configuration of social relations. In this sense, it can be seen as showing how corruption depends not only on institutional factors and agency problems but also on particular expressions of social capital; that is, it seeks to recognise the existence of forms of negative social capital.

On the one hand, there is a clear relationship between general social capital and the absence of corruption. However, there is also a causality of corruption itself in particular forms of social capital. Some norms, values and networks facilitate the emergence of this type of behaviour contrary to the general norm, which can make it persistent in the face of any attempt at reform.

Particularistic norms and trust result in closed networks that facilitate and reinforce behaviours contrary to the norm and may even constitute a form of negative social capital. This is the case with amoral familism or rent-seeking behaviour by interest groups. Both are examples of bonding and bridging; more proper, micro levels and meso level not necessarily associated with the development of social capital. This "paradoxical" relationship is expressed in the well-known "Olson-Putnam" controversy. Not every form of association is conducive to the expansion of social capital. As Paxton proposes, horizontal open associationism is more favourable to extending networks and, therefore, positive for generating general social capital. The small empirical exercise showed evidence of this result considering a set of 60 economies.

Finally, this problem brings us back to the need to consider the character or content of the networks that make up the micro and meso levels. Their interrelationship with the macro level is not independent of the values and norms underlying them. This might lead us to the need to define what constitutes a certain form of moral capital.

Notes

1 Some studies have shown that the relationships between corruption levels and output are not monotonic. In fact, under certain circumstances of inefficiencies in the functioning of public administrations, corruption could be a second-best allocator that compensates for the bureaucracy's shortcomings (Kaufman & Kraay, 2002; Canavese, 2006).

2 This empirical exercise is based on previous methodological studies of Pena-López & Sanchez-Santos, (2009, 2014).

8 Well-being and relational goods. The intrinsic value of social relations

> For friendship is a virtue, or involves virtue; and also it is one of the most indispensable requirements of life. For no one would choose to live without friends but possessing all other good things.
>
> (Aristotle, *NE* VIII, 1)

One of the criticisms of the concept of social capital that we have been dealing with refers to the sociality of the term capital. From some areas of sociology, psychology and even economics, it has been pointed out that this research programme is an attempt to economically instrumentalise aspects that have to do with human beings (Fine, 1999). In a way, this criticism is justified if what is exhibited is a reductionist vision in which the social is taken into account if and only if it serves as an asset in the process of maximising agents' utility or as a factor in a production function (Etzioni, 2007).

This economistic approach is short-sighted because instrumentality is not the only dimension in social interaction. Moreover, intrinsic or expressive sociability is essential to a person's subjective well-being (Figure 8.1). Returning to Chapter 5, when we proposed our micro model, we pointed out the existence of two types of

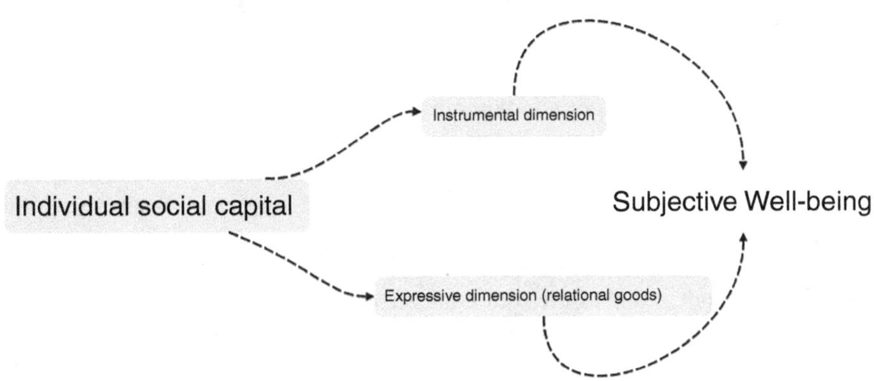

Figure 8.1 The double effect of social capital on well-being.

Source: Own elaboration.

DOI: 10.4324/9781003375302-12

mobilisation and effects of social capital: "instrumental" and "expressive" or "intrinsic" (Membiela-Pollán, 2016). The instrumental dimension has been mentioned repeatedly in previous chapters. It is linked to those uses of social capital that provide a functional "benefit" for the individual and the group in terms of income or status, translatable into the other forms of capital, economic or human. At the micro level, the individual in a network accesses and potentially mobilises resources such as information and influence, opportunities, economic and physical support, expert advice, education, and portfolio of contacts.

Notwithstanding, the expressive and intrinsic dimension of social capital is also a reality that must be contemplated to the extent that this is the most related to sociality itself. When referring to social network resources, we must speak of emotional support, authentic sociability, and identity. Whether in a family, community, association or social circle, the person might find help, opportunities, or advice. However, instrumentalising these relationships would be unwise and mean losing what is specifically human. It would be discarding the love between parents and children, the friendship between friends, and the sense of belonging experienced within a community.

Addressing the expressive is as relevant as pointing out that both effects of social capital – instrumental and expressive – are essential for well-being. Nevertheless, while the instrumental dimension provides a more objective or "material" type of well-being, the expressive dimension provides a more subjective well-being. The latter means that the intrinsic value of social relationships and the social climate affect happiness or, what economists prefer to call, revealed subjective well-being (Pena-López et al., 2017; Hommerich & Tiefenbach, 2018). This final chapter studies the expressive or intrinsic dimension of individual social capital, the relational goods. Specifically, it examines the paradoxes in the relationship between income and happiness and the role played by the stock of personal relations. We will try to answer these questions: What are intrinsic or expressive needs? What are relational goods, and how are they produced? How do social networks and relational goods affect happiness?

1 Relational goods or the expressive dimension of social capital

From the "instrumentalist" perspective, membership in a social network is evaluated quantitatively and materially without paying sufficient attention to its psychological, sociological, and moral effects. Nevertheless, much of the reward of social interaction has intrinsic value (Arrow, 2000). Although interpersonal ties may have instrumental purposes, the relationship can be a good, not just a means to achieve other goals.

The intrinsic value of the social network is made explicit in the concept of relational good, understood as the communicative and affective side of interpersonal relationships (Becchetti et al., 2008) or as the "expressive dimension of social capital" (Membiela-Pollán, 2016). This approach to relationships as an intrinsic good parallels what happened with the concept of social capital. It arises in response to the insufficiency of traditional economic theory in addressing the growing dissatisfaction in affluent societies and the need to consider the social dimension and ethical and moral codes in the economic system (Bartolini, 2007).

Research on relational goods is intertwined with Social Capital Theory and Socioeconomics. It also falls under Happiness Economics, a discipline that studies happiness by combining economics with other fields such as psychology and sociology. In the field of schools, for some years now, relational goods have been a line of research within the "Economia di Comunione", led by researchers such as Benedetto Gui, Luigino Bruni and Stefano Zamagni.

As with the concept of social capital, studying the communicative-affective dimension of interpersonal relationships is not new and has been addressed by some classical and modern authors. From Aristotle to Keynes and Sen, the intrinsic value of sociability for human happiness is recognised. However, economic theory in the 19th and 20th centuries, influenced by the marginalist revolution, reduced happiness to pleasure and ultimately to utility, relegating broader considerations of the importance interpersonal relationships. This simplification has led to a failure to adequately analyse the value of the social dimension, especially the effects of the expressive dimension on individual well-being.

In this context, the notion of relational good emerges as a crucial component of "social environment" and social capital, contributing to the analysis of the intrinsic value provided by interpersonal relationships and fostering the integration of sociability into "more human" (Bruni & Stanca, 2007, p. 508) and more real economic models (Robison & Oliver, 2023).

2 The concept of relational good and its characteristics

One of its meanings, possibly the most prominent in our context, is that the word *good* refers to the satisfaction of a need, to something that has a positive and appreciable value, something that generates benefit or utility (Encyclopedia Britannica, 2023; Real Academia Española, 2024a). In economics, an infinite number of categorisations are offered: private goods, public goods, preferential goods, material and immaterial goods, consumer goods and capital goods, among others.

In a clear materialistic bias, the specificity of the good that social relationships represent is often overlooked, not only because of their instrumental value but also because of their intrinsic component. In simple terms, how do I emphasise the importance of the company and love of my friends and family?

Four relevant contributions to defining relational good are made by the neo-Aristotelian philosopher Martha Nussbaum (1995 [1986], 1987), the sociologist Pierpaolo Donati (1986), and the economists Benedetto Gui (1987) and Carole Uhlaner (1989). All four introduced the notion of relational good practically at the same time. However, each did so from different approaches and contributed fundamental aspects to the theoretical development (Donati, 2019).

Martha Nussbaum (1995 [1986], ch. 12) defines relational goods as those human experiences in which the relationship is a good in itself. This stresses the protagonism of the relationship as a capacity for satisfaction. Donati (1986, 1997) pays more attention to the productive process to emphasise its simultaneity. Relational goods must be considered an "effect" of concrete social relations. They arise from relationships so that the relational good is produced simultaneously by the participating subjects, who are both producers and consumers. Gui (1987) emphasises the immaterial character linked to interpersonal relations and, like Uhlaner (1989), expresses that these immaterial goods can only be possessed through a reciprocal agreement following a joint action of several people. These agreements do not have to be explicit but are neither casual nor arbitrary. In other words, their production requires specific contexts.

Let us give a trivial example, "friendship". It is unnecessary to quote Aristotle's extensive analysis of friendship (books VIII and XIX of the *Nicomachean Ethics*) to show that one component of happiness is the enjoyment of friendship, which does not require any exchange but mutual recognition. It is expressive, and both participants are producers and consumers simultaneously. The good is the relationship itself, is immaterial and is produced simultaneously by producers and consumers at the same time; friendship requires a particular context for its cultivation.

However, beyond mutual love and friendship, relational goods can be extended to civil commitment, belonging to a group, identity, social approval, companionship, emotional support, solidarity, and mutual recognition. These elements are, in principle, desirable for every individual. They are typified as "inherent human needs", the third step (need for esteem and affection) and – partially – the fourth step (need for recognition) of Maslow's pyramid (1943).

As for where these goods are produced and consumed, the list is endless (Gui, 2000, 2005; Membiela-Pollán, 2016; Bruni et al., 2021). Some examples may be illustrative: In the love between a mother and her child; in a relaxed conversation between a salesperson and a shopper at the supermarket; in the relationship between colleagues in an association, mediated by recognition and trust; in the friendly interaction between a doctor and a patient; in a family meal, and a coffee with friends; and even in the social atmosphere that the subject experiences in a public square. They are omnipresent in social interactions or a potential part of every interaction.

Thus, relational goods are located beyond the stage of strong ties, and every social and even economic relationship could encompass their production and consumption. Interaction between people, or between "agents", can be understood as a productive process called "encounter" (Gui, 2005), which derives outputs of a disparate nature. In the above cases, one set of traditional outputs would have to do with group work in a company, collective action in an association, the economic transaction in a supermarket or the execution of specific functions in a household. Therefore, Gui's (2000) definition of relational goods as intangible outputs or products of a communicative and affective nature that originate in interactions seems correct.

From the above, a reflection on the quality of an encounter or relationship arises. There is the possibility that this intangible output of the interaction may be negative. This situation means that relational goods are "fragile" (Nussbaum, 1995 [1986]), and there is also the real possibility that what is produced and consumed are even relational bads (Putzel, 1997; Gui, 2005, p. 37). In this sense, Adam Smith himself, in *The Theory of Moral Sentiments* (1759), already compared the cases in which interpersonal relations involve "correspondence in sentiment" with those in which "dissonant sentiments" are induced.

2.1 The characteristics of relational goods

As we have remarked, the relational good is a notable output of the interpersonal relationship and the social capital, constituting its expressive or intrinsic dimension. Its relevance is significant both for subjective well-being and even for the operation of social capital. All this requires specifying the characteristics that define the relational good and make it unique.

By way of systematisation, they can be summarised as follows:

a. *Relational goods have the properties of a good but are not comparable to a "commodity".* They are social interactions that generate intangibles that satisfy expressive needs such as a sense of belonging, identity, or friendship. However, they lack a market price due to their nature based on gratuitousness, which can also be interpreted as authenticity (Bruni, 2008, p. 95).
b. *They do not coincide with the relationship itself.* Being produced through interactions, they emerge as a result of the relationship. For example, a business dinner may be merely instrumental, or a relational good may emerge through a relaxed conversation (Gui, 2000, p. 155).
c. *They require reciprocity and cannot be consumed or produced individually.* They can only be enjoyed if shared with others. For this reason, the identity of the parties involved – for example, in a mother-child relationship – is crucial for the existence of the relational good (Sacco et al., 2006).
d. *They involve simultaneity*, being co-produced and co-consumed during participation in a joint activity (Gui, 2000, p. 155). Although the contribution may be asymmetrical, all participants experience it simultaneously.
e. *They require motivation, authenticity, and gratuitousness* since their value is based on sincerity and authenticity. These goods are "non-contractual" and cannot be bought or imposed (Bruni, 2008, p. 94).
f. *They are a form of local public good*, shared in the context of the relationship without rivalry or exclusion (Becchetti et al., 2020, p. 539). However, unlike traditional public goods, which can be enjoyed in solitude, their production and consumption are, as we say, simultaneous and joint (Uhlaner, 1989) (Table 8.1).
g. *They are vulnerable and fragile* because they depend on reciprocity and are subject to others' decisions (Bruni & Porta, 2007). Influenced by socio-cultural, institutional, economic, contextual, and personal factors, they are susceptible to negative experiences that can affect their subsequent disposition towards others (Pugno, 2007). They are also highly susceptible to problems of free riding.

2.2 The relationship between relational goods and social capital

Limiting the definition of relational goods as a mere by-product of social capital restricts the analysis of the link between the two concepts.

We are returning to the complex dimensions that constitute the social capital we discussed in the third chapter. "Assets [...] provide benefit streams that make future productive processes more efficient, effective, and innovative [...]. Social capital accumulates various social, psychological, cultural, cognitive, and institutional

Table 8.1 Taxonomy of private, public, and relational goods

	Private property	*Public good*	*Relational good*
Rivalrousness	Rival	Non-rival	Anti-rivalry (between the participants in the interaction)
Excludability	Excludable	Non-excludable	Non-excludable (between the participants in the interaction)
Marginal profit	Decreasing		Constant or increasing
Investment, production and consumption	Separate actions	Separate actions	Coincide

Source: own elaboration based on Becchetti, Bruni and Zamagni (2010).

assets, increasing the sum [or probability] of mutually beneficial cooperative behaviour. This behaviour is productive for others as well as for oneself. It benefits others and not only oneself, following the Latin origin of the word "social"" (Uphoff, 2000, p. 216).

Relational goods are assets that form part of social capital because they favour cooperative behaviours that induce mutual benefit. Part of this reduction in transaction costs is associated with the relational and expressive component of the social bond. Hence, relational goods are economic goods that contribute to individuals' subjective well-being through social interactions inside and outside the market (Bruni, 2010). As Macneil (1987) points out, virtually all real-life contracts are somehow relational. In other words, all economic interactions are social, and what facilitates social interactions also facilitates economic ones.

Thus, the quality of relationships and the human and social environment matters (Zamagni, 2004; Williamson, 1996, p. 275) both in interpersonal relationships, whether in spheres of reciprocity and cooperation such as family, community, association, and business or in the market where goods and services are exchanged (Corsi et al., 2022).

These have intrinsic value in terms of well-being as well as instrumental value. Agents are also interested in intrinsically agreeable ties, and the outcomes of these interactions can affect their activity (Bruni, 2008; Becchetti et al., 2010a, p. 415). If a relationship does not promote a relational good, a fellow feeling or correspondence of feelings (Sugden, 2005, p. 66), even if a relational bad could occur, the bond that provided instrumental and economic value could dissolve. It follows that participants value interpersonal encounters in terms of all inputs and outputs, including those of a communicative and affective nature (Gui, 2005; Pugno, 2007).

In sum, the instrumental functionality of social relations is also influenced by assets with intrinsic value. This is why authors such as Sacco and Vanin (2000) and Nussbaum (1995 [1986]) point to the "instrumental value" of relational goods, in line with Amatya Sen (1997 [1987]), who mentions the "instrumental value of ethics". Relational goods, with trust, norms, values, and the social network, can thus be considered "assets" of social capital.

In this context, relational goods are first approached as an output. Then, as an asset of social capital, they can also be apprehended as an input or input factor influencing other assets.

Let us see how:

a. *Relational goods contribute to the internalisation and strengthening of cooperative norms and trust* (cognitive assets of social capital) (Sacco and Vanin, 2000, p. 232; Donati and Prandini, 2007, p. 220). At the same time, the enjoyment of relational goods reinforces the value attributed to social, family, friendship, organisational or knowledge relationships (structural asset of social capital) (see Laville and Nyssens, 2001, p. 319; Brablec, 2019).
b. *Relational goods positively influence an individual's happiness*. Those with higher well-being tend to show a greater inclination towards sociability, which ultimately increases the accumulation and stock of social capital (Stutzer & Frey, 2006). Moreover, they generate what Meade (1952) called "environmental externality". Everyone benefits when others produce relational goods.
c. *Civic participation may be driven by the expectation of positive relationships* or, in other words, by the potential enjoyment of relational goods (Gui, 2000; Mosca et al., 2006). The anticipation of positive effects on well-being acts as a motivator for social participation.

Having exposed the contribution of relational goods to other social capital assets, it is worth returning now to the concept of relational badness, which, let us recall, refers to the case in which interpersonal interaction is perceived as negative. In this case, in contrast to the previous one, friction is created in other assets. A bad relational experience causes the individual's disposition towards sociability to be reduced. Moreover, the danger of this effect is not only one-off but may have implications for the future, leading to a vicious circle and the loss of all contact (Pugno, 2007).

On the other hand, in contrast to the view of relational good as a local public good, relational badness derives an environmental externality that goes beyond the limits of the individual relationship, giving rise to a local "public badness" (Caruso, 2011, p. 457) with repercussions on the social capital of the network. Tangibly, the bad relationship between two family members, between two workers or between two members of an association not only affects the social capital between the two nodes but also has repercussions on the collective social capital of the network in which they are inserted (the family, the company, the civic organisation).

2.3 All relations matter, bonding, bridging, or linking

Relational goods are produced and consumed in various spheres of social life, but some actors and contexts play a prominent role. Thus, they seem most directly linked to bonding social capital (a social network of strong ties or primary social relations) (Donati, 2019). However, bridging social capital (weak ties) is also linked to these assets, sometimes decisively.

Relational goods are especially evident in bonding social capital. The criterion used to classify social capital is based on the closeness of a reference contact and the frequency of interaction with that contact (Fennema & Tillie, 2008, p. 353). Bonding-type social capital is associated with "strong ties", encompassing relationships with family, close friends, and close social circle, with high trust and emotional involvement (Raiser, 2008, p. 495).

The significance of bonding social capital in the production of these goods is due to the following:

a. Closeness and frequency of interpersonal contact exist in the family and close social circle, which makes it, by nature, a potential main stage in the production and consumption of relational goods.
b. Family and friendship ties are characterised by high expressiveness, emotional involvement, and reciprocity. Intrinsic motivations, authenticity and trust operate to a greater degree in this primary social group.
c. Bonding-type social capital implies a certain homogeneity in the subjects, either morally or socioeconomically, thus facilitating interpersonal interaction and the production and consumption of relational goods (Castiglione, 2008).

However, in the previous section, we have seen that relational goods are not only an intangible output from interpersonal encounters and the social network. They also act as an input and asset of social capital. Relational goods are an input to social bonding capital because they enhance internal cohesion, trust, and virtuous disposition. In this sense, some authors highlight the importance of the relational web surrounding the individual, stressing that positive sociability in the context of strong ties drives prosocial behaviour (Donati & Prandini, 2007, p. 209; Caruso, 2011, p. 457). These act on beneficial cooperative behaviours. The socioeconomic resources and functions carried out by the family, such as physical, economic, and emotional support, socialisation, and education, emerge from cooperation and reciprocity, and these goods reinforce such cooperation, improving the quality of interpersonal interaction and the satisfaction of the subjects involved (Sacco & Vanin, 2000; Lee et al., 2018).

Building on the previous sections, there is also a link to bridging social capital. This relies on relationships that transcend the family and the closest social circle and tend to be more socioeconomically and culturally disparate (Putnam, 2000; Durlauf, 2008). The frequency of interaction, emotional closeness, and the degree of reciprocity and altruism are also lower (Membiela-Pollán, 2016). As we have already analysed, bridging is configured from different spheres of life, such as work, the neighbourhood, school, associations, clubs, commerce, or the business network. Contexts where weak ties predominate. However, it also plays a crucial role in the generation of relational goods (Sabatini, 2009, p. 433) and can be decisive in contexts in which the individual lacks strong ties; they are of low quality, or, for example, in the case of widowhood (Nakagomi et al., 2020). Even so, the connection based on weak ties is not always immediate due to its more instrumental and often casual or time-limited character.

Nevertheless, as in the case of bonding social capital, relational goods are not only an output of bridging social capital but also an input and an asset of it. They are an input because they affect the continuity and strength of the link with weak ties. They are also an asset because they increase the probability of cooperative behaviour and exchange between subjects, reducing transaction costs. For example, in work, associative, school, community or market environments, relational goods act as non-monetary incentives (Dur & Sol, 2009; Mosca et al., 2006; Robison et al., 2020), potentially improving productivity, information exchange, cooperation and understanding, collective action and performance.

At a third level, we could include expressions of relational good related to linking social capital. These present particular characteristics that deserve to be addressed in a specific field (Box 8.1) linked to a recently expanding field, identity economics.

Box 8.1 Economics of identity: the importance of I belong at...

Relational good arises, in principle, as a product of interpersonal interaction. Despite this, the literature establishes that identity and a sense of belonging are also examples of relational good (Nussbaum, 1995 [1986]; Uhlaner, 1989). This means that it is possible for an individual to experience these feelings – albeit in a more diluted way – without direct and timely participation in tangible, personal interaction.

For example, a person may feel happy walking down a street in a village where he is rooted, enjoying a more abstract relational good than he experiences at home with his family or at a gathering with friends. In this case, he perceives a socio-cultural climate or atmosphere with which he identifies and belongs. Similarly, estrangement, perceived alienation, or the loss of a sense of belonging that generates a hostile or problematic social climate (poor relationality) negatively affects their well-being and a general loss of confidence (Puntscher et al., 2015).

Identity implies that people recognise and associate themselves with certain behaviours because of shared beliefs in different social, religious, ethnic, or occupational contexts (Akerlof &Kranton, 2010, p. 4). This concept is closely linked to social norms and motivations and affects economic and social behaviour. People feel happier when they comply with social expectations and follow patterns influencing their decisions. Similarly, happiness is also experienced by the subject when he or she feels part of that social context, identifying motivationally.

In short, collective identity and sense of belonging, at micro, meso or macro levels, are considered a relational good because of their distinctive characteristics: they are experienced reciprocally, they are produced and consumed simultaneously, they are based on intrinsic motivations such as norms and values, they involve recognisable subjects, they resemble a "local public good" as they are non-rivalrous and non-excludable, and they cannot be enjoyed in solitude. Moreover, they do not coincide with the relationship itself but represent an intangible experience of a communicative and affective nature.

All the above manifests in the concept of belonging social capital (Figure 8.2), which refers precisely to the identity that emerges from institutions and communities; that is, it can be considered a form of linking. This identity provides a "sense of belonging" to its members (Lin, 2008, p. 60) and can generate benefits in terms of generalised cooperative behaviours (Delhey & Dragolov, 2016) and, as we say, in terms of the production and consumption of relational goods.

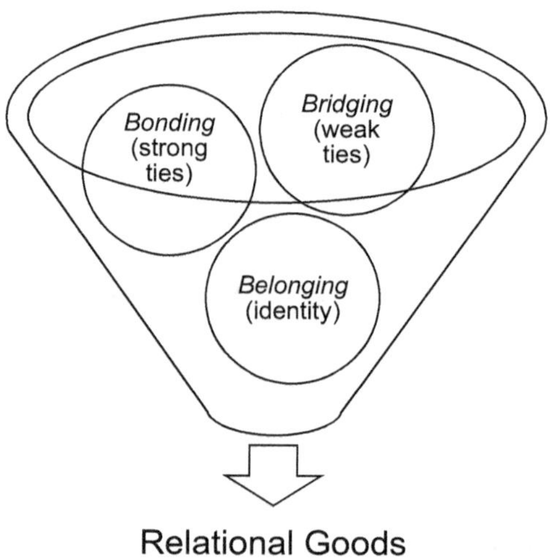

Figure 8.2 Relational goods as a product of bonding, bridging and belonging social capital.

Source: Own elaboration.

Using the business level as a specific example, what is known as organisational culture is considered relevant because the company's employees share a mission, vision, values, and a way of working. A shared identity potentially favours productivity, efficiency, and the group's human capital (instrumental output). However, it can also build a social climate appropriate for personal development and subjective well-being (expressive and intrinsic output) through common references.

As a recent research branch, identity economics considers how a personal identity conditions economic decision-making beyond the usual determinants. It is based on the evidence that individuals make decisions based on monetary incentives and their identity; more put, monetary incentives are constant, and people avoid actions that conflict with their self-concept. Moreover, they may manifest a clear trade-off with monetary benefits and opt for their identity values. The authors demonstrate the importance of identity in economics by showing how predictions change in classical principal-agent problems, preferences for redistribution and social identities and, in general, a wide range of economic behaviours (Shayo, 2009).

3 The paradoxes of the production function of relational goods

From the above, interpersonal encounters seem essential in generating relational goods. We have said that such an encounter occurs with strong ties (bonding social capital) with weak ties (bridging social capital), and it can also occur in the spontaneous interaction between individuals or in the perception of a group identity (linking and belonging social capital).

However, one of the characteristics of this type of good is "gratuitousness", which means that it emerges without instrumentality. This means the relationship cannot be interpreted as an instrument for goals outside itself. This is easy to understand when considering friendship, companionship, and love.

For this reason, it is worth delving deeper into what induces these feelings. In other words, why do we feel good around relational goods? Ideas such as trust or the degree of empathy and sympathy with the other person come up. Nevertheless, what are the factors that drive these elements at the same time? Then we go further, and values, disposition, and attitude come forth. It is logical to think that it will be easier to enjoy the relational good with a person in whom we perceive generosity, fairness, kindness, and sincerity (Nussbaum, 1995 [1986], p. 432; Gui, 2000, p. 155) than with another who is somehow surlier, whose degree of disposition is lower and who behaves in a somewhat utilitarian way or who instrumentalises personal relationships.

In this sense, we could affirm that the production of relational goods is rooted in universalistic values and attitudes that are prosocial because they somehow incline human beings towards cooperation, coordination, and contribution to the common good (Membiela-Pollán, 2013; Helliwell et al., 2017) (Figure 8.3).

In addition, there is a need for mutual understanding, and thus, sharing a specific system of values, ideas, and interests must be considered. Because "identification" with the other(s) plays a decisive role. This does not negate the above but operates in a complementary way. A subject can be kind, generous and honest and this context will always be helpful for the induction of relational good. However, some people will find it easier to produce and consume relational goods with others that are more akin to their cultural system and their tastes and interests because of this identification issue and the perception that interests are interchangeable and reliable (Sugden, 2005). In this case, utility functions are more interdependent, increasing communication and sympathy between individuals.

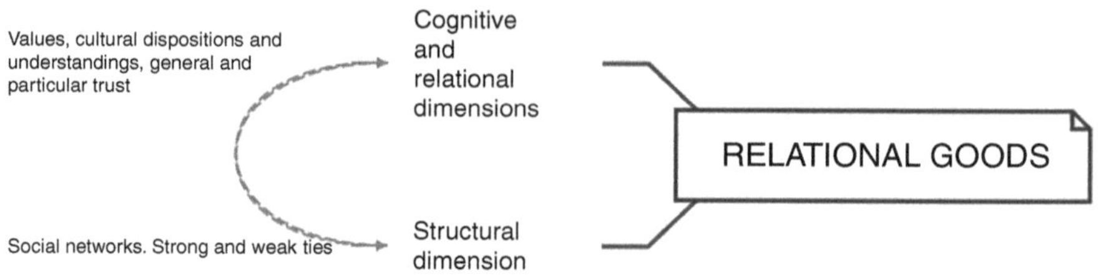

Figure 8.3 Relational goods as output or product of social capital's cognitive and structural dimensions.

Source: Own elaboration.

Several ideas come out from the above, all linked to social capital's structural and cognitive dimensions. The first is that relational goods emerge from the interpersonal encounter. The second is that values influence its emergence by the degree of prosociality and identification with the interests and cultural system of the other. Finally, the general structural network framework surrounding the individual ultimately shapes the possibility of producing and consuming relational goods. A trusting society and group facilitate the production of relational goods.

4 A foray into the paradoxes of the economics of happiness

At this point, we are touching on something essential. If we go back again to Aristotle, happiness is considered to be the supreme good of the human being (*EN*, I, 2) and the ultimate goal of all human action. Naturally, this topic has been the subject of analysis in various disciplines. It has been a central issue for philosophers, writers and researchers in psychology, sociology, economics, and health sciences (Diener, 2000, p. 34).

Social scientists use a variety of indicators to describe the well-being and quality of life of individuals, communities, and society, depending on their approach and theoretical orientations. To avoid expanding on the obvious, we touch on the background of any human action and, ultimately, the meaning of existence.

Although influenced by objective factors, happiness is subjective, and its definition and measurement entail some problems. Theorists disagree about its meaning, as it can refer to pleasure, life satisfaction, positive emotions, a meaningful life or a sense of fulfilment. Economists who are part of the so-called Economics of Happiness choose to avoid a priori definitions that presuppose what individuals need to be happy, such as the calculation of the HDI, and prefer to measure it by giving individuals a leading role through a survey study of so-called revealed Subjective Well-being, to determine which factors directly influence it.

Revealed subjective well-being (RSW) is the degree to which individuals judge the overall quality of their life as favourable (Veenhoven, 1991). An overall self-assessment of a person's life can present two significant measurement methods: experiential methods, which focus on recording positive and negative emotions, and evaluative methods, which focus on the overall judgement of the personal situation (Diener, 2009, 2012). Both sources are interrelated and complementary.

The former, known as hedonic, focuses on the moment's feelings (positive and negative). Conversely, the evaluative ones focus on the evaluation that subjects make of these experiences over long periods; that is, they introduce the cognitive analysis of the perceived experiences. Thus, it is necessary to distinguish the experience of utility, satisfaction, pleasure, or pain from global evaluations of happiness or satisfaction (Kahneman et al., 2004). The latter emphasises a mode of realising human potential (Henderson & Knight, 2012) and is a form of balance or skill, while the former or experiential is associated with a perception of life flow, relief or joy that places the subject outside their problems (Waterman et al., 2008). They are different subjective states with specificities but sensitively linked since the development of potentials is related to positive experiences (Delle Fave et al., 2011). However, both are diversely affected by personal and socioeconomic variables.

If we adopt a temporal dimension, both modes of measurement can be considered in a continuum from the immediate assessment of an experience or emotional state to the assessment of life satisfaction considering the long term or life in general. In order to delimit them conceptually, we can establish a threefold division of the set of indicators (Table 8.2) according to the time reference and the characteristics of the questions used in each indicator.

Experiential indicators consider immediacy or periods no longer than a day and focus on sets of positive or negative feelings; evaluative indicators consider the whole of life or particular domains of life without defined time references. Finally, the eudaimonic ones, like the previous ones, do not delimit time, but in this case, they allude to an evaluation of life in terms of meaning or personal fulfilment (Nikolova & Graham, 2020; Pena-López and de Juan, 2024). In short, although it is a subjective experience, it is measurable and opens up a crucial field of research into its determinants.

4.1 Economics and revealed subjective well-being

Economic studies have renewed their interest in "happiness", mainly because of a paradox between improving living conditions and increasing unhappiness in affluent societies. This paradox breaks one of the basic assumptions of microeconomics,

Table 8.2 Indicators of subjective well-being

	Definition	*Measurement*
Experiential indicators hedonic	Perception of positive and negative feelings on the previous day	Affective-emotional aspects associated with particular activities
Evaluative indicators	Life satisfaction	Satisfaction with life in general and life sub-domains: health, work, income, environment, children
Eudaimonic indicators	Perception of meaning in one's existence	Vital rewards of certain activities linked to self-fulfilment

Source: Own elaboration.

namely that of "non-satiability", from which we would derive that any increase in purchasing power is correlated with improvements in subjective well-being.

The "Happiness Paradox" or "Easterlin Paradox" challenges the idea that material prosperity guarantees happiness by highlighting the lack of connection between rising per capita income and the evolution of overall subjective well-being (Bartolini et al., 2016).

In 1974, Easterlin examined the relationship between income and happiness using survey data from 19 countries between 1946 and 1970. His results, corroborated in subsequent research (Frey & Stutzer, 2002; Blachflower & Oswald, 2004), indicate that, although within a country and at a given point in time, there is a positive correlation between income and happiness, this association is not consistent when comparing different countries (Figure 8.4). Additionally, over time, variation in income has little impact on people's happiness (Easterlin, 1974).

Then, "Happiness Paradox" highlights that, over a lifetime, income and happiness do not vary together, showing a low correlation (Bruni, 2008). The study discrepancy persists, especially in the association between income and happiness across nations. Although people with higher incomes tend to be happier than those with lower incomes, a general increase in income does not guarantee greater happiness beyond a certain threshold (Frey & Stutzer, 2002).

The open debate in the Economics of Happiness takes up the idea that happiness is not always a synonymous with economic income and growth. This reconsideration of elements unrelated to material well-being involves questioning basic assumptions of Economics (Bartolini, 2007; Becchetti et al., 2023), in

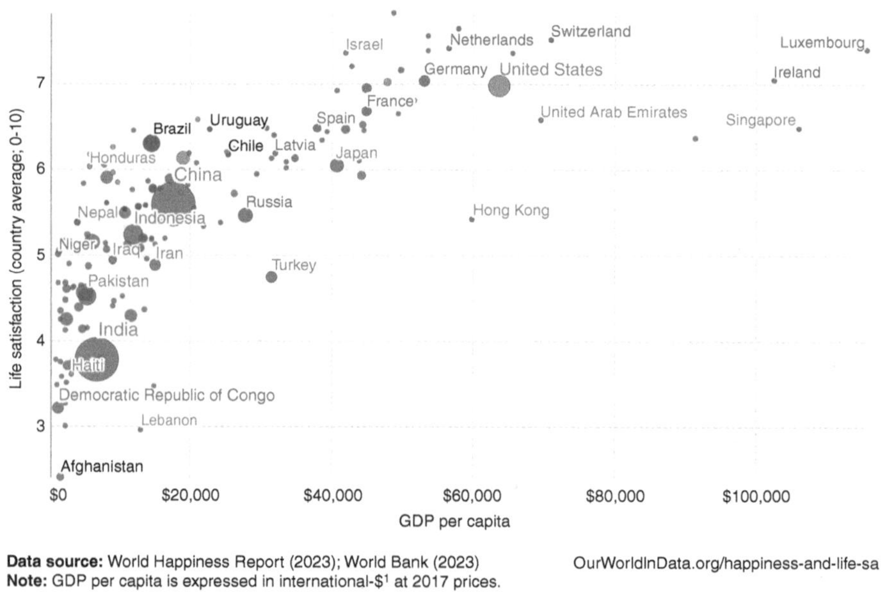

Figure 8.4 Income and happiness 2022.

Source: Own elaboration from data https://ourworldindata.org/grapher/gdp-vs-happiness?xScale=linear.

particular, neoclassical postulates rooted in traditional economic theory, which assumes that subjective well-being depends on income levels (Membiela-Pollán et al., 2019a). Many theoretical proposals explain the paradox mentioned above, and we will briefly review them before focusing on the interrelationship between relational dimensions and happiness. Although innovative, this perspective has its roots in authors such as Genovesi and Verri in the 18th century, who considered economics the "science of public happiness" (Becchetti et al., 2010a, p. 390).

The explanatory hypotheses of the Paradox of Happiness can be classified into four main groups: (1) relative position theory, (2) adaptation theory, (3) theory of the diminishing marginal utility of money, (4) personality theory. In contrast to these, relational goods could offer an alternative since they influence subjective well-being differently from income.

1. The relative position hypothesis focuses on the existence of a social reference system to evaluate one's well-being. For this point of view, subjective well-being does not depend directly on income or consumption but on the relative position with others (Duesenberry, 1952). Social comparison, influenced by norms and standards, generates positional competition so that an increase in income increases happiness, but if everyone increases at the same time, happiness remains stable (Bartolini, 2007, p. 347; Dolan et al., 2007, p. 98). Formally, as we illustrate in expression (1), the utility of an individual would depend on his income and, at the same time, on the relation between his income and an income adopted as a reference (Y*), the general income of society or, as is usually the case, that of the social environment that the individual considers as belonging to ("keeping up with the Joneses"):

$$U_t = \left(u_1\left(Y_t\right) + u_2\left(Y_t / Y_t^*\right)\right) \tag{1}$$

2. The adaptation hypothesis holds that improvements in objective circumstances have temporary effects on subjective well-being due to adaptation (Brickman & Campbell, 1971; Bruni, 2008, p. 82). The "hedonic treadmill" assumes an adaptation to the new situation and a reformulation, after some time, of aspirations that counteracts the initial positive effects (Kahneman, 2004).
3. The diminishing marginal utility of money hypothesis states that additional income is valuable in overcoming poverty, but marginal returns diminish once a certain level is reached (Duesenberry, 1952). The latter applies to income and what income can buy (Iglesias Vázquez et al., 2013). In developed societies, where material satiation has been achieved, the positive impact of income increases on welfare is limited.
4. The personality hypothesis argues that subjective well-being depends mainly on the genetic dispositions to happiness or unhappiness in the individual's personality (Lykken & Tellegen, 1996; Haller and Hadler, 2006, p. 172; Anglim et al., 2020). Accepting this perspective implies that happiness remains virtually constant throughout the life cycle, only being affected in the short term by changes in variables such as income and health.

4.2 Relational goods and intrinsic well-being

In this case we are dealing with a hypothesis of a different nature related to the particularities of the production function of relational goods and the effects of these on welfare. People's lives go far beyond their income and consumption. Individuals have families, children, partners, friends and colleagues, a job, neighbours, and hobbies.

The theory of social capital and relational goods have their place in explaining Easterlin's paradox. Both concepts concern sociability and, as we have already analysed, are linked to the production of a double output: the economic-instrumental (stable socioeconomic cooperation) and the expressive-intrinsic (subjective well-being).

This relational explanation highlights the importance of changes in "sociability" in developed societies. As income has risen, there has been a deterioration in the social fabric and a considerable decline in the production and consumption of relational goods (communicative and affective aspects of interpersonal relationships such as friendship, companionship, mutual love, and social approval). This relational failure is attributed to a range of reasons, including intra-economic, extra-economic, and cultural, as well as changes in social norms, customs, and even social structures. This decline has an effect in subjective well-being at individual and global levels.

The relational hypothesis's theoretical basis focuses on the trade-off between work, excessive preoccupation with income, and time devoted to interpersonal relationships. A disproportionate dedication to achieving material goals detriments other non-material aspects of life, such as family and health.

The relational hypothesis does not reject the theories put forward; they can be considered complementary (Pena-López et al., 2017). Positional theory suggests that income increases only raise welfare when the reference group does not experience a similar increase. Constant social comparison and positional competition generate a continuous striving for higher income, contributing to "overwork". In addition, hedonic adaptation drives changing aspirations and a greater focus on material goods, creating dependency and undervaluing relational goods.

However, as psychology has shown, the relevance of non-instrumental relationality (relational goods) for well-being and happiness, in line with studies of the economics of happiness, is crucial. Some experts argue that people's intrinsic needs have been underestimated and play a more significant role than expected. Relationality is presented as a basic human need and crucial for well-being (Ryan & Deci, 2001), and "relational goods" are highlighted as a critical variable in the role of happiness (Becchetti et al., 2020).

The historical lack of attention to this aspect is attributed to the tendency towards individualism in Western societies, which often lose sight of the importance of sociability in subjective well-being. Although many happiness studies do not explicitly consider relational variables, research demonstrates the influence of socio-demographic factors on intrinsic sociability and subjective well-being. Thus, for example, well-being tends to be higher in married people and decreases in those who declare themselves separated or widowed. Furthermore, the presence of children, close friendships and strong family ties are positively associated with well-being (Helliwell & Putnam, 2004; Alesina & Giuliano, 2010). The importance of time spent with family and friends and social activities in happiness and life satisfaction is highlighted (Oshio, 2017). Participation in religious, sporting, and charitable organisations – all of which are expressive-intrinsic – is also positively linked to subjective well-being.

In the same vein, Kahneman et al. (2004) emphasise that shared activities generate greater satisfaction than those performed alone. Moreover, psychologists consistently observe that happier people show positive social relationships (Diener et al., 2003).

Concretising the reasoning behind the relational hypothesis, relational goods, such as creative activities and interpersonal relationships, offer long-term utility. However, the higher cost of production hampers their consumption (long-term investments) and competition with comfort and positional goods. Overvaluation of the latter leads to inefficient resource allocation, material accumulation, and wealth destruction, resulting in increased social unrest (Membiela-Pollán et al., 2019a, 2019b).

An apparent "optimising" behaviour can lead to a suboptimal outcome. This arises from recognising that "other goods" not strictly associated with material wealth might hold greater relative significance than initially presumed. Allocating more time to family life and health could enhance subjective well-being. To reflect this interrelation, we can amend the preceding expression as follows (2), where l represents the time allocated to work, and Z denotes a vector comprising socioeconomic and demographic variables:

$$U_t = \left(u_1\left(Y_t\right) + u_2\left(Y_t / Y_t^*\right)\right) + u_3\left(T - l_t, Z_t\right) \tag{2}$$

One possible explanation for the trade-off between material and relational goods lies in the nature of the latter. Since relational goods can be considered public goods, they tend to be under-supplied, leading individuals to undervalue them. This phenomenon represents a characteristic market failure, which can be conceptualised using the prisoner's dilemma and mitigated through the implementation of social institutions (Frey & Stutzer, 2005).

Simultaneously, it is essential to note that the decision-making process often exhibits a bias towards overestimating the satisfaction derived from extrinsic desires, such as income, while underestimating the impact of intrinsic sources of satisfaction, like family and hobbies. This bias occurs due to various distorting factors. Unlike relational goods, extrinsic desires, such as income and material possessions, are subject to unpredictable adjustment processes post-decision-making. Additionally, decisions tend to be influenced by psychological impulses favouring extrinsic goals over intrinsic ones, as intrinsic goals often involve long-term benefits. Furthermore, cultural and contextual factors, such as conspicuous consumption and social trends, can influence decision-making. In Western cultures, decisions based on extrinsic factors are typically more socially acceptable than those based on intrinsic factors (Becchetti et al., 2013).

In sum, it is foreseeable that the consumption of relational goods is inefficiently low; that is, it would be feasible to increase well-being by substituting income with relational goods. The relational hypothesis addresses the Easterlin Paradox by highlighting the importance of sociability for subjective well-being. It warns that the decline in interpersonal relationships is a relevant cause of societal malaise despite economic growth and objective improvements in material living conditions.

5 Subjective well-being and relational goods in Spanish society: an empirical proposal

To illustrate and deepen the relational hypothesis in this chapter, we propose a study carried out for Spanish society on the determinants of revealed subjective well-being. In this case, we introduced among the explanatory variables the individual social capital indicators analysed in Chapter 5, where we had already derived the distinction between an individual indicator of instrumental social capital and one of expressive social capital.[1] The latter is probably the best indicator of relational goods so that we can identify the weight of this variable on subjective well-being and, at the same time, the interrelation with other variables (Pena-López et al., 2017).

Regarding the choice of the dependent variable, the survey included two ordinal questions that followed the World Values Survey standard. In the first, participants were asked: "In general, would you say that you are…?" with the options of very happy, fairly happy, not very happy, or not happy. In the second question, respondents were asked to rate their overall life satisfaction on a scale of 1–10. Life satisfaction has a more cognitive focus than happiness, as it involves the positive appraisal of various aspects of life, such as family, work, health, and friends (Diener, 2013). This subjective appraisal results from the comparison between individual expectations and achievements, encompassing micro-social (marital status, family, social support) and macro-social (income, culture) factors (Veenhoven, 1994). It is a classical evaluative measurement where individuals adopt a long-term perspective.

For the independent variables, we included personal networks (their accessibility and mobilisation), which we studied in Chapter 4, and other indicators of social capital, such as membership in associations and different socio-demographic and macro-social variables. As we have already seen, we determined individual social capital endowments through the position and resource generators by distinguishing those relationships that can be classified as expressive and instrumental.

The analysis of endowments already reveals a crucial result: the existence of a trade-off between the endowment of instrumental and expressive relations (see Table 8.3). That is, a more significant investment in the more typically instrumental relations linked to status entails a form of "Baumol cost disease", a reduction in the provision of relational goods that become comparatively "expensive", practically a "luxury good" (Becchetti & Santoro, 2007). Explained in more everyday terminology, the pursuit of status and increased income entails instrumentalising most relationships or increasing the endowment of instrumental relationships. The relative scarcity of relational goods and the difficulty involved in their production make them "comparatively expensive".

Table 8.3 Correlations of individual social capital indicators

	Accessibility	Mobilisation		Associationism	
		Instrumental	*Expressive*	*Secular associat.*	*Religious associat.*
Socioeconomic variables					
Municipality size	0.03	0.097**	0.013	0.021	0.022
Length of residency	−0.177**	−0.139**	−0.207**	−0.131**	0.033
Work activity	0.241**	0.137**	0.243**	0.215**	−0.058**
Age	−0.165**	−0.153**	−0.267**	−0.085**	0.084**
Sex	0.064**	0.045**	0.050**	0.106**	−0.013
Marital status	0.075**	−0.009	0.052**	0.079**	0.003
Number of household members	0.135**	0.087**	0.176**	0.068**	−0.024
Level studies	0.368**	0.296**	0.328**	0.247**	0.050**
Income	0.263**	0.175**	0.183**	0.250**	0.050*
Well-being indicators					
Life satisfaction	0.071**	0.120**	0.161**	0.050**	0.064**
Physical health	0.095**	0.120**	0.208**	0.056**	0.023
Mental health	0.041*	0.094**	0.117**	0.046**	0.067**
Subjective well-being (Happiness)	0.071**	0.088**	0.157**	0.058**	0.049**
General social capital indicators					
Generalised trust	0.152**	0.127**	0.521**	0.131**	0.040*
Safety in residency	0.058**	0.046**	0.106**	0.015	0.022
Security at night	0.130**	0.107**	0.162**	0.072**	−0.002
Individual social capital indicators					
Instrumental mobilisation	0.484**	1	−0.258**	0.187**	0.113**
Expressive mobilisation	0.430**	−0.258**	1	0.201**	0.074**
Secular-ideological associationism	0.283**	0.187**	0.201**	1	−0.155**
Religious-expressive associationism	0.168**	0.113**	0.074**	−0.155**	1
Accessibility	1	0.484**	0.430**	0.283**	0.168**

*Significant at 0.1, **significant at the 0.05.

Source: Own elaboration.

We are now entering the realm of functional relationships with subjective well-being. The regression analysis showed that subjective well-being is affected, as expected, along with the personal networks of relationships with the socioeconomic variables. Both the networks of expressive ties and the networks of weak-instrumental ties available and membership of the two forms of associationism are relevant.

Thus, the regression conducted on the response to the question on the level of happiness using ordered logit showed results that align with our starting position on the importance of relationality:

$$SW_i = \alpha + \beta_1 X_{1it} + \beta_2 X_{2it} + \cdots + \varepsilon_{it}$$

The high weight of the coefficients of expressive relationships and the low explanatory power of income are noteworthy. Relationality has a decisive influence on the levels of subjective well-being, including associative membership (see Table 8.4).

Table 8.4 Social capital and subjective well-being

Ordered Logit, using observations 1-3401
Dependent variable: happiness

	Model I	*Model II*	*Model III*
Municipality size	−0.003844		
General trust	0.22851**		
Physical health	0.180249 ***	0.186744***	
Mental health	0.297311***	0.306433***	
Night safety	0.326940***	0.379684***	0.47413***
Labour activity	0.105664	0.094945	0.143493**
Age	−1.13176***	−1.03320***	−1.24177***
Age2	0.1411926***	0.130975***	0.1536***
Sex	−0.0759093		
Marital status	0.938830***	0.822170***	0.85424***
Level of studies	0.043639	0.081804***	0.09771***
Instrumental mobilisation	0.309915**	0.12336	0.24979***
Expressive mobilisation	0.347824**	0.24546***	0.38556***
Secular-ideological association	0.145322**	0.091030	0.084919
Religious-expressive association	0.249454 *	0.130059	0.221574**
Accessibility	−0.283504 *		
Income	0.0236896		
Cut1	−1.31804***	−0.885972***	−4.15225***
Cut2	1.38679***	1.7425***	−1.70985***
Cut3	5.84935***	6.2217***	2.3585***
Pseudo-R^2 McFadden	0.3851	0.1603	0.102
Log-likelihood	−1675.784	−2288.910	−2466.957
Schwarz criterion	3,506.948	4,699.070	5,046.508
Akaike criteria	3,391.569	4,607.820	4,967.337
Crit. Hannan-Quinn	3,433.574	4,640.514	4,995.693

Source: Own elaboration.

As its results summarise, this research's interest lies in assessing the explanatory power of relational goods. Specifically, it aims to test the hypothesis that individuals who engage more with relational goods or effectively address the challenges linked to their production experience higher levels of subjective well-being. Moreover, by comparing the explanatory ability of income-related variables, the study aims to offer evidence regarding the constrained substitutability between material goods associated with income and relational goods.

Hence, income, educational attainment, or labour market participation are less impactful. In contrast, relational stability (represented by strong ties or bonding) and feelings of security (associated with group relational goods or a sense of belonging) exhibit vital significance. Notably, general trust, seen as a perception of security within the environment, has demonstrated considerable influence in prior research (Rodríguez-Pose & Von Berlepsch, 2012; Righi & Masserini, 2023).

Expressive mobilisation, dominated by non-instrumental relational assets of social capital, has a relevant causal relationship with subjective well-being. At the same time, instrumental relations, mainly composed of weak ties or bridging social capital, also have a significant influence. Only expressive associations (sports organisations, cultural organisations, and NGOs) are significant if we focus on associations. Political, trade union and professional organisations are irrelevant. This result is consistent with Rodriguez-Pose and Von Berlepsch's (2012) work on the negative nature of interactions in Olsonian groups (associations that can act as lobbies). At the same time, the models point to the influence of variables with which there is an apparent relationship (perception of safety and health). These results can also be interpreted in terms of capabilities. The variables that show an apparent influence imply more personal autonomy and control of the social environment.

Consequently, the empirical analysis of Spanish society underscores the relational hypothesis of the Easterlin paradox. Specifically, what we have identified as relational goods – like family stability, participation in associations, feelings of security, and trust in the environment – emerge as strongly significant. Individuals who engage more in relational goods or effectively address the challenges related to their cultivation tend to exhibit higher levels of revealed subjective satisfaction. Notably, these satisfaction levels are largely independent of income in the Spanish context, but the production of this kind of relational goods has a trade-off with instrumental ones.

5 Recapping

In this chapter, we have introduced the concept of relational good. It tries to capture the communicative or affective dimension of interpersonal relationships. Examples of relational goods are friendship, mutual love, companionship, belonging to a group, recognition, identity, and social approval. These goods, with unique attributes, are characterised by authenticity and absence of instrumentality and will not be equated with the relationship itself but emerge from it. They can be defined as the expressive-intrinsic dimension of social capital. Nonetheless, the link between the two concepts – relational goods and social capital – is neither unique nor unidirectional. Relational goods are an output of social capital because they arise from interpersonal relationships (structural dimension) and depend on values, disposition, attitude, and trust (cognitive dimension). At the same time, they are an input of social capital because they reinforce its stock and accumulation, and they can also be qualified as an asset because they favour cooperation and socioeconomic exchange.

The features mentioned above imply the need to study the scenarios in which they are produced and consumed, both in the case of bonding social capital (social network of strong ties) and bridging social capital (social network of weak ties). Strong ties, or domestic-expressive networks, play a significant role in their production and consumption, but weak ties can play a prominent role depending on the circumstances of each individual. Similarly, linking social capital covers a relevant role that could be identified as a relational good when we refer to the influence on the individual of notions such as identity and belonging, which we could also call belonging.

One of the most essential effects of relational goods relates to their relationship with subjective well-being. Relational goods are components of the good life and society (Donati, 2019). In this context, we have introduced the fundamental concepts of the so-called Economics of Happiness. This branch of research criticises the reductionism of the neoclassical mainstream when considering the determinants of individuals' subjective well-being. Specifically, the so-called Easterlin paradox, which occupies a central position, evidences the absence of a clear link between income progression and improvements in satisfaction revealed at the aggregate level, calling into question the assumption of non-satiety. A wide range of explanatory hypotheses have been proposed, from relative income to the hedonic treadmill. In this chapter, taking up previous research, we have presented the "relational hypothesis", which is complementary to the previous ones. It is linked to the theory of social capital and the concept of relational good, and its theoretical basis focuses on the trade-off between work, excessive concern for income, and time devoted to interpersonal relationships. The disproportionate dedication to achieving monetary and material goals and their translation into purely instrumental relationships is detrimental to other non-material aspects of life, such as family and health and, in relational terms, expressive relationships, that is, relational goods. The results of the empirical study for the Spanish case are evidence in this sense.

Note

1 Logically, the data source is the same as the one used in Chapter 5, so for simplicity's sake we do not describe the survey characteristics again.

Bibliography

Acket, S., Borsenberger, M., Dickes, P., & Sarracino, F. (2011). Measuring and validating social cohesion: A bottom-up approach (Working paper no 2011–08, CEPS/INSTEAD).

Adam, F., & Roncevic, B. (2003). Social capital: Recent debates and research trends. *Social Science Information, 42*(2), 151–183.

Addis, E., & Joxhe, M. (2017). Gender gaps in social capital: A theoretical interpretation of evidence from Italy. *Feminist Economics, 23*(2), 146–171.

Adler, P. A., & Kwon, S. W. (2002). Social capital: Prospects for a new concept. *The Academy of Management Review, 27*(1), 17–40.

Ahn, T. K., & Ostrom, E. (2008). Social capital and collective action. In D. Castiglione, J. van Deth, & G. Wolleb (Eds.), *The handbook of social capital* (pp. 70–100). Oxford: Oxford University Press.

Akçay, S. (2006). Corruption and human development. *Cato Journal, 26*(1), 29–48.

Akerlof, G. A., & Kranton, R. E. (2010). *Identity economics: How our identities shape our work, wages, and well-being*. Princeton, NJ: Princeton University Press.

Akram, W., & Kumar, R. (2017). A study on positive and negative effects of social media on society. *International Journal of Computer Sciences and Engineering, 5*(10), 347–354.

Aktipis, A., & Kurzban, R. (2005). Is homo economicus extinct? In R. Koppl (Ed.), *Evolutionary psychology and economic theory* (pp. 135–154). Stamford: JAI Press Inc.

Aldrich, D. P. (2017). The importance of social capital in building community resilience. In W. Yan & W. Galloway (Eds.), *Rethinking resilience adaptation and transformation in a time of change* (pp. 357–364). Berlin: Springer.

Alesina, A., & Giuliano, P. (2010). The power of the family. *Journal of Economic Growth, 15*(2), 93–125.

Allen, T. D., Herst, D. E. L., Bruck, C. S., & Sutton, M. (2000). Consequences associated with work-to-family conflict: A review and agenda for future research. *Journal of Occupational Health Psychology, 5*(2), 278–308.

Almond, G. A., & Verba, S. (1963). *The civic culture: Political attitudes and democracy in five nations*. Princeton, NJ: Princeton University Press.

Anderson, E. (1993). *Value in ethics and economics*. Cambridge, MA: Harvard University Press.

Anderson, E. (2001). Unstrapping the straitjacket of preference. *Economics and Philosophy, 17*, 21–38.

Anderson, E., & Jap, S. (2005). The dark side of close relationships. *MIT Sloan Management Review, 46*(3), 75–82.

Andersson, A. B. (2021). Social capital and leaving the nest: Channels and housing tenures. *Social Networks, 65*, 8–18.

Andreoni, A. (1990). Impure altruism and donations to public goods: A theory of warm glow giving. *Economic Journal, 100*, 464–477.

Andriani, L., & Christoforou, A. (2016). Social capital: A roadmap of theoretical and empirical contributions and limitations. *Journal of Economic Issues, 50*(1), 4–22.

Anglim, J., Horwood, S., Smillie, L. D., Marrero, R. J., & Wood, J. K. (2020). Predicting psychological and subjective well-being from personality: A meta-analysis. *Psychological Bulletin, 146*(4), 279.

Anheier, H. K. (2014). Civil society research: Ten years on. *Journal of Civil Society, 10*(4), 335–339.

Anheier, H. K., & Stares, S. (2002). Introducing the Global Civil Society Index. In M. Glasius, M. Kaldor & H. Anheier (Eds), *Global Civil Society 2002* (pp. 241–254). Oxford: Oxford University Press.

Antoci, A., Bonelli, L., Paglieri, F., Reggiani, T., & Sabatini, F. (2019). Civility and trust in social media. *Journal of Economic Behavior & Organization, 160*, 83–99.

Argentiero, A., Cerqueti, R., & Sabatini, F. (2021). Does social capital explain the Solow residual? A DSGE approach. *Structural Change and Economic Dynamics, 58*, 35–53.

Aristóteles. (2004). *Ética a Nicómaco*. Madrid: Alianza Editorial.

Aristotle. (s.f.). *Politics, Book 1, section 1253a*. Recuperado el 12 de abril de 2021, de www.perseus.tufts.edu.

Arrow, K. J. (1972). Gifts and exchanges. *Philosophy and Public Affairs, 1*(4), 343–362.

Arrow, K. J. (2000). Observations on social capital. In P. Dasgupta & I. Serageldin (Eds.), *Social capital: A multifaceted perspective* (pp. 3–5). Washington, DC: World Bank.

Arrow, K. J., & Borzekowski, R. (2004). Limited network connections and the distribution of wages. *Finance and Economics Discussion Series 2004-41*. Board of Governors of the Federal Reserve System (U.S.).

Arrow, K. J., & Debreu, D. (1954). Existence of an equilibrium for a competitive economy. *Econometrica, 22*(3), 265–290.

Atkinson, A. B., & Morelli, S. (2014). *Chartbook of economic inequality*. Recuperado de http://www.chartbookofeconomicinequality.com/

Ayala Espino, J. (2005). *Instituciones y economía: una introducción al neoinstitucionalismo económico*. México: Fondo de Cultura Económica.

Aybas, Y. C., & Jackson, M. O. (2021). *Social learning and homophily-induced herding*. Stanford: mimeo Stanford.

Bacharach, M., & Gambetta, D. (2001). Trust in signs. In K. Cook (Ed.), *Trust in Society* (pp. 148–184). Nueva York: Russell Sage Foundation.

Bae, S. M. (2019). The relationship between smartphone use for communication, social capital, and subjective well-being in Korean adolescents: Verification using multiple latent growth modeling. *Children and Youth Services Review, 96*, 93–99.

Baker, W. E. (1984). The social structure of a national securities market. *American Journal of Sociology, 89*(4), 775–811.

Baker, W. E. (1990). Market networks and corporate behavior. *American Journal of Sociology, 96*(3), 589–625.

Bankston, C. L., & Zhou, M. (2002). Social capital as process: The meanings and problems of a theoretical metaphor? *Sociological Inquiry, 72*(2), 285–317.

Barro, R. (1997). *Determinants of economic growth: A cross-country empirical study*. Cambridge: The MIT Press.

Barro, R. (2001). Human capital and growth. *American Economic Review, 91*(2), 12–17.

Bartolini, S. (2007). Why are people so unhappy? Why do they strive so hard for money? Competing explanations of the broken promises of economic growth. In L. Bruni & P. L.

Porta (Eds.), *Handbook of economics and happiness* (pp. 337–364). Cheltenham: Edward Elgar Publishing.

Bartolini, S., Bilancini, E., & Sarracino, F. (2016). Social capital predicts happiness: World-wide evidence from time series. In S. Bartolini, E. Bilancini, L. Bruni, & P. Porta (Eds.), *Policies for happiness* (pp. 175–198). Oxford: Oxford University Press.

Batson, C. D. (2011). *Altruismo en Humanos*. Nueva York: Oxford Prensa Universitaria.

Baycan, T., & Öner, Ö. (2023). The dark side of social capital: A contextual perspective. *The Annals of Regional Science, 70*(3), 779–798.

Beasley-Murray, J. (2000). Value and capital in Bourdieu and Marx. In N. Brown & I. Szeman (Eds.), *Pierre Bourdieu: Fieldwork in culture*. Lanham, MD: Rowman & Littlefield Publishers.

Becchetti, L., Bruni, L., & Zamagni, S. (2010a). *Microeconomia*. il Mulino.

Becchetti, L., Bruni, L., Carmelli, M., Zamagni, S. (2020). *Manual de economía civil*. Bilbao, España: Desclée de Brouwer.

Becchetti, L., Cermelli, M., & Rosa, D. (2023). *Three times more than money: Generativity, relational goods and life satisfaction*. Durham, NC: Research Square.

Becchetti, L., Corrado, L., & Conzo, P. (2013). Sociability, altruism and subjective well-being (AICCON Working Paper No. 120. Associazione italiana per la cultura della cooperazione e del Non Profit).

Becchetti, L., Degli Antoni, G., & Faillo, M. (2010b). Let's meet up! The role of relational goods in promoting cooperation. *The Journal of Socio-Economics, 39*(6), 661–669.

Becchetti, L., Pelloni, A., & Rossetti, F. (2008). Relational goods, sociability, and happiness (Working Paper No. 39, Department of Communication, University of Teramo, Teramo).

Becchetti, L., & Santoro, M. (2007). The income–unhappiness Paradox: A relational goods/Baumol disease explanation. In L. Bruni & P. L. Porta (Eds.), *Handbook on the economics of happiness* (capítulo 13). Cheltenham: Edward Elgar Publishing.

Becker, G. (1957). *The economics of discrimination*. Chicago, IL: University of Chicago Press.

Becker, G. (1964). *Human capital: A theoretical and empirical analysis, with special reference to education*. Londres: National Bureau of Economic Research.

Becker, G. (1968). Crime and punishment: An economic approach. *The Journal of Political Economy, 76*, 169–217.

Becker, G. (1974). A theory of social interactions. *Journal of Political Economy, 82*(6), 1063–1093.

Becker, G. (1976). *The economic approach to human behavior*. Chicago, IL: University of Chicago Press.

Becker, G. (1981). *A treatise on the family*. Cambridge, MA: Harvard University Press.

Becker, G. (1987). *Tratado sobre la familia*. Madrid: Alianza Universidad.

Becker, G. (1996). *Accounting for tastes*. Cambridge, MA: Harvard University Press.

Belliveau, M. A., O'Reilly, C. A., & Wade, J. B. (1996). Social capital at the top: Effects of social similarity and status on CEO compensation. *Academy of Management Journal, 39*(6), 1568–1593.

Bennett, T., Savage, M., Silva, E. B., Warde, A., Gayo-Cal, M., & Wright, D. (2008). *Class, culture, distinction*. Londres: Routledge.

Berger, P., & Luckmann, T. (1966). *The social construction of reality: A treatise in the sociology of knowledge*. New York: First Anchor Books.

Bertrand, M., & Duflo, E. (2016). Field experiments on discrimination (Working Paper No. 22014). National Bureau of Economic Research.

Bertrand, M., & Duflo, E. (2017). Field experiments on discrimination. In A. V. Banerjee & E. Duflo (Eds.), *Handbook of economic field experiments* (Vol. 1, pp. 309–393). Amsterdam, Netherlands: North-Holland.

Bezanson, K. (2006). *Gender, the state and social reproduction*. Toronto: University of Toronto Press.

Bhaskar, R. (2008). *A realist theory of science*. London and New York: Routledge.

Bian, M., & Leung, L. (2015). Linking loneliness, shyness, smartphone addiction symptoms, and patterns of smartphone use to social capital. *Social Science Computer Review, 33*(1), 61–79.

Bjørnskov, Ch. (2006). The many facets of social capital. *European Journal of Political Economy, 22*(1), 22–40.

Bjørnskov, Ch., & Svendsen, G. T. (2003). Measuring social capital – Is there a single underlying explanation? (Working Paper No. 5, Department of Economics. University of Aarhus, Aarhus School of Business).

Blanchflower, D. G., & Oswald, A. J. (2004). Well-being over time in Britain and the USA. *Journal of Public Economics, 88*, 1359–1386.

Blaug, M. (1980). *La metodología de la economía*. Madrid: Alianza.

Bobbio, N., & García, L. S. (2001). *Estado, gobierno, sociedad* (pp. 39–67). Burgos, España: Movimiento Cultural Cristiano.

Böhm-Bawerk, E. V. (1889). *The positive theory of capital*. New York: Stechert.

Boix, C., & Posner, D. N. (1998). Social capital: Explaining its origins and effects on government performance. *British Journal of Political Science, 28*, 686–693.

Bolancé, C., Caïs, J., & Torrente, D. (2018). Trust in times of economic crisis in Spain: Paradoxes for social capital theory (IREA Working Papers No. 201830). University of Barcelona, Research Institute of Applied Economics.

Bolte, L., Immorlica, N., & Jackson, M. O. (2020). The role of referrals in immobility, inequality, and inefficiency in labor markets. *Papers*, 2012.15753. arXiv.org

Bolton, R. (2006). Habermas's theory of communicative action and the theory of social capital (In Department of Economics Working Papers. Department of Economics, Williams College).

Botterman, S., Hooghe, M., & Reeskens, T. (2012). 'One size fits all'? An empirical study into the multidimensionality of social cohesion indicators in Belgian local communities. *Urban Studies, 49*(1), 185–202.

Boulding, K. (1973). *The economy of love and fear: A preface to grants economics*. Belmont, CA: Wadsworth Publishing Company.

Bourdieu, P. (1980). Le capital social: Notes provisoires. *Actes de la Recherche en Sciences Sociales, 31*, 2–25.

Bourdieu, P. (1983). Economic capital, cultural capital, social capital. *Soziale-Welt, Supplement, 2*(13), 183–198.

Bourdieu, P. (1984). *Die feinen Unterschiede: Kritik der gesellschaftlichen Urteilskraft*. Frankfurt/Main: Suhrkamp.

Bourdieu, P. (1986). The forms of capital. In J. Richardson (Ed.), *Handbook of theory and research for the sociology of education* (pp. 241–258). New York: Greenwood.

Bourdieu, P. (1991). *Language and symbolic power*. Cambridge, MA: Harvard University Press.

Bourdieu, P. (2001). The forms of capital. In M. Granovetter & R. Swedberg (Eds.), *The sociology of economic life* (2nd ed., pp. 97–111). Oxford: Westview Press.

Bourdieu, P. (2003). *Las estructuras sociales de la economía*. Barcelona: Anagrama.

Bourdieu, P., & Passeron, J. (1970). *La Reproduction*. Paris: Les Editions de Minuit.

Bourdieu, P., & Wacquant, L. (1992). *An invitation to reflexive sociology*. Chicago, IL: The University of Chicago Press.

Bowles, S. (2016). *The moral economy: Why good incentives are no substitute for good citizens*. New Haven, CT: Yale University Press.

Bowles, S., & Gintis, H. (2002). Social capital and community governance. *The Economic Journal, 112*(483), 419–436.

Bowles, S., Loury, G. C., & Sethi, R. (2009). Group inequality (Economics Working Papers, 0088).

Boxman, E. A. W., De Graaf, P. M., & Flap, H. D. (1991). The impact of social and human capital on the income attainment of Dutch managers. *Social Networks, 13*(1), 51–73.

Boyer, R. (2003). L'anthropologie économique de Pierre Bourdieu. *Actes de la recherche en sciences sociales, 150*, 65–78.

Boytsun, A., Deloof, M., & Matthyssens, P. (2011). Social norms, social cohesion, and corporate governance. *Corporate Governance: An International Review, 19*(1), 41–60.

Brablec, D. (2019). Relational goods and endurance of voluntary associational participation: The case of the Indigenous Mapuche in Santiago de Chile. *Bulletin of Latin American Research, 38*(2), 222–236.

Brehm, J., & Rahn, W. (1997). Individual-level evidence for the causes and consequences of social capital. *American Journal of Political Science, 41*(3), 999–1023.

Brewer, A. (1984). *A guide to Marx's capital*. Cambridge: Cambridge University Press.

Brickman, P., & Campbell, D. T. (1971). Hedonic relativism and planning the good society. In M. H. Apley (Ed.), *Adaptation-level theory: A symposium* (pp. 287–302). New York: Academic Press.

Brighouse, H., & Swift, A. (2014). *Family values: The ethics of parent-child relationships*. Princeton, NJ: Princeton University Press.

Brinton, M., & Nee, V. (2001). *The new institutionalism in sociology*. New York: Russell Sage Foundation.

Bruni, L. (2008). *El precio de la gratuidad*. Madrid: Editorial Ciudad Nueva.

Bruni, L. (2010). The happiness of sociality. Economics and Eudaimonia: A necessary encounter. *Rationality and Society, 22*(4), 383–406.

Bruni, L., De Rosa, D., & Ferri, G. (2021). Cooperatives and happiness: Cross-country evidence on the role of relational capital. In L. Bruni, & S. Zamagni (Eds.), *A modern guide to the economics of happiness* (pp. 243–278). Cheltenham: Edward Elgar Publishing.

Bruni, L., & Porta, P. L. (2007). *Handbook of economics of the happiness*. Cheltenham: Edward Elgar.

Bruni, L., & Stanca, L. (2007). Watching alone: Relational goods, television and happiness. *Journal of Economic Behaviour & Organization, 65*(3–4), 506–528.

Brzeżicka, J., & Wisniewski, R. (2014). Homo oeconomicus and behavioral economics. *Contemporary Economics, 8*(4), 353–364.

Bubolz, M. M. (2001). Family as a source, user, and builder of social capital. *Journal of Socio-Economics, 30*, 129–131.

Buchmann, C., & Dalton, B. (2002). Interpersonal influences and educational aspirations in 12 countries: The importance of institutional context. *Sociology of Education, 72*(2), 99–122.

Burt, R. (1992). *Structural holds: The social structure of competition*. Cambridge, MA: Harvard University Press.

Burt, R. (2001). Structural holes versus network closure as social capital. In N. Lin, K. Cook, & R. S. Burt (Eds.), *Social capital: Theory and research* (pp. 31–56). Hawthorne, NY: Aldine de Gruyter.

Caïs, J., Torrente, D., & Bolancé, C. (2021). The effects of economic crisis on trust: Paradoxes for social capital theory. *Social Indicators Research, 153*, 173–192.

Calcagnini, G., & Perugini, F. (2019). Social capital and well-being in the Italian provinces. *Socio-Economic Planning Sciences, 68*, 100668.

Camerer, C. F. (1997). Progress in behavioral game theory. *Journal of Economic Perspectives, 11*(4), 167–188.

Cameron, R., & Neal, L. (2005). *Historia económica mundial: desde el Paleolítico hasta el presente* (4th ed.). Madrid: Alianza Editorial.

Canavese, A. J. (2006). Corrupción organizativa y asignación de recursos. *Desarrollo Económico, 45*(180), 473–485.

Carbonell, X., & Oberst, U. (2015). Las redes sociales en línea no son adictivas. *Aloma: revista de psicologia, ciències de l'educació i de l'esport Blanquerna*, *33*(2), 13–19.

Carr, C. T., & Hayes, R. A. (2015). Social media: Defining, developing, and divining. *Atlantic Journal of Communication, 23*(1), 46–65.

Carter, M., & Barrett, C. (2006). The economics of poverty traps and persistent poverty: An asset-based approach. *Journal of Development Studies, 42*(2), 178–199.

Caruso, R. (2011). Crime and sport participation: Evidence from Italian regions over the period 1997–2003. *The Journal of Socio-Economics, 40*, 455–463.

Cason, M. C. (1990). Economic man. In J. Creedy (Ed.), *Foundations of economic thought* (p. 10). Oxford: Blackwell.

Castells, M. (2008). Comunicación, poder y contrapoder en la sociedad red (II). Los nuevos espacios de la comunicación. *Telos, 75*, 11–23.

Castiglione, D. (2008). Introduction: Social capital between community and society. In D. Castiglione, J. W. Van Deth, & G. Wolleb (Eds.), *The handbook of social capital* (pp. 555–567). New York: Oxford University Press.

Castiglione, D., Van Deth, J. W., & Wolleb, G. (Eds.) (2008a). Social capital's fortune: An introduction. In D. Castiglione, J. W. Van Deth, & G. Wolleb (Eds.), *The handbook of social capital* (pp. 1–12). New York: Oxford University Press.

Castiglione, D., Van Deth, J. W., & Wolleb, G. (Eds.) (2008b). *The handbook of social capital*. New York: Oxford University Press.

Chan, M. (2015). Mobile phones and the good life: Examining the relationships among mobile use, social capital and subjective well-being. *New Media & Society*, *17*(1), 96–113.

Chen, H. T., & Li, X. (2017). The contribution of mobile social media to social capital and psychological well-being: Examining the role of communicative use, friending and self-disclosure. *Computers in Human Behavior, 75*, 958–965.

Chesterton, G. K. (2023). *Muchos vicios y algunas virtudes*. Madrid, España: Encuentro Ediciones.

Chetty, R. (2021). Improving equality of opportunity: New insights from big data. *Contemporary Economic Policy, 39*(1), 7–41.

Chetty, R., Hendren, N., Jones, M. R., & Porter, S. R. (2020). Race and economic opportunity in the United States: An intergenerational perspective. *The Quarterly Journal of Economics, 135*(2), 711–783.

Chetty, R., Jackson, M. O., Kuchler, T., & Stroebel, J. (2022a). Social capital II: Determinants of economic connectedness. *Nature, 608*(7921), 122–134.

Chetty, R., Jackson, M. O., Kuchler, T., Stroebel, J., Hendren, N., Fluegge, R. B.,…, & Wernerfelt, N. (2022b). Social capital I: Measurement and associations with economic mobility. *Nature, 608*(7921), 108–121.

Christoforou, A. (2011). Social capital: A manifestation of neoclassical prominence or a path to a more pluralistic economics? *Journal of Economic Issues, 45*(3), 685–702.

Christoforou, A., & Davis, J. B. (2014a). *Social capital and economics*. Nueva York: Routledge.
Christoforou, A., & Davis, J. B. (2014b). Social capital: Social values, power, and social identity. In A. Christoforou & J. B. Davis (Eds.), *Social capital and economics* (pp. 25–34). London and New York: Routledge.
Christoforou, A., & Lainé, M. (2014). *Re-thinking economics: Exploring the work of Pierre Bourdieu*. Londres: Routledge.
Claibourn, M. P., & Martin, P. S. (2000). Trusting and joining? An empirical test of the reciprocal nature of social capital. *Political Behaviour, 22*(4), 267–291.
Claridge, T. (2018a). Criticisms of social capital theory: And lessons for improving practice. *Social Capital Research, 4*(2), 1–8.
Claridge, T. (2018b). Dimensions of social capital – structural, cognitive, and relational. *Social Capital Research, 1*, 1–4.
Claridge, T. (2020). Social capital at different levels and dimensions: A typology of social capital. *Social Capital Research, 1*, 1–8.
Claridge, T. (2023). Social capital. In K. P. Kearns, & W. Wang (Eds.), *Elgar Encyclopedia of nonprofit management, leadership and governance* (pp. 525–528). Cheltenham: Edward Elgar Publishing.
Coase, R. H. (1937). The nature of the firm. *Economica, 4*(16), 386–405.
Coase, R. (1988). *The firm, the market and the law*. Chicago, IL: University.
Cockburn, T., & Cockburn-Wootten, C. (2022). Redefining social capital and social networks in global civil society. In R. Oberoi, J. P. Halsall, & M. Snowden (Eds.), *Contestations in global civil society* (pp. 119–156). Bingley: Emerald Publishing Limited.
Coffé, H., & Geys, B. (2005). Institutional performance and social capital: An application to the local government level. *Journal of Urban Affairs, 27*(5), 485–501.
Colander, D., Holt, R., & Rosser Jr, B. (2004). The changing face of mainstream economics. *Review of Political Economy, 16*(4), 485–499.
Coleman, J. S. (1988). Social capital in the creation of human capital. *The American Journal of Sociology, 94*, 95–120.
Coleman, J. S. (1990). *Foundations of social theory*. Cambridge: Harvard University Press.
Coleman, J. S. (1995). *Grundlagen der Sozialtheorie. Band 1: Handlungen und Handlungssysteme. Band 2: Körperschaften und die moderne Gesellschaft*. München: Oldenbourg.
Coleman, J. S. (1998). Social capital in the creation of human capital. *American Journal of Sociology, 94*, S95–S120.
Collard, D. (1975). Edgeworth's propositions on altruism. *Economic Journal, 85*(338), 355–360.
Conill Sancho, J. (2004). *Horizontes de economía ética*. Madrid: Editorial Tecnos.
Cook, K. S. (2003a). Trust in society. In K. S. Cook (Coord.), *Trust in society* (pp. XI–XVIII). New York: Russell Sage Foundation.
Cook, K. S. (Coord.) (2003b). *Trust in society*. New York: Russell Sage Foundation.
Cooley, C. H. (1909). *Social organization: A study of the larger mind*. New York: Charles Scribner's Sons.
Corak, M. (2016). *Inequality from generation to generation: The United States in comparison (No. 9929)*. Bonn: Institute for the Study of Labor (IZA).
Corsi, A., Frontuto, V., & Novelli, S. (2022). Relational goods and direct purchase from farmers: Estimating the value of the relationship between consumers and producers. *International Food and Agribusiness Management Review, 25*(2), 245–262.

Dahlman, C. J. (1979). The problem of externality. *The Journal of Law and Economics, 22*(1), 141–162.

Dakin, B. C., Tan, N. P., Conner, T. S., & Bastian, B. (2022). The relationship between prosociality, meaning, and happiness in everyday life. *Journal of Happiness Studies, 23*(6), 2787–2804.

Das, R. (2006). Putting social capital in its place. *Capital and Class, 30*(3), 65–92.

Dasgupta, P. (2000). Economic progress and the idea of social capital. In P. Dasgupta, & I. Serageldin (Eds.), *Social capital: A multifaceted perspective*. Washington, DC: World Bank.

Dasgupta, P. (2005). The economics of social capital. *The Economic Record, 81*(S1), S58–S70.

Dasgupta, P., & Serageldin, I. (Eds.) (2000). *Social capital: A multifaceted perspective*. Washington, DC: World Bank.

Datareportal. (2023). Digital 2023: Global overview report. Recuperado de https://datareportal.com/reports/digital-2023-global-overview-report

Davenport, S., & Daellenbach, U. (2011). 'Belonging' to a virtual research centre: Exploring the influence of social capital formation processes on member identification in a virtual organization. *British Journal of Management, 22*(1), 54–76.

Dederichs, K. (2024). Join to connect? Voluntary involvement, social capital, and socioeconomic inequalities. *Social Networks, 76*, 42–50.

Delhey, J., & Dragolov, G. (2016). Happier together. Social cohesion and subjective well-being in Europe. *International Journal of Psychology, 51*(3), 163–176.

Delhey, J., & Newton, K. (2003). Who trusts? The origins of social trust in seven societies. *European Societies, 5*(2), 93–137.

Delhey, J., & Newton, K. (2005). Predicting cross-national levels of social trust: Global pattern or Nordic exceptionalism? *European Sociological Review, 21*(4), 311–327.

Delhey, J., Newton, K., & Welzel, C. (2011). How is general trust in "most people"?: Solving the radius trust problem. *American Sociological Review, 76*, 786–807.

Delle Fave, A., Brdar, I., Freire, T., Vella-Brodrick, D., & Wissing, M. (2011). The Eudaimonic and Hedonic components of happiness: Qualitative and quantitative findings. *Social Indicators Research, 100*(2), 185–207.

Deller, S. C., Conroy, T., & Markeson, B. (2018). Social capital, religion and small business activity. *Journal of Economic Behavior & Organization, 155*, 365–381.

Dépelteau, F., & Powell, C. (Eds.) (2013). *Applying relational sociology: Relations, networks and society*. New York: Palgrave Macmillan.

Dickes, P., Valentova, M., & Borsenberger, M. (2010). Construct validation and application of a common measure of social cohesion in 33 European countries. *Social Indicators Research, 98*, 451–473.

Diener, E. (2000). Subjective well-being: The science of happiness and a proposal for a national index. *American Psychologist, 55*, 34–43.

Diener, E. (2009). Subjective well-being. In E. Diener (Ed.), *The science of well-being: The collected works of Ed Diener* (pp. 11–58). New York: Springer Science + Business Media.

Diener, E. (2012). New findings and future directions for subjective well-being research. *American Psychologist, 67*(8), 590–597.

Diener, E. (2013). The remarkable changes in the science of subjective well-being. *Perspectives on Psychological Science, 8*(6), 663–666.

Diener, E., Oishi, S., & Lucas, R. E. (2003). Personality, culture and subjective well-being: Emotional and cognitive evaluations of life. *Annual Review of Psychology, 54*, 403–425.

Dodd, M. D. (2016). Intangible resource management: Social capital theory development for public relations. *Journal of Communication Management, 20*(4), 289–311.

Doh, S., & McNeely, C. L. (2012). A multi-dimensional perspective on social capital and economic development: An exploratory analysis. *The Annals of Regional Science, 49*, 821–843.

Dolan, P., Peasgood, T., & White, M. (2007). Do we really know what makes us happy? A review of the economic literature on the factors associated with subjective well-being. *Journal of Economic Psychology, 29*(1), 94–122.

Donaldson, T. (2001). The ethical wealth of nations. *Journal of Business Ethics, 31*, 25–36.

Donati, P. (1986). *Introduzione alla sociologia relazionale*. Milán: Franco Angeli.

Donati, P. (1997). El desarrollo de las organizaciones del tercer sector en el proceso de modernización y más allá. *Reis, 79*, 113–141.

Donati, P. (2019). Discovering the relational goods: Their nature, genesis and effects. *International Review of Sociology, 29*(2), 238–259.

Donati, P., & Prandini, R. (2007). The family in the light of a new relational theory of primary, secondary and generalized social capital. *International Review of Sociology: Revue Internationale de Sociologie, 17*(2), 209–223.

Doob, C. (2013). *Social stratification and social inequality in US society*. Nueva York: Routledge.

Downs, A. (1957). *An economic theory of democracy*. Nueva York: Harper.

Duesenberry, J. S. (1952). *Income, saving and the theory of consumer behaviour*. Cambridge, MA: Harvard University Press.

Dufur, M. J., Hoffmann, J. P., Braudt, D. B., Parcel, T. L., & Spence, K. R. (2015). Examining the effects of family and school social capital on delinquent behavior. *Deviant Behavior, 36*(7), 511–526.

Dur, R., & Sol, J. (2009). Social interaction, co-worker altruism, and incentives. *Games and Economic Behavior, 69*, 293–301.

Durkheim, E. (1984 [1893]). *The division of labor in society*. New York: The Free Press.

Durlauf, S. N. (1999). The case "against" social capital (Working papers 29, Wisconsin Madison – Social Systems).

Durlauf, S. N. (2002). On the empirics of social capital. *The Economic Journal, 112*(483), 459–479.

Durlauf, S. N. (2008). Membership and inequality. In D. Castiglione, J. W. Van Deth, & G. Wolleb (Eds.), *The handbook of social capital* (pp. 594–623). New York: Oxford University Press.

Easterlin, R. (1974). Does economic growth improve the human lot? In P. A. David y M. W. Reder (Eds.), *Nations and households in economic growth: Essays in honour of Moses Abramovitz* (pp. 89–125). New York: Academic Press, Inc.

Eccles, R. G. (1981). The quasifirm in the construction industry. *Journal of Economic Behavior & Organization, 2*(4), 335–357.

Edyvane, D. (2017). The passion for civility. *Political Studies Review, 15*(3), 344–354.

Eloire, F. (2017). The Bourdieusian conception of social capital: A methodological reflection and application. *Forum for Social Economics, 1*(1), 1–24.

Emirbayer, M. (1997). Manifesto for a relational sociology. *The American Journal of Sociology, 103*(2), 281–317.

Encyclopedia Britannica (2023). Society. In *Encyclopedia Britannica*. Britannica Group. https://www.britannica.com/topic/society

Engbers, T. A., Thompson, M. F., & Slaper, T. F. (2017). Theory and measurement in social capital research. *Social Indicators Research, 132*, 537–558.

Erickson, B. H. (1996). Culture, class and connections. *American Journal of Sociology, 102*(1), 217–251.
Erickson, B. H. (2001). Good networks and good jobs: The value of social capital to employers and employees. In N. Lin, K. Cook, & R. S. Burt (Eds.), *Social capital* (pp. 127–158). New York: Routledge.
Ermisch, J., & Gambetta, D. (2010). Do strong family ties inhibit trust? *Journal of Economic Behavior & Organization, 75*(3), 365–376.
Etzioni, A. (1988). *The moral dimension: Towards a new economics*. New York: Free Press.
Etzioni, A. (2007). *La dimensión moral: Hacia una nueva economía*. Madrid: Ediciones Palabra, S. A.
Etzioni, A. (2011). Behavioral economics: Toward a new paradigm. *American Behavioral Scientist, 55*(8), 1099–1119.
Fang, H., & Loury, G. (2005). Dysfunctional identities' can be rational. *American Economic Review, 95*(2), 104–111.
Fehr, D., Rau, H., Trautmann, S. T., & Xu, Y. (2020). Inequality, fairness and social capital. *European Economic Review, 129*, 103566.
Feher, A., & Tremblay, P. F. (2018). Estudio de la influencia de los rasgos y el individualismo en la satisfacción vital entre naciones: un modelo multinivel. *Acción Psicológica, 15*(2), 15–26.
Fennema, M., & Tillie, J. (2008). Social capital in multicultural societies. In D. Castiglione, J. W. Van Deth, & G. Wolleb (Eds.), *The handbook of social capital* (pp. 349–370). New York: Oxford University Press.
Ferragina, E., & Arrigoni, A. (2017). The rise and fall of social capital: Requiem for a theory? *Political Studies Review, 15*(3), 355–367.
Festinger, L., Schachter, S., & Back, K. (1950). Social pressures in informal groups; a study of human factors in housing. Stanford: Stanford University.
Field, J. (2016). *Social capital*. New York: Routledge.
Fine, B. (1999). The developmental state is dead – Long life social capital? *Development and Change, 30*(1), 1–19.
Fine, B. (2001a). It ain't social and it ain't capital. *Research in Progress*, (1), 11–15.
Fine, B. (2001b). *Social capital vs. social theory: Political economy and social science at the turn of the millennium*. London, Routledge.
Fine, B. (2002a). They F**k You up Those Social Capitalists. *Antipode, 34*(4), 796–9.
Fine, B. (2002b). "Economic imperialism": A view from the periphery. *Review of Radical Political Economics, 34*(2), 187–201.
Fine, B. (2003). Social capital: The World Bank's fungible friend. *Journal of Agrarian Change, 3*(4), 586–603.
Fine, B. (2010). *Theories of social capital: Researchers behaving badly*. New York: Pluto Press.
Fitzgerald, S. (1925). *The great Gatsby*. New York: Charles Scribner´s Sons.
Flap, H. D. (1991). Social capital in the reproduction of inequality. *Comparative Sociology of Family, Health and Education, 20*, 61–79.
Flap, H. D. (1999). Creation and returns of social capital: A new research program. *La Revue Tocqueville, 20*, 5–26.
Flap, H. D. (2002). No man is an island: The research programme of a social capital theory. In O. Favereau & E. Lazega (Eds.), *Conventions and structures. Markets, networks and hierarchies* (pp. 29–59). Cheltenham: Edward Elgar.
Flap, H. D. (2004). Creation and returns of social capital. In H. Flap & B. Völker (Eds.), *Creation and returns of social capital* (pp. 3–24). London: Routledge.

Flap, H. D., & Boxman, E. (2001). Getting started: The influence of social capital on the start of the occupational career. In N. Lin, K. Cook, & R. S. Burt (Eds.), *Social capital: Theory and research* (pp. 159–181). Londres: Routledge.

Flap, H. D., & Volker, B. (2001). Goal specific social capital and job satisfaction: Effects of different types of networks on instrumental and social aspects of work. *Social Networks, 23*(4), 297–320.

Folbre, N., & Nelson, J. A. (2000). For love or money–or both? *Journal of Economic Perspectives, 14*(4), 123–140.

Fontaine, P. (1997). Identification and economic behaviour; sympathy and empathy in historical perspective. *Economics and Philosophy, 13*(1997), 271.

Fontaine, P. (2000). Making use of the past: Theorists and historians on the economics of altruism. *European Journal of the History of Economic Thought, 7*(3), 407–422.

Frederiksen, M. (2019). On the inside of generalized trust: Trust dispositions as perceptions of self and others. *Current Sociology, 67*(1), 3–26.

Freitag, M., & Traunmüller, R. (2009). Spheres of trust: An empirical analysis of the foundations of particularised and generalised trust. *European Journal of Political Research, 48*(6), 782–803.

Frey, B. S., & Stutzer, A. (2002). *Happiness and economics*. Princeton, NJ: University Press.

Friedman, M. (1953). *Essays in positive economics*. Chicago, IL: University of Chicago Press.

Fukuyama, F. (1995a). *Trust: The social virtues and the creation of prosperity*. New York: Free Press.

Fukuyama, F. (1995b). The primacy of culture. *Journal of Democracy, 6*(1), 7–14.

Fukuyama, F. (1997). Social capital and the modern capitalist economy: Creating a high trust workplace. *Stern Business Magazine, 4*(1), 4–17.

Fukuyama, F. (2001). Social capital, civil society and development. *Third World Quarterly, 22*(1), 7–20.

Fundación BBVA (2007). *El capital social en España y los países de la OCDE*. Cuadernos de Divulgación. Recuperado de www.fbbva.es

Gaag, M. P. J. V. D. (2005). *Measurement of individual social capital* [Thesis fully internal (DIV), Rijksuniversiteit Groningen] [S.n.].

Gannon, B., & Roberts, J. (2020). Social capital: Exploring the theory and empirical divide. *Empirical Economics, 58*(3), 899–919.

Gemici, K. (2008). Karl Polanyi and the antinomies of embeddedness. *Socio-Economic Review, 6*(1), 5–33.

Gheorghiu, M. A., Vignoles, V. L., & Smith, P. B. (2009). Beyond the United States and Japan: Testing Yamagishi's emancipation theory of trust across 31 nations. *Social Psychology Quarterly, 72*(4), 365–383.

Gibbons, R. (1998). Incentives in organizations. *Journal of Economic Perspectives, 12*(4), 115–132.

Gidengil, E., & O'Neill, B. (Eds.) (2006). *Gender and social capital*. Nueva York: Routledge.

Glaeser, E. L. (2001). The formation of social capital. *Canadian Journal of Policy Research, 2*(1), 34–40.

Glaeser, E. L., Laibson, D., & Sacerdote, B. (2002). An economic approach to social capital. *The Economic Journal, 112*(483), 437–458.

Glanville, J. L., & Paxton, P. (2007). How do we learn to trust?: A confirmatory tetrad analysis of the sources of generalized trust. *Social Psychology Quarterly, 70*, 230–242.

Glanville, J. L., Paxton, P., & Wang, Y. (2016). Social capital and generosity: A multilevel analysis. *Nonprofit and Voluntary Sector Quarterly, 45*(3), 526–547.

Glasman, N. S., & Biniaminov, I. (1981). Input-output analysis of schools. *Review of Educational Research, 51*(4), 509–539.

Goddard, R. D. (2003). Relational networks, social trust, and norms: A social capital perspective on students chances of academic success. *Educational Evaluation and Policy Analysis, 25*(1), 59–74.

Godelier, M. (1982). *La production des grands hommes: pouvoir et domination masculine chez les Baruya de Nouvelle-Guinée*. Paris: Fayard.

Godelier, M. (1984). *L'idée et le Matériel: Pensée, Économies, Sociétés*. París: Flamarion.

González, W. J. (2004). *Racionalidad, historicidad y predicción en H. Simon*. A Coruña: Netbiblo.

González Heras, A. (2023). Los tipos de capital social bonding, bridging y linking: una revisión de los indicadores cuantitativos utilizados para su operacionalización. *EMPIRIA. Revista de Metodología de las Ciencias Sociales, 58*, 75–97.

Goode, R. (1984). *Government finance in developing countries*. Washington, DC: Brookings Institute.

Gooderham, Paul N. (2007). Enhancing knowledge transfer in multinational corporations: A dynamic capabilities driven model. *Knowledge Management Research & Practice, 5*(1), 34–43.

Graeber, D. (2001). *Toward an anthropological theory of value*. New York: Palgrave.

Graeff, P. (2005). Why should corruption be trusted? The linkage between corruption, norms and social capital. In J. Lambsdorff, M. Taube, & M. Schramm (Eds.), *The new institutional economics of corruption* (pp. 21–42). London and New York: Routledge.

Graeff, P., & Svendsen, G. T. (2013). Trust and corruption: The influence of positive and negative social capital on the economic development in the European Union. *Quality & Quantity, 47*(5), 2829–2846.

Granovetter, M. S. (1973). The strength of weak ties. *American Journal of Sociology, 78*(6), 1360–1380.

Granovetter, M. S. (1983). The strength of weak ties: A network theory revisited. *Sociological Theory, 1*, 201–233.

Granovetter, M. S. (1985). Economic action and social structure: The problem of embeddedness. *American Journal of Sociology, 91*(3), 481–510.

Granovetter, M. S. (2005). *The social construction of corruption*. Stanford: Stanford University.

Griesshaber, N., & Geys, B. (2011). *Civic engagement and corruption in 20 European democracies: Separating the bright form the dark side*. Berlín: Documento de debate, WZB.

Grootaert, Ch., Narayan, D., Nyhan, V., & Woolcock, M. (2004). *Measuring social capital: An integrated questionnaire* (Working Paper, No. 18, World Bank, Washington).

Grootaert, C., & Van Bastelar, T. (Eds.). (2002). *Understanding and measuring social capital: A multi-disciplinary tool for practitioners*. Washington: The World Bank.

Gui, B. (1987). Éléments por une définition d''économie communautaire. *Notes et Documents, 19–20*, 32–42.

Gui, B. (1996). On "relational goods": Strategic implications of investment in relationships. *International Journal of Social Economics, 23*(10/11), 260–278.

Gui, B. (2000). Beyond transactions: On the impersonal dimension of economic reality. *Annals of Public and Cooperative Economics, 71*(2), 139–169.

Gui, B. (2001). Organizaciones productivas con fines ideales y realización de la persona: Relaciones interpersonales y horizontes de sentido. In L. Bruni (Ed.), *Economía de Comunión* (pp. 149–168). Madrid: Editorial Ciudad Nueva.

Gui, B. (2005). From transactions to encounters: The joint generation of relational goods and conventional values. In B. Gui, & R. Sugden (Eds.), *Economics and social interactions: Accounting for interpersonal relations* (pp. 23–51). Cambridge: Cambridge University Press.

Gui, B., & Sugden, R. (2005). *Economics and social interactions: Accounting for interpersonal relations*. Cambridge: Cambridge University Press.

Guiso, L., Sapienza, P., & Zingales, L. (2011). Civic capital as the missing link. *Handbook of Social Economics*, *1*, 417–480.

Guribye, E. (2018). Co-creation of linking social capital in 'municipality 3.0'. *Journal of Civil Society, 14*(1), 77–93.

Habermas, J. (1986). *Law and morality: Tanner lectures on human values*. Cambridge, MA: Harvard.

Hall, P. (1999). Social capital in Britain. *British Journal of Political Science, 29*(3), 417–464.

Haller, M., & Hadler, M. (2006). How social relations and structures can produce happiness and unhappiness: An international comparative analysis. *Social Indicators Research, 75*, 169–216.

Halstead, J. M., & Deller, S. C. (2015). Social capital and community development: An introduction. In S. C. Deller & J. M. Halstead (Eds.), *Social capital at the community level* (pp. 1–13). New York: Routledge.

Hämmerle, V., Braundwalder, R., Pauli, C., & Misoch, S. (2020). Shaping social relationships digitally: WhatsApp's influence on social relationships of older adults. In *International conference on human-computer interaction* (pp. 42–49). Cham: Springer.

Hangartner, D., Kopp, D., & Siegenthaler. (2021). Monitoring hiring discrimination through online recruiting platforms. *Nature, 589*, 572–576.

Hanifan, L. J. (1916). The rural school community center. *The Annals of the American Academy of Political and Social Science, 67*(1), 130–138.

Hanifan, L. J. (1920). *The community center*. Boston, MA: Silver, Burdett & Company.

Hanushek, E. A. (1972). *Education and race: An analysis of the education production process*. Cambridge: Heath-Lexington.

Hardin, R. (2001). Conceptions and explanations of trust. In K. S. Cook (Ed.), *Trust in society* (Vol. 2, pp. 3–39). Nueva York: Russell Sage Foundation.

Hardin, R. (2002). *Trust and trustworthiness*. London: Russell Sage Foundation.

Hardin, W. (1999). Do we want trust in government? In M. E. Warren (Ed.), *Democracy and trust* (pp. 22–41). Cambridge: Cambridge University Press.

Häuberer, J. (2011). *Social capital theory: Towards a methodological foundation*. Wiesbaden: VS Verlag für Sozialwissenschaften.

Hausman, D. M., & M. Mcpherson (2007). *El análisis económico y la filosofía moral*. México D. F.: Fondo de Cultura Económica.

Hechter, M., & Kanazawa, S. (1997). Sociological rational choice theory. *Annual Review of Sociology, 23*, 191–214.

Hedström, P. (2005). *Dissecting the social: On the principles of analytical sociology*. Cambridge: Cambridge University Press.

Hedström, P., & Swedberg, R. (Eds.) (1998). *Social mechanisms: An analytical approach to social theory*. Cambridge: Cambridge University Press.

Hedström, P., & Ylikoski, P. (2010). Causal mechanisms in the social sciences. *Annual Review of Sociology, 36*, 49–67.

Heinrich, V. F. (2005). Studying civil society across the world: Exploring the thorny issues of conceptualization and measurement. *Journal of Civil Society, 1*(3), 211–228.

Hellerstein, J. K., & Neumark, D. (2020). Social capital, networks, and economic wellbeing. *The Future of Children, 30*(1), 127–152.
Helliwell, J. F., Aknin, L. B., Shiplett, H., Huang, H., & Wang, S. (2017). *Social capital and prosocial behaviour as sources of well-being (no. w23761).* Cambridge, MA: National Bureau of Economic Research.
Helliwell, J. F., & Putnam, R. D. (2004). The social context of well-being. *Philosophical Transactions of the Royal Society of London, 359*, 1425–1446.
Henderson, L. W., & Knight, T. (2012). Integrating the hedonic and eudaimonic perspectives to more comprehensively understand wellbeing and pathways to wellbeing. *International Journal of Wellbeing, 2*(3), 196–221.
Henrich, J., Boyd, R., Bowles, S., Gintis, H., Camerer, C., Fehr, E., & McElreath, R. (2001). In search of Homo economicus: Experiments in 15 small-scale societies. *American Economic Review, 91*, 73–78.
Herreros, F. (2004). ¿Por qué confiar? Formas de creación de confianza social. *Revista Mexicana de Sociología, 66*(4), 605–626.
Herreros, F., & Criado, H. (2008). The state and the development of social trust. *International Political Science Review, 29*(1), 53–71.
Herreros Vázquez, F. (2002). *¿Por qué confiar?: El problema de la creación del capital social.* Madrid: Centro de Estudios Avanzados en Ciencias Sociales. Instituto Juan March.
Hirschman, A. O. (1985). *Shifting involvements: Private interest and public action*. Oxford: Basil Blackwell.
Hodgson, B. (2001). *Economics as moral science*. Heidelberg: Springer Verlag.
Howells, W. D. (1890). *A hazard of new fortunes*. New York: Harper & Brothers.
Huber, K., Lindenthal, V., & Waldinger, F. (2021). Discrimination, managers, and firm performance: Evidence from "Aryanizations" in Nazi Germany. *Journal of Political Economy, 129*(9), 2455–2503.
Huberts, L. (1998). What can be done against public corruption and fraud: Expert views on strategies to protect public integrity. *Crime, Law & Social Change, 29*, 209–224.
Hulbert, J. S., Beggs, J. J., & Haines, V. A. (2001). Social networks and social capital in extreme environments. In N. Lin, K. Cook y R. S. Burt (Eds.), *Social capital: Theory and research* (pp. 209–232). New York: Aldine de Gruyter.
Husted, B. W. (1999). Wealth, culture and corruption. *Journal of International Business Studies, 30*, 339–359.
Iglesias Vázquez, E., Pena-López, A., & Sánchez Santos, J. M. (2013). Bienestar subjetivo, renta y bienes relacionales: Los determinantes de la felicidad en España. *Revista Internacional de Sociología, 71*(3), 567–592.
Inglehart, R. (1990). *Culture shift*. New Jersey: Princeton University Press.
Inglehart, R. (1997). *Modernization and post-modernization: Cultural, economic, and political change in 43 societies*. New Jersey: Princeton University Press.
Iyer, S., Kitson, M., & Toh, B. (2005). Social capital, economic growth and regional development. *Regional Studies, 39*(8), 1015–1040.
Jackson, M. O. (2020). A typology of social capital and associated network measures. *Social Choice and Welfare, 54*(2), 311–336.
Jackson, M. O. (2021). Inequality's economic and social roots: The role of social networks and homophily. *SSRN Electronic Journal*. Publicación anticipada en línea.
Jacobs, J. (1961). *The life and death of great American cities*. New York: Random House.
Jain, A. K. (2001a). Corruption: A review. *Journal of Economic Surveys, 15*, 71–121.
Jain, A. K. (Ed.). (2001b). *The political economy of corruption* (Vol. 2). Routledge.

Jaraiz, G., & Vidal Fernández, F. (2014). *VII Informe sobre exclusión y desarrollo social en España* (pp. 451–532). Madrid: Fundación Foessa.

Jenson, J. (2010). Defining and measuring social cohesion (No. 1). Commonwealth Secretariat and United Nations Research Institute for Social Development.

Jon, E. (1989). Social norms and economic theory. *The Journal of Economic Perspectives, 3*(4), 99–117.

Josten, S. D. (2013). Middle-class consensus, social capital and the fundamental causes of economic growth and development. *Journal of Economic Development, 38*(1), 1.

Kadushin, C. (2004). Too much investment in social capital? *Social Networks, 26*, 75–90.

Kahneman, D. (2003). A psychological perspective on economics. *American Economic Review, 93*(2), 162–168.

Kahneman, D., Krueger, A. B., Schkade, D. A., Schwarz, N., & Stone, A. A. (2004). A survey method for characterizing daily life experience: The Day Reconstruction Method. *Science, 306*(5702), 1776–780.

Kahneman, D., & Netsch, J. (1992). Valuing public goods: The purchase of moral satisfaction. *Journal of Environmental Economics and Management, 22*(1), 57–70.

Kaiser, M., Barnhart, S., & Huber-Krum, S. (2020). Measuring social cohesion and social capital within the context of community food security: A confirmatory factor analysis. *Journal of Hunger & Environmental Nutrition, 15*(5), 591–612.

Karapanos, E., Teixeira, P., & Gouveia, R. (2016). Need fulfillment and experiences on social media: A case on Facebook and WhatsApp. *Computers in Human Behavior, 55*, 888–897.

Kaufmann, D., & Kraay, A. (2002). *Growth without governance* (World Bank Policy Research Working Paper No. 2928). Washington, DC: The World Bank.

Kawachi, I., Kennedy, B. P., Lochner, K., & Prothrow-Stith, D. (1997). Social capital, income inequality, and mortality. *American Journal of Public Health, 87*(9), 1491–1497.

Khalil, E. L. (2001). A. Smith and three theories of altruism. *Louvain Economic Review, 67*, 421–435.

Khalil, E. L. (2004). What is altruism? *Journal of Economic Psychology, 25*(1), 97–123.

Klein, C. (2013). Social capital or social cohesion: What matters for subjective well-being? *Social Indicators Research, 110*, 891–911.

Kleiner, T. M. (2021). The isolating side effect of civic participation. *Journal of Sociology, 57*(4), 877–897.

Kliksberg, B. (2000). *Capital social y cultura: Las claves olvidadas del desarrollo*, New York: Bid-Intal.

Knack, S. (2002). Social capital and the quality of government: Evidence from the States. *American Journal of Political Science, 46*(4), 772–785.

Knack, S. (2003). Groups, growth and trust: Cross-country evidence on the Olson and Putnam hypotheses. *Public Choice, 117*, 341–355.

Knack, S., & Keefer, P. (1997). Does social capital have an economic payoff? *The Quarterly Journal of Economics, 112*(4), 1252–1288.

Knoke, D. (1999). Organizational networks and corporate social capital. In R. Th. A. J. Leenders & S. M. Gabbay (Eds.), *Corporate social capital and liability* (pp. 17–42). Boston: Kluwer.

Kobayashi, T., Kawachi, I., Iwase, T., Suzuki, E., & Takao, S. (2013). Individual-level social capital and self-rated health in Japan: An application of the Resource Generator. *Social Science & Medicine, 85*, 32–37.

Koslowski, P. (1991). Ethical economy as synthesis of economic and ethical theory. In P. Koslowski (Ed.), *Ethics in economics, business and economic policy* (pp. 1–15). Berlin: Springer.

Koslowski, P. (1999). *Contemporary economic ethics and business ethics*. Berlin: Springer.

Kotzé, H., & du Toit, P. (2005). Civil society and democracy. In H. Kotzé & P. du Toit (Eds.), *Democracy under construction, Patterns from four continents* (pp. 243–258). Opladen: Verlag Barbara Budrich.

Kranton, R. E. (1996). Reciprocal exchange: A self-sustaining system. *American Economic Review, 86*, 830–851.

Kraufmann, D., & Kraay, A. (2002). Growth without governance. *The World Bank Discussion Paper*. Washington, DC.

Kraufmann, D., Kraay, A., & Mastruzzi, M. (2006). Measuring corruption: Myths and realities. *The World Bank Discussion Paper*. Washington, DC.

Kripper, G. R. (2001). The elusive market: Embeddedness and the paradigm of economic sociology. *Theory and Society, 30*, 775–810.

Krishna, A., & Shrader, E. (1999, June 22-24). Social capital assessment tool. Paper presented at the Conference on social capital and poverty reduction, Washington, DC.

Kuhn, T. S. (1962). *The structure of scientific revolutions*. Chicago, IL: University of Chicago Press.

Kurz, M. (1978). Altruism as an outcome of social interactions. *American Economic Review, 68*, 216–222.

La Porta, R., López-de-Silanes, F., Schleifer, A., & Vishny, R. W. (2000). Trust in large organizations. In P. Dasgupta & I. Serageldin (Eds.), *Social capital: A multifaceted perspective* (pp. 310–324). Washington, DC: World Bank.

Lambsdorff, J. G. (2002). Corruption and rent-seeking. *Public Choice, 113*, 97–125.

Lambsdorff, J. G., Taube, M., & Schramm, M. (2005). *Contratación corrupta: Exploring the Economics of Corruption*. Boston, MA: Kluwer.

Lanier, J. (2018). *Diez Razones para Borrar tus Redes Sociales de Inmediato*. Madrid: Debate.

Laumann, E. (1966). *Prestige and association in an urban community*. New York: Bobbs-Merrill.

Laville, J.-L., & Nyssens, M. (2001). The social enterprise: Towards a theoretical socio-economic approach. In C. Borzaga & J. Defourny (Eds.), *The emergence of social enterprise* (pp. 312–332). London: Routledge.

Law, A., & Mooney, G. (2006). The Maladies of social capital I: The missing 'capital' in theories of social capital. *Critique, 34*(2), 127–143.

Lawndes, V., & Pratchett, L. (2008). Public policy and social capital. In D. Castiglione, J. W. Van Deth, & G. Wolleb (Eds.), *The handbook of social capital* (pp. 677–707), New York: Oxford University Press.

Lawson, T. (1997). *Economics and reality*. London: Routledge.

Lawson, T. (1999). Critical realism. In P. O'Hara (Ed.), *The encyclopedia of political economy* (166–167). London: Routledge.

Lawson, T. (2003). *Reorienting economics*. Abingdon: Routledge.

Lazarova, M., & Taylor, S. (2009). Boundaryless careers, social capital, and knowledge management: Implications for organizational performance. *Journal of Organizational Behavior, 30*(1), 119–139.

Lazenby, H. (2016). What is equality of opportunity in education? *Theory and Research in Education, 14*(1), 65–76.

Lee, S., Chung, J. E., & Park, N. (2018). Network environments and well-being: An examination of personal network structure, social capital, and perceived social support. *Health Communication, 33*(1), 22–31.

Leeves, G. D., & Herbert, R. (2014). Gender differences in social capital investment: Theory and evidence. *Economic Modelling, 37*, 377–385.

Lefebvre, V., Sorenson, D., Henchion, M., & Gellynck, X. (2016). Social capital and knowledge sharing performance of learning networks. *International Journal of Information Management, 36*(4), 570–579.

Leipert, C. (1989). National income and economic growth: The conceptual side of defensive expenditures. *Journal of Economic Issues, 23*(3), 843–856.

Levi, M. (1996). Social and unsocial capital: A review essay of Robert Putnam's making democracy work. *Politics and Society, 24*(1), 45–55.

Light, I. (2004). Cultural capital. In M. C. Horowitz (Ed.), *The New Dictionary of the History of Ideas* (Vol. 2, pp. 511–512). New York: Scribner's.

Li, Y., Savage, M., & Pickles, A. (2003). Social capital and social exclusion in England and Wales (1972–1999). *Sociology: A Journal of the British Sociological Association, 54*(4), 497–526.

Lin, N. (1982). Social resources and instrumental action. In P. V. Marsden & N. Lin (Eds.), *Social structure and network analysis* (pp. 131–145). Beverly Hills, CA: Sage.

Lin, N. (1990). Social resources and social mobility: A structural theory of status attainment. In R. L. Breiger (Ed.), *Social mobility and social structure* (pp. 247–271). Cambridge: Cambridge University Press.

Lin, N. (1999a). Building a network theory of social capital. *Connections, 22*(1), 28–51.

Lin, N. (1999b). Social networks and status attainment. *American Review of Sociology, 25*(1), 467–487.

Lin, N. (2000). Inequality in social capital. *Contemporary Sociology, 29*(6), 785–795.

Lin, N. (2001). *Social capital: A theory of social structure and action*. Cambridge: Cambridge University Press.

Lin, N. (2008). A network theory of social capital. In D. Castiglione, J. van Deth, & G. Wolleb (Eds.), *The handbook of social capital* (pp. 50–70). Oxford: Oxford University Press.

Lin, N., Cook, K., & Burt, R. S. (Eds.) (2001). *Social capital: Theory and research*. New York: de Gruyter.

Lin, N., Dean, A., & Ensel, W. M. (1981a). Social support scales: A methodological note. *Schizophrenia Bulletin, 7*(1), 73–89.

Lin, N., Ensel, W. M., & Vaughn, J. C. (1981b). Social resources and strength of ties: Structural factors in occupational status attainment. *American Sociological Review, 46*(4), 393–405.

Lin, N., & Erickson, B. (Eds.) (2008). *Social capital: An international research program*. Oxford: Oxford University Press.

Lin, N., Yang-chih, F., & Hsung, R.-M. (2001). The position generator: Measurement techniques of investigations of social capital. In N Lin., K. Cook, & R. S. Burt (Eds.), *Social capital: Theory and research* (pp. 57–81). New Brunswick, NJ: Aldine Transaction.

Lindenberg, S. (1996). Continuities is the theory of social production functions. In H. Ganzeboom & S. Lindenberg (Eds.), *Verklarende sociologie; opstellen voor Reinhart Wippler* (Thesis Publications, Amsterdam).

Lins, K. V., Servaes, H., & Tamayo, A. (2017). Social capital, trust, and firm performance: The value of corporate social responsibility during the financial crisis. *The Journal of Finance, 72*(4), 1785–1824.

Little, D. (1998). *Microfoundations, method and causation: On the philosophy of the social sciences*. New Brunswick, NJ: Transaction Publishers.

Llano Ortiz, J. C. (2015). El estado de la pobreza, 5° informe EAPN. Recuperado de https://www.eapn.es/estadodepobreza/descargas.php (consultado el 4 de mayo de 2021).

Lobel, I., & Sadler, E. (2016). Preferences, homophily, and social learning. *Operations Research, 64*(3), 564–584.

Loury, G. (1977). Women, minorities, and employment discrimination. In P. A. Wallace & A. Le Mund (Eds.), *A dynamic theory of racial income differences* (pp. 153–186). Lexington, MA: Lexington Books.

Loury, G. (2002). *The anatomy of racial inequality.* Cambridge, MA: Harvard University Press.

Lowndes, V. (2004). Getting on or getting by? Women, social capital and political participation. *The British Journal of Politics & International Relations, 6*, 45–65.

Lowndes, V. (2006). It's not what you've got, but what you do with it: Women, social capital and political participation. In B. O'Neill & E. Gidengil (Eds.), *Gender and social capital* (pp. 213–240). New York: Routledge.

Luhmann, N. (1988). Familiarity, confidence and trust: Problems and alternative. In D. Gambetta (Ed.), *Making and breaking cooperative relations* (pp. 94–107). Oxford: Blackwell.

Lykken, D., & Tellegen, A. (1996). Happiness is a stochastic phenomenon. *Psychological Science, 7*(3), 180–189.

Macneil, I. R. (1987). Relational contract theory as sociology: A reply to professors Lindenberg and de Vos. *Journal of Institutional and Theoretical Economics, 143*, 272–290.

Maki, U. (2000). Imperialismo da economia: conceitos e restrições. *Economica, 2*(3), 5–36.

Malecki, E. J. (2012). Regional social capital: Why it matters. *Regional Studies, 46*(8), 1023–1039.

Manski, C. F. (2000). Economic analysis of social interactions. *Journal of Economic Perspectives, 14*(3), 115–136.

Marsden, P. V. (1990). Network data and measurement. *American Review of Sociology, 16*, 435–463.

Martin, N. (2012). The privilege of ease: Social class and campus life at highly selective, private universities. *Research in Higher Education, 53*(4), 426–452.

Martin, N. D. (2009). Quantifying social class: A latent clustering approach. In K. Robson & C. Sanders (Eds.), *Quantifying theory: Pierre Bourdieu* (pp. 161–174). Toronto: Springer.

Martínez-García, J. S. (2023). Karl Marx, Erik O. Wright y Pierre Bourdieu: Hacia una generalización de la teoría del capital. *Revista Española de Sociología, 32*(1), 1–17.

Maslow, A. H. (1943). A theory of human motivation. *Psychological Review, 50*(4), 370–396.

Maslow, A. H. (1954). *Motivation and personality.* New York: Harper and Row.

Mata, T., & Louçã, F. (2009). The Solow residual as a black box: Attempts at integrating business cycle and growth theories. *History of Political Economy, 41*(Suppl_1), 334–355.

Mauro, P. (1995). Corruption and growth. *Quarterly Journal of Economics, 110*, 681–712.

Mauss, M. (1977). *Obras* (3 vols.). Barcelona: Seix Barral.

Mayol, A., & T. Pénard (2017). Facebook use and individual well-being: Like me to make me happier! *Revue d'économie industrielle, 158*, 101–127.

McDonald, S., Lin, N., & Ao, D. (2009). Networks of opportunity: Gender, race, and job leads. *Social Problems, 56*, 385–402.

McPherson, J., Smith-Lovin, L., & Cook, J. M. (2001). Birds of a feather: Homophily in social networks. *Annual Review of Sociology, 27*, 415–444.

Meade, J. E. (1952). External economies and diseconomies in a competitive situation. *The Economic Journal, 62*(245), 54–67.

Membiela-Pollán, M. (2013). *Capital social: Glosario. El valor económico de la dimensión social.* A Coruña: Editorial Camiño do Faro, S. L.

Membiela-Pollán, M. (2016). *La teoría del capital social.* A Coruña: Editorial Camiño do Faro.

Membiela-Pollán, M., Alló-Pazos, M., Pateiro-Rodríguez, C., & Blázquez-Lozano, F. (2019a). The inefficiency of the neoclassical paradigm in the promotion of subjective well-being and socioeconomic, and environmental sustainability: An empirical test for the Spanish case. *Sustainability, 11*(24), 7102.

Membiela-Pollán, M., & Pena-López, J. A. (2017). Clarifying the concept of social capital through its three perspectives: Individualistic, communitarian and macrosocial. *European Journal of Government and Economics (EJGE), 6*(2), 146–170.

Membiela-Pollán, M., Pena López, J. A., & Sánchez-Amboage, E. (2019b). La interrelación entre el "capital humano" y el "capital social": Una aproximación al caso español. *Atlantic Review of Economics (ARoEc), 2*(2), 1–18.

Membiela-Pollán, M., Picatoste, X., & Blázquez-Lozano, F. (2023). Social capital's role in SDG 3 of 2030 agenda: Promoting health and well-being. In W. Leal Filho, M.A.P. Dinis, S. Moggi, E. Price, A. Hope (Eds.), *SDGs in the European region* (pp. 1–25). Cham: Springer International Publishing.

Membiela-Pollán, M., Rodríguez-Vázquez, C., & Sánchez-Amboage, E. (2021, June). Effects of social media on structural social capital and subjective well-being: Insights from a review of the literature. In 2021 16th Iberian Conference on Information Systems and Technologies (CISTI) (pp. 1–6). IEEE.

Membiela-Pollán, M., Sánchez-Amboage, E., & Rodríguez-Vázquez, C. (2020). The media and its influence in three dimensions of social capital, an opportunity for social marketing? *Revista de la Asociación Española de Investigación de la Comunicación, 7*(14), 258–289.

Merton, R. K. (1988). The Matthew effect in Science II: Cumulative advantage and the symbolism of intellectual property. *ISIS, 79*(1), 606–623.

Meshi, D., & Ellithorpe, M. E. (2021). Problematic social media use and social support received in real-life versus on social media: Associations with depression, anxiety and social isolation. *Addictive Behaviors, 119*, 1–6.

Migheli, M. (2017). Ubuntu and social capital: A strong relationship and a possible instrument of socio-economic development. *Cambridge Journal of Economics, 41*(4), 1213–1235.

Millán, R., & Gordon, S. (2004). Capital social: una lectura de tres perspectivas clásicas. *Revista Mexicana de Sociología, 66*(4), 711–747.

Mishra, S. (2020). Social networks, social capital, social support and academic success in higher education: A systematic review with a special focus on 'underrepresented' students. *Educational Research Review, 29*, 100307.

Misztal, B. A. (1996). *Trust in modern societies*. Cambridge: Polity Press.

Miu, T. A. (2019). The mass media and the Christian values. *International Journal of Theology, Philosophy and Science, 3*(5), 62–68.

Molina, J. L. (2001). *El análisis de redes sociales. Una introducción.* Barcelona: Editorial Bellaterra.

Monteiro, C., & Lima, R. (2021). Embeddedness and disembeddedness in economic sociology in three time periods. *Sociologia & Antropologia, 11*, 43–67.

Moore, M. D., & Recker, N. L. (2016). Social capital, type of crime, and social control. *Crime & Delinquency, 62*(6), 728–747.

Morales, L., & Mota, F. (2006). El asociacionismo en España. In J. R. Montero, J. Font, & M. Torcal (Eds.), *Ciudadanos, asociaciones y participación en España* (pp. 77–104). Madrid: CIS.

Mosca, M., Musella, M., & Pastore, F. (2006). Relational goods, monitoring and non-pecuniary compensations in the nonprofit sector: the case of Italian social services. IZA Discussion Papers, 2254, IZA, Bonn.

Myrdal, G. (1957). *Rich lands and poor*. New York: Harper & Brothers.

Nahapiet, J., & Ghoshal, S. (1998). Social capital, intellectual capital and the organizational advantage. *Academy of Management Review, 23*(2), 242–266.

Nakagomi, A., Shiba, K., Hanazato, M., Kondo, K., & Kawachi, I. (2020). Does community-level social capital mitigate the impact of widowhood & living alone on depressive symptoms?: A prospective, multi-level study. *Social Science & Medicine, 259*, 113140.

Narayan, D., & Cassidy, M. F. (2001). A dimensional approach to measuring social capital: development and validation of a social capital inventory. *Current Sociology*, *49*(2), 59–102.

Nee, V., & Sanders, J. (2003). Trust in ethnic ties: Social capital and immigrants. In K. S. Cook (Ed.), *Trust in society* (pp. 374–392). New York: Russell Sage Foundation.

Neira, I., Vázquez, E., & Portela, M. (2009). An empirical analysis of social capital and economic growth in Europe (1980–2000). *Social Indicators Research, 92*, 111–129.

Neveu, E. (2018). Bourdieu's capital(s): Sociologizing an economic concept. In T. Medvetz & J. J. Sallaz (Eds.), *The Oxford handbook of Pierre Bourdieu* (pp. 347–374). Oxford: Oxford University Press.

Newton, K. (2001). Trust, social capital, civil society, and democracy. *International Political Science Review, 22*(2), 201–214.

Nieli, R. (1986). Spheres of intimacy and the A. Smith problem. *Journal of the History of Ideas, 47*(4), 611–624.

Nikolova, M., & Graham, C. (2020). The economics of happiness. GLO Discussion Paper Series 640. Global Labor Organization (GLO).

North, D. (1990). *Institutions, institutional change, and economic performance*. Cambridge, RU: Cambridge University Press.

Nowak, M., & Highfield, R. (2012). *Supercooperators: Altruism, evolution, and why we need each other to succeed*. New York: Simon and Schuster.

Nussbaum, M. (1987). The stoics on the extirpation of the passions. *Apeiron: A Journal for Ancient Philosophy and Science, 20*(2), 129–177.

Nussbaum, M. (1995 [1986]). *La fragilidad del bien: Fortuna y ética en la tragedia y la filosofía griega*. Madrid: Visor.

Nussbaum, M. (2001). *Upheavals of thought: The intelligence of emotions*. Cambridge: Cambridge University Press.

O'Keeffe, G. S., & Clarke-Pearson, K. (2011). The impact of social media on children, adolescents, and families. *Paediatrics, 127*(4), 800–804.

Odabas, M., & Adaman, F. (2014). Engaging with social networks: The Bourdieu-Becker encounter revisited. *Forum for Social Economics, 47*(3–4), 305–323.

OECD. (2007). *How what you know shapes your life*. París: OECD Insights.

Olson, M. (1965). *The logic of collective action*. Cambridge, MA: Harvard University Press.

Olson, M. (1982). *The rise and decline of nations: Economic growth, stagflation, and social rigidities*. New Haven, CT: Yale University Press.

Ormel, J., Lindenberg, S., Steverink, N., & Verbrugge, L. M. (1999). Subjective well-being and social production functions. *Social Indicators Research, 46*(1), 61–90.

Oshio, T. (2017). Which is more relevant for perceived happiness, individual-level or area-level social capital? A multilevel mediation analysis. *Journal of Happiness Studies, 18*, 765–783.

Ostrom, E. (1990). *Governing the commons: The evolution of institutions for collective action*. Cambridge: Cambridge University Press.

Ostrom, E., & Ahn, T. K. (2003). A social science perspective on social capital: Social capital and collective action. *Revista Mexicana de Sociología, 65*(1), 155–233.

Ostrom, E., & Ahn, T. K. (2009). The meaning of social capital and its links to collective action. In G. T. Svendsen & G. L. Svendsen (Eds.), *Handbook of social capital: The troika of sociology, political science, and economics* (pp. 17–35). Northampton: Elgar.

Oxoby, R. J. (2004). Cognitive dissonance, status and growth of the underclass. *Economic Journal, 114*, 727–749. https://doi.org/10.1111/j.1468-0297.2004.00241.x

Oyarzun, D. A., Gavaldón Hernández, G., & García de Sotelsek, L. M. (2007). Educación y desarrollo: ¿capital humano o capital social? *Revista de educación, 344*, 221–222.

Paldam, M. (2000). Social capital, one or many? Definition and measurement. *Journal of Economic Surveys, 14*(5), 629–653.

Paldam, M. (2002). The cross-country pattern of corruption: Economics, culture and the seesaw dynamics. *European Journal of Political Economy, 18*, 215–240.

Pang, H. (2022). Connecting mobile social media with psychosocial well-being: Understanding relationship between WeChat involvement, network characteristics, online capital and life satisfaction. *Social Networks, 68*, 256–263.

Paterson, L. (2000). Civil society and democratic renewal. In S. Baron, J. Field, & T. Schuller (Eds.), *Social capital: Critical perspectives* (pp. 39–55). Oxford: Oxford University Press.

Paxton, P. (2002). Social capital and democracy: An interdependent relationship. *American Sociological Review, 67*, 254–277.

Paxton, P. (2007). Association memberships and generalized trust: A multilevel model across 31 countries. *Social Forces, 86*, 47–76.

Payne, G. T., Moore, C. B., Griffis, S. E., & Autry, C. W. (2011). Multilevel challenges and opportunities in social capital research. *Journal of Management, 37*(2), 491–520.

Pena-López, J. A., & Sánchez-Santos, J. M. (2007). The Olson-Putnam controversy: Some empirical evidence. *Economics Bulletin, 26*(4), 1–10.

Pena-López, J. A., & Sánchez-Santos, J. M. (2008a). Los fundamentos morales de la economía: una relectura del problema de Adam Smith. *Revista de economía institucional, 9*(16), 63–87.

Pena-López, J. A., & Sanchez-Santos, J. M. (2008b). Social capital, trust and models of associationism in Spain. *Papers-Revista de Sociologia, 103*(2), 153–173.

Pena-López, J. A., & Sánchez-Santos, J. M. (2009). La dotación de capital social como factor determinante de la corrupción. *Revista de Economía Mundial*, (22), 197–219.

Pena-López, J. A., & Sánchez-Santos, J. M. (2011). *El capital social como recurso de la empresa familiar: La familiness*. Colección Materiales Docentes, 3. Coruña: Netbiblo.

Pena-López, J. A., & Sánchez-Santos, J. M. (2013). El capital social individual: lo micro y lo macro en las relaciones sociales. In J. L. Veira Veira (Ed.), *Desigualdad y capital social en España* (pp. 11–31). Oleiros: Netbiblo.

Pena-López, J. A., & Sánchez-Santos, J. M. (2014). Does corruption have social roots? The role of culture and social capital. *Journal of Business Ethics, 122*, 697–708.

Pena-López, J. A., & Sánchez-Santos, J. M. (2017). Individual social capital: Accessibility and mobilization of resources embedded in social Networks. *Social Networks, 49*, 1–11.

Pena-López, J. A., Sánchez-Santos, J. M., & Membiela-Pollán, M. (2017). Individual social capital and subjective wellbeing: The relational goods. *Journal of Happiness Studies, 18*, 881–901.

Pena-López, J. M., Rungo, P., & Sánchez-Santos, J. M. (2021). Inequality and individuals' social networks: The other face of social capital. *Cambridge Journal of Economics, 45*(4), 675–694.

Pena-López, A., & De Juan-Díaz, R. (2024). Indicadores de bienestar subjetivo y sus determinantes socioeconómicos: un estudio para la sociedad española. *EMPIRIA. Revista de Metodología de Ciencias Sociales*, (61), 123-147.
Pérez Adán, J. (1997). *Socioeconomía*. Madrid: Editorial Trotta, S. A. University Press.
Phillips, D. (2006). *Quality of life: Concept, policy and practice*. London: Routledge.
Philp M. (2006). Corruption, definition and measurement. In C. Sampford, A. Shacklock, C. Connors, & F. Galtung (Eds.), *Measuring corruption* (pp. 45–56). Aldershot: Ashgate.
Pichler, F., & Wallace, C. (2007). Patterns of formal and informal social capital in Europe. *European Sociological Review, 23*(4), 423–435.
Pichler, F., & Wallace, C. (2009). Social capital and social class in Europe: The role of social networks in social stratification. *European Sociological Review, 25*(3), 319–332.
Piketty, T. (2014). *Capital in the twenty-first century*. Cambridge: Harvard University Press.
Plattner, S. (Ed.) (1991). *Antropología económica*. Madrid: Alianza Editorial.
Polanyi, K. (1944). *The great transformation*. New York: Rinehart (1968 ed.).
Polanyi, K. (1977). *The livelihood of man* (H. W. Pearson, Ed.). New York: Academic Press.
Polanyi, K., Arensberg, C. M., & Pearson, H. W. (1957). *Trade and markets in the early empires*. Glencoe: The Free Press.
Portes, A. (1998). Social capital: Its origins and applications in modern sociology. *Annual Review of Sociology, 24*(1), 1–24.
Portes, A. (2000). The two meanings of social capital. *Sociological Forum, 15*(1), 1–12.
Portes, A. (2018). Social capital: Its origins and applications in modern sociology. *Annual Review of Sociology, 24*(1), 1–24.
Portes, A., & Vickstrom, E. (2015). Diversity, social capital, and cohesion. *Series Etudes europeennes, 41*. Brussels: Institut de D'Etudes Europeennes.
Pugno, M. (2007). The subjective well-being paradox: A suggested solution based on relational goods. In L. Bruni, & P. L. Porta (Eds.), *Handbook of economics of the happiness* (pp. 263–290). Cheltenham: Edward Elgar.
Punch, M. (2000). Police corruption and its prevention. *European Journal on Criminal Policy and Research, 8*, 301–324.
Puntscher, S., Hauser, C., Walde, J., & Tappeiner, G. (2015). The impact of social capital on subjective well-being: A regional perspective. *Journal of Happiness Studies, 16*, 1231–1246.
Putnam, R. D. (1993). *Making democracy work: Civic traditions in modern Italy*. Princeton, NJ: Princeton University Press.
Putnam, R. D. (1995). Bowling alone: America's declining social capital. *Journal of Democracy, 6*(1), 65–78.
Putnam, R. D. (2000). *Bowling alone, the collapse and revival of American community*. New York: Simon and Schuster.
Putnam, R. D. (2001). Social capital: Measurement and consequences. *Canadian Journal of Policy Research, 2*, 41–51.
Putnam, R. D. (Ed.) (2002). *Democracies in flux: The evolution of social capital in contemporary society*. New York: Oxford University Press.
Putnam, R.D., & Goss, K. A. (2001). Einleitung. In *Gesellschaft und Gemeinsinn – Sozialkapital im internationalen Vergleich* (pp. 15–43). Gütersloh: Verlag Bertelsmann Stiftung.
Putzel, J. (1997). Accounting for the 'dark side' of social capital: Reading Robert Putnam on democracy. *Journal of International Development, 9*(7), 939–949.
Quibria, M. G. (2003). The puzzle of social capital: A critical review. *Asian Development Review, 20*(2), 19–39.

Rahn, W. M., & Transue, J. E. (1998). Social trust and value change: The decline of social capital in American youth, 1976–1995. *Political Psychology, 19*(3), 545–565.

Raiser, M. (2008). Social capital in transition economies. In D. Castiglione, J. W. Van Deth, & G. Wolleb (Eds.), *The handbook of social capital* (pp. 491–519). New York: Oxford University Press.

Ramos-Pinto, P. (2012). Social capital as a capacity for collective action. In P. Ramos-Pinto (Ed.), *Assessing social capital: Concept, policy and practice* (Vol. 53, No. 69, pp. 53–69). Newcastle upon Tyne: Cambridge Scholars Publishing in association with GSE Research.

Ratnapala, S. (2003). Moral capital and commercial society. *The Independent Review, 8*(2), 213–233.

Real Academia Española (2024a). Diccionario de la lengua española. Sociedad. Recuperado de https://dle.rae.es/sociedad?m=form

Real Academia Española (2024b). Diccionario de la lengua española. Bien. Recuperado de https://dle.rae.es/bien?m=form

Righi, A., & Masserini, L. (2023). Measuring relational factors underlying subjective happiness. *Current Psychology, 42*(11), 9225–9236.

Rigney, D. (2010). *The Matthew effect*. New York: Columbia University Press.

Robison, L. J., Malone, T., Oliver, J. O., Bali, V., & Winder, R. E. (2020). Social capital, relational goods, and terms and level of exchange. *Modern Economy, 11*(07), 1288.

Robison, L. J., & Oliver, J. R. (2023). Rationalizing predictably irrational choices: The social capital synthesis. *The Annals of Regional Science, 70*(3), 611–631.

Robison, L. J., & Ritchie, B. K. (2010). *Relationship economics: The social capital paradigm and its application to business, politics, and other transactions*. New York: Routledge.

Robison, L. J., Schmid, A. A., & Siles, M. E. (2002). Is social capital really capital? *Review of Social Economy, 60*, 1–24.

Roche, M. (2004). Social policy and social capital: A clear case of putting merit before method? *Social Policy and Society, 3*(2), 97–111.

Rodríguez-Pose, A., & Von Berlepsch, V. (2012). Social capital and individual happiness in Europe. *Bruges European Economic Research Papers, 25*, 1–45.

Roemer, J. E. (1989). *Teoría general de la explotación y las clases*. Madrid: Siglo XXI.

Rose-Ackerman, S. (1975). The economics of corruption. *Journal of Public Economics, 4*, 187–203.

Rose-Ackerman, S. (1978). *Corruption: A study in political economy*. New York, San Francisco, CA, London: Academic Press.

Rose-Ackerman, S. (1999). *Corruption and government: Causes, consequences and reform*. Cambridge: Cambridge University Press.

Rose-Ackerman, S. (2001). Trust and honesty in post-socialist societies. *Kyklos, 54*, 415–444.

Roth, F. (2022). *Intangible capital and growth*. Cham: Springer.

Rothstein, B., & Uslaner, E. M. (2005). All for all: Equality, corruption and social trust. *World Politics, 58*, 41–72.

Rotter, J. B. (1980). Interpersonal trust, trustworthiness, and gullibility. *American Psychologist, 35*, 1–7.

Rubineau, B., & Fernandez, R. M. (2013). Missing links: Referrer behavior and job segregation. *Management Science, 59*(11), 2470–2489.

Rungo, P., &Pena-López, J. A. (2019). Persistent inequalities and social relations: An intergenerational model. *The Journal of Mathematical Sociology, 43*(1), 23–39.

Rungo, P., Sánchez-Santos, J. M., & Pena López, A. (2024). Individual social capital and expectations of career advancement. *The Economic and Labour Relations Review, 35*(1), 118–139.

Ryan, R. M., & Deci, E. L. (2001). On happiness and human potentials: A review of research on hedonic and eudaimonic well-being. *Annual Review of Psychology, 52*, 141–146.

Sabatini, F. (2009). Social capital as social networks: A new framework for measurement and an empirical analysis of its determinants and consequences. *The Journal of Socio-Economics, 38*, 429–442.

Sacco, P. L., & Vanin, P. (2000). Network interaction with material and relational goods: An exploratory simulation. *Annals of Public and Cooperative Economics, 71*(2), 229–259.

Sacco, P. L., Vanin, P., & Zamagni, S. (2006). The economics of human relationships. In S.-C. Kolm & J. Mercier Ythier (Eds.), *Handbook of the economics of giving, altruism and reciprocity* (vol. 1, pp. 695–730). Amsterdam: Elsevier North Holland.

Sacco, P. L., & Zamagni, S. (2002). *Complessità Relazionale e Comportamento Economico.* Bologna: Il Mulino.

Sally, D. (1995). Conversation and cooperation in social dilemmas: A meta-analysis of experiments from 1958 to 1992. *Rationality and Society, 7*, 58–92.

Sánchez-Santos, J. M., & Pena López, J. A. (2005). Actividad asociativa, confianza y generación de capital social: Evidencia empírica. *Ekonomiaz: Revista Vasca de Economía, 59*, 136–159.

Sandel, M. (2013). Market reasoning as moral reasoning: Why economists should reengage with political philosophy. *Journal of Economic Perspectives, 27*(4), 121–140.

Savage, M., Devine, F., & Cunningham, N. (2013). A new model of social class: Findings from the BBC's Great British Class Survey experiment. *Sociology, 47*(2), 219–250.

Savvides, A., & Stengos, T. (2009). *Human capital and economic growth.* Stanford: Stanford University Press.

Sayer, A. (2000). Moral economy and political economy. *Studies in Political Economy, 61*, 79–103.

Sayer, A. (2004). *Moral economy*. Lancaster: Lancaster University.

Schiefer, D., & Van der Noll, J. (2017). The essentials of social cohesion: A literature review. *Social Indicators Research, 132*, 579–603.

Schiff, M. (1992). Social capital, labor mobility, and welfare: The impact of Uniting States. *Rationality and Society, 4*(2), 157–175.

Schinkel, W. (2004). The will to violence. *Theoretical Criminology, 8*(1), 5–31.

Schultz, T. W. (1961). Investment in human capital. *The American Economic Review, 51*(1), 1–17.

Schultz, T. W. (1982). *Investing in people: The economics of population quality*. Berkeley: University of California Press.

Schweitzer, H. (2005). Corruption, its spread and decline. In J. Lambsdorff, M. Taube, & M. Schramm (Eds.), *The new institutional economics of corruption: Norms, trust, and reciprocity* (pp. 16–40). Londres: Routledge.

Scopus (2023). Recuperado de https://www.scopus.com/term/analyzer.uri?sort=plf-f&src=s&sid=d00d7a2bbb55b085d9aacd8331e3525a&sot=a&sdt=a&sl=69&s=TITLE-ABS-KEY%28%22social+capital%22%29+AND+PUBYEAR+%3e+1984+AND+PUBYEAR+%3c+2023&origin=resultslist&count=10&analyzeResults=Analyze+results

Scott, D., & Usher, R. (2011). *Researching education: Data, methods and theory in educational enquiry* (2nd ed.). London: Continuum International Publishing Group.

Semmann, D., Krambeck, H.-J., & Milinski, M. (2005). Reputation is valuable within and outside one's own social group. *Behavioral Ecology and Sociobiology, 57*(6), 611–616.

Sen, A. (1977). Rational fools: A critique of the behavioural foundations of economic theory. *Philosophy and Public Affairs, 6*(4), 317–344.

Sen, A. (1995). Goals, commitment and identity. In S. Zamagni (Ed.), *Economics of altruism* (pp. 79–93). Aldershot: E. Elgar.

Sen, A. (1997 [1987]). *Sobre ética y economía*. Madrid: Alianza Universidad, S. A.

Sen, A. (1999). *Desarrollo y Libertad*. Barcelona: Editorial Planeta.

Sen, A. K. (1985). The moral standing of the market. In E. F. Paul et al. (Eds.), *Ethics and economics* (pp. 1–19). Oxford: Blackwell.

Serageldin, I. (1996). Sustainability as opportunity and the problem of social capital. *Brown Journal of World Affairs, 3*(2), 187–203.

Shane-Simpson, C., Manago, A., Gaggi, N., & Gillespie-Lynch, K. (2018). Why do college students prefer Facebook, Twitter, or Instagram? Site affordances, tensions between privacy and self-expression, and implications for social capital. *Computers in Human Behavior, 86*, 276–288.

Shayo, M. (2009). A model of social identity with an application to political economy: Nation, class and redistribution. *American Political Science Review, 103*(2), 147–174.

Sheer, V. C., & Rice, R. E. (2017). Mobile instant messaging use and social capital: Direct and indirect associations with employee outcomes. *Information & Management, 54*(1), 90–102.

Simmel, G. (1950). *The sociology of Georg Simmel*. New York: Simon and Schuster.

Simon, H. A. (1993). Altruism and economics. *American Economic Review, 83*, 156–161.

Simon, H. A. (2000). Bounded rationality in social science. *Mind and Society, 1*, 25–39.

Skidelsky, R. (2009). *El regreso de Keynes*. Barcelona: Crítica.

Slovic, P., Finucane, M., Peters, E., & MacGregor, D. G. (2002). Rational actors or rational fools: Implications of the affect heuristic for behavioral economics. *The Journal of Socio-Economics, 31*(4), 329–342.

Smith, A. (1994). *La riqueza de las naciones* [The wealth of nations]. (Ed. C. Rodríguez Braun). Madrid: Alianza Editorial. (Trabajo original publicado en 1776).

Smith, A. (1997). *La teoría de los sentimientos morales* [The theory of moral sentiments]. (Ed. C. Rodríguez Braun). Madrid: Alianza Editorial. (Trabajo original publicado en 1759).

Snijders, T. A. B. (1999). Prologue to the measurement of social capital. *La Revue Tocqueville, 20*, 27–44.

Sobel, J. (2002). Can we trust social capital? *Journal of Economic Literature, 40*(1), 139–154.

Solow, R. (1956). A contribution to the theory of economic growth. *The Quarterly Journal of Economics, 70*(1), 65–94.

Solow, R. M. (1957). Technical change and the aggregate production function. *The Review of Economics and Statistics, 39*(3), 312–320.

Solow, R. (1963). *Capital theory and the rate of return*. Amsterdam: North Holland.

Solow, R. M. (2000). Notes on social capital and economic performance. In P. Dasgupta & I. Serageldin (Eds.), *Social capital: A multifaceted perspective* (pp. 6–10). Washington, DC: World Bank.

Sommer, C. (2019). *Social cohesion and economic development: Unpacking the relationship* (Briefing Paper No. 16/2019). Bonn: Deutsches Institut für Entwicklungspolitik (DIE).

Sønderskov, K. M. (2011). Does generalized social trust lead to associational membership?: Unraveling a bowl of well-tossed spaghetti. *European Sociological Review, 27*(4), 419–434.

Spottswood, E. L., & Wohn, D. Y. (2020). Online social capital: Recent trends in research. *Current Opinion in Psychology, 36*, 147–152.

Stigler, J., & Becker, G. (1977). De gustibus non est disputandum. *American Economic Review, 67*(2), 76–90.

Stolle, D. (2001). Getting to trust: An analysis of the importance of institutions, families, personal experiences and group membership. In P. Dekker & E. M. Uslaner (Eds.), *Politics in everyday life: Social capital and participation* (pp. 118–133). London: Routledge.

Stolle, D., & Rochon, T. (1999). The myth of American exceptionalism: A three-nation comparison of associational membership and social capital. In J. Van Deth, M. Maraffi, K. Newton, & P. Whiteley (Eds.), *Social capital and European democracy* (pp. 192–209). London: Routledge.

Stone, W. (2001). Measuring social capital: Towards a theoretically informed measurement framework for researching social capital in family and community life (Research Paper No. 24). Australian Institute of Family Studies, Melbourne.

Storberg, J. (2002). The evolution of capital theory: A critique of a theory of social capital and implications for HRD. *Human Resource Development Review, 1*(4), 468–499.

Stutzer, A., & Frey, B. S. (2006). Does marriage make people happy, or do happy people get married? *The Journal of Socio-Economics, 35*(2), 326–347.

Sugden, R. (2002). Beyond sympathy and empathy: Adam's Smith's concept of fellow-feeling. *Economics and Philosophy, 18*, 63–87.

Sugden, R. (2005). Fellow-feeling. In B. Gui, & R. Sugden: *Economics and social interactions: Accounting for interpersonal relations* (pp. 52–95). Cambridge: Cambridge University Press.

Sullivan, A. (2002). Bourdieu and education: How useful is Bourdieu's theory for researchers? *The Netherlands Journal of Social Science, 38*, 144–166.

Suzuki Hillyer, R. (2021). Staying connected: Effects of online platforms on transnational family relations and social capital. *Contemporary Japan, 33*(1), 3–23.

Svendsen, G. L., & Svendsen, G. T. (2004). On the wealth of nations: Bourdieuconomics and social capital. In D. L. Swartz, & V. L. Zolberg, *After Bourdieu: Influence, Critique, Elaboration* (pp. 607–631). Netherlands: Springer Science and Business Media.

Svendsen, G. T. (2003). Social capital, corruption and economic growth: Eastern and Western Europe (Working Papers 03-21, University of Aarhus, Aarhus School of Business, Department of Economics).

Swedberg, R. (2011). The economic sociologies of Pierre Bourdieu. *Cultural Sociology, 5*(1), 67–82.

Swedberg, R., & Granovetter, M. (1992). *The sociology of economic life*. Oxford: Westview Press.

Szreter, S. (2002). The state of social capital: Bringing back in power, politics and history. *Theory and Society, 31*(5), 573–621.

Tanzi, V. (1994). Corruption, government activities, and markets. Documento de trabajo del FMI No. 94/99.

Tanzi, V. (1998). Corruption around the world causes, consequences, scope, and cures. *IMF Staff Papers, 45*(4), 559–594.

Tarrow, S. (1996). Making social science work across space and time: A critical reflection on Robert Putnam's Making Democracy Work. *American Political Science Review, 90*(2), 389–397.

Thomas, C. Y. (1996). Capital markets, financial markets and social capital. *Social and Economic Studies, 45*(23), 1–23.

Thompson, M. (2018). Social capital, innovation and economic growth. *Journal of Behavioral and Experimental Economics, 73*, 46–52.

Tilly, C. (1999). *Durable inequality*. Berkeley: University of California Press.

Tocqueville, A. (1987). *La democracia en América*. México: Fondo de Cultura Económica.

Tönnies, F. (1947 [1887]). *Comunidad y sociedad*. Buenos Aires: Losada.

Torpe, L., & Lolle, H. (2011). Identifying social trust in cross-country analysis: Do we really measure the same? *Social Indicators Research, 103*, 481–500.

Treisman, D. (2000). The causes of corruption: A cross-national study. *Journal of Public Economics, 73*, 399–457.

Tsai, W., & Ghoshal, S. (1998). Social capital and value creation: The role of Intrafirm networks. *The Academy of Management Journal, 41*(4), 464–476.

Tulin, M., Lancee, B., & Volker, B. (2018). Personality and social capital. *Social Psychology Quarterly, 81*(4), 295–318.

Turner, J. H. (2000). The formation of social capital. In P. Dasgupta & I. Serageldin (Eds.), *Social capital: A multifaceted perspective* (pp. 94–116). Washington, DC: World Bank.

Uhlaner, C. J. (1989). 'Relational goods' and participation: Incorporating sociability into a theory of rational action. *Public Choice, 62*(3), 253–285.

Uhlaner, L. M., Matser, I. A., Berent-Braun, M. M., & Flören, R. H. (2015). Linking bonding and bridging ownership social capital in private firms. *Family Business Review, 28*(3), 260–277.

Uphoff, N. (2000). Understanding social capital: Learning from the analysis and experience of participation. In I. Serageldin & P. Dasgupta (Eds.), *Social capital: A multifaceted perspective* (pp. 215–249). Washington, DC: World Bank.

Urbina, D. A., & Ruiz-Villaverde, A. (2019). A critical review of homo economicus from five approaches. *American Journal of Economics and Sociology, 78*(1), 63–93.

Uslaner, E. M. (1999). Democracy and social capital. In Warren, M. E. (Ed.), *Democracy and trust* (pp. 121–150). Cambridge: Cambridge University Press.

Uslaner, E. M. (2002). *The moral foundations of trust*. Nueva York: Universidad de Cambridge.

Uslaner, E. M. (2005). Trust and corruption. In J. Lambsdorff, M. Taube, & M. Schramm (Eds.), *The new institutional economics of corruption* (pp. 76–92). Londres, Nueva York: Routledge.

Uslaner, E. M. (2008). Trust as a moral value. In D. Castiglione & J. W. Van Deth (Eds.), *The handbook of social capital* (pp. 101–121). New York: Oxford University Press.

Van Der Gaag, M., & Snijders, T. (2004). Proposals for the measurement of individual social capital. In H. D. Flap & B. Volker (Eds.), *Creation and returns of Social Capital* (pp. 199–218). London: Routledge.

Van Der Gaag, M., & Snijders, T. (2005). The resource generator: Measurement of individual social capital with concrete items. *Social Networks, 27*, 1–29.

Van Der Gaag, M., & Snijders, T. (2008). Position generator measures and their relationship to other social capital measures. In N. Lin & B. Erickson (Eds.), *Social capital: An international research program*. Oxford: Oxford University Press.

Van Deth, J. W. (2008). Measuring social capital. In D. Castiglione, J. W. Van Deth, & G. Wolleb (Eds.), *The handbook of social capital* (pp. 150–176). New York: Oxford University Press.

Van Ingen, E., & Bekkers, R. (2015). Generalized trust through civic engagement? Evidence from five national panel studies. *Political Psychology, 36*(3), 277–294.

Van Oorschot, W., & Arts, W. (2005). The social capital of European welfare states: The crowding-out hypothesis revisited. *Journal of European Social Policy, 15*(1), 5–26.

Van Staveren, I., & Pervaiz, Z. (2017). Is it ethnic fractionalization or social exclusion, which affects social cohesion? *Social Indicators Research, 130*, 711–731.

Van Tubergen, F., & Volker, B. (2015). Inequality in access to social capital in the Netherlands. *Sociology, 49*(3), 521–538.

Veenhoven, R. (1991). Is happiness relative? *Social Indicators Research, 24*, 1–34.

Veenhoven, R. (1994). Is happiness a trait? Tests of the theory that a better society does not make people any happier. *Social Indicators Research, 32*, 101–160.

Verbrugge, R. (1977). The structure of adult friendship choices. *Social Forces, 56*, 576–597.

Verhaeghe, P. (2015). Inequalities in social capital and their longitudinal effects on the labour market entry. *Social Networks, 40*, 174–184.

Villalonga-Olives, E., Almansa, J., Shaya, F., & Kawachi, I. (2020). Perceived social capital and binge drinking in older adults: The Health and Retirement Study, US data from 2006–2014. *Drug and Alcohol Dependence, 214*, 108099.

Villalonga-Olives, E., & Kawachi, I. (2017). The dark side of social capital: A systematic review of the negative health effects of social capital. *Social Science & Medicine, 194*, 105–127.

Volker, B., & Flap, H. (1997). The comrades' belief: Intended and unintended consequences of communism for neighbourhood relations in the former GDR. *European Sociological Review, 13*(3), 241–265.

von Böhm-Bawerk, E. (1884). *Kapital und Kapitalzins: Geschichte und Kritik der Kapitalzins-Theorieen* (Vol. 1). Leipzig: Wagner.

Vorhaus, J. (2014). Function and functional explanation in social capital theory: A philosophical appraisal. *Studies in Philosophy and Education, 33*, 185–199.

Waldstrøm, C., & Svendsen, G. (2008). On the capitalization and cultivation of social capital: Towards a neo-capital general science? *The Journal of Socio-Economics, 37*(4), 1495–1514.

Warren, M. E. (1999). Democratic theory and trust. In M. E. Warren (Ed.), *Democracy and trust* (pp. 310–345). Cambridge: Cambridge University Press.

Warren, M. E. (2008). The nature and logic of bad social capital. In D. Castiglione, J. W. Van Deth, & G. Wolleb (Eds.), *The handbook of social capital* (pp. 122–149). New York: Oxford University Press.

Waterman, A. S. (2008). Reconsidering happiness: A eudaimonist's perspective. *The Journal of Positive Psychology, 3*(4), 234–252.

Weber, M. (1964 [1922]). *Economía y Sociedad*. México: FCE.

Weber, M. (1993 [1922]). *Economía y sociedad*. México: Fondo de Cultura Económica.

Weber, M. (1994 [1905]). *La ética protestante y el espíritu del capitalismo*. Barcelona: Península.

Welch, M. R., Rivera, R., Conway, B. P., Yonkoski, J., Lupton, P. M., & Giancola, R. (2005). Determinants and consequences of social trust. *Sociological Inquiry, 75*(4), 453–473.

Wellman, B., & Wortley, S. (1990). Different strokes from different folks: Community ties and social support. *American Journal of Sociology, 96*, 558–588.

Westlund, H., & Adam, F. (2009). Social capital and economic performance: A meta-analysis of 65 studies. *European Planning Studies, 18*(6), 893–919.

Westlund, H., & Larsson, J. P. (2021). Local social capital and regional development. In M. M. Fischer, P. Nijkamp (Eds.), *Handbook of regional science* (pp. 721–735). Berlin: Springer-Verlag.

Whiteley, P. F. (2000). Economic growth and social capital. *Political Studies, 48*(3), 443–466.

Wilber, K. (1996). *The Atman project, a transpersonal view of human development*. Wheaton: Quest books.

Williamson, O. (1981). The economics of organization: The transaction cost approach. *The American Journal of Sociology, 87*(3), 548–577.
Williamson, O. (1985). *The economics institutions of capitalism: Firms, markets, relational contracting*. London: Macmillan.
Williamson, O. (1996). *The mechanisms of governance*. Oxford: Oxford University Press.
Williamson, O. (2000). The new institutional economics: Taking stock, looking ahead. *Journal of Economic Literature, 38*(3), 595–613.
Wilson, J., & Musick, M. (1998). The contribution of social resources to volunteering. *Social Science Quarterly, 79*(4), 799–814.
Wilson, T. D. (2004). *Strangers to ourselves: Discovering the adaptive unconscious*. Cambridge, MA: Harvard University Press.
Winter, I. (2001). Toward a theorized understanding of family life and social capital. (Working Paper 21, Melbourne University).
Winthrop, R. H. (1991). *Dictionary of concepts in cultural anthropology*. New York: Greenwood Press.
Wolleb, G. (2008). Introduction: Social capital and economic development. In D. Castiglione, J. W. Van Deth, & G. Wolleb (Eds.), *The handbook of social capital* (pp. 373–385). New York: Oxford University Press.
Wong, A. (2023). How social capital builds online brand advocacy in luxury social media brand communities. *Journal of Retailing and Consumer Services, 70*, 103–143.
Woolcock, M. (1998). Social capital and economic development: Toward a theoretical synthesis and policy framework. *Theory and Society, 27*(2), 151–208.
Woolcock, M. (2001). The place of social capital in understanding social and economic outcomes. *Canadian Journal of Policy Research, 2*(1), 1492–1525.
Woolcock, M. (2010). The rise and routinization of social capital, 1988–2008. *Annual Review of Political Science, 13*, 469–487.
Woolcock, M. (2021). The social life of academic articles: Some reflections on the making and impact of "social capital and economic development". *Theory and Society, 50*, 381–392.
Woolcock, M., & Narayan, D. (2000). Social capital: Implications for development theory, research, and policy. *World Bank Research Observer, 15*(2), 225–250.
Woolcock, M., & Radin, E. (2008). A relational approach to the theory and practices of economic development. In D. Castiglione, J. W. Van Deth, & G. Wolleb (Eds.), *The handbook of social capital* (pp. 411–437). New York: Oxford University Press.
World Bank (2001). ¿Qué es el capital social? Documento en línea, http://www.worldbank.org/poverty/spanish/scapital/ index.htm, agosto de 2001.
World Bank (21/03/2017). Overview: Social capital. Recuperado de http://www.worldbank.org/en/webarchives/archive/
Wright, E. O. (2015). *Understanding class*. London: Verso.
Yamagishi, T., & Yamagishi, M. (1994). Trust and commitment in the United States and Japan. *Motivation and Emotion, 18*(2), 129–166.
Yang, K. (2007). Individual social capital and its measurement in social surveys. *Survey Research Methods, 1*(1), 19–27.
Yosano, A., & Hayashi, N. (2005). Social stratification, intermediary groups, and creation of trustfulness. *Sociological Theory and Methods, 20*, 27–44.
Young, J. T. (1997). *Economics as a moral science: The political economy of A. Smith*. Cheltenham: E. Elgar Pub.
Zak, P. J., & Knack, S. (2001). Trust and growth. *Economic Journal, 111*, 295–321.
Zamagni, S. (Ed.) (1995). *Economics of altruism*. Aldershot: E. Elgar.

Zamagni, S. (2004). Towards an economics of human relations: On the role of psychology in economics. *Group Analysis, 37*(1), 17–32.

Zelizer, V. A. (1983). *Morals and markets: The development of life insurance in the United States*. New Brunswick: Transaction Press.

Zelizer, V. A. (2007). *Undeafening the dialogue between sociology and economics*. Princeton: Princeton University.

Zeltzer, D. (2020). Gender homophily in referral networks: Consequences for the Medicare Physician Earnings Gap. *American Economic Journal: Applied Economics, 12*(2), 169–197.

Zucker, L. G. (1986). Production of trust: Institutional sources of economic structure, 1840-1920. In B. M. Straw, & L. L. Cumming (Eds.), *Research in Organizational Behavior* (pp. 53–111). Greenwich: JAI Press.

Index

Note: **Bold** page numbers refer to tables; *italic* page numbers refer to figures and page numbers followed by "n" denote endnotes.

Kolibri 360 GmbH
Ferdinand-Jühlke-Straße 7
99095 Erfurt, Deutschland
produktsicherheit@kolibri360.de